The Tennessee Valley Authority: Design and Persuasion

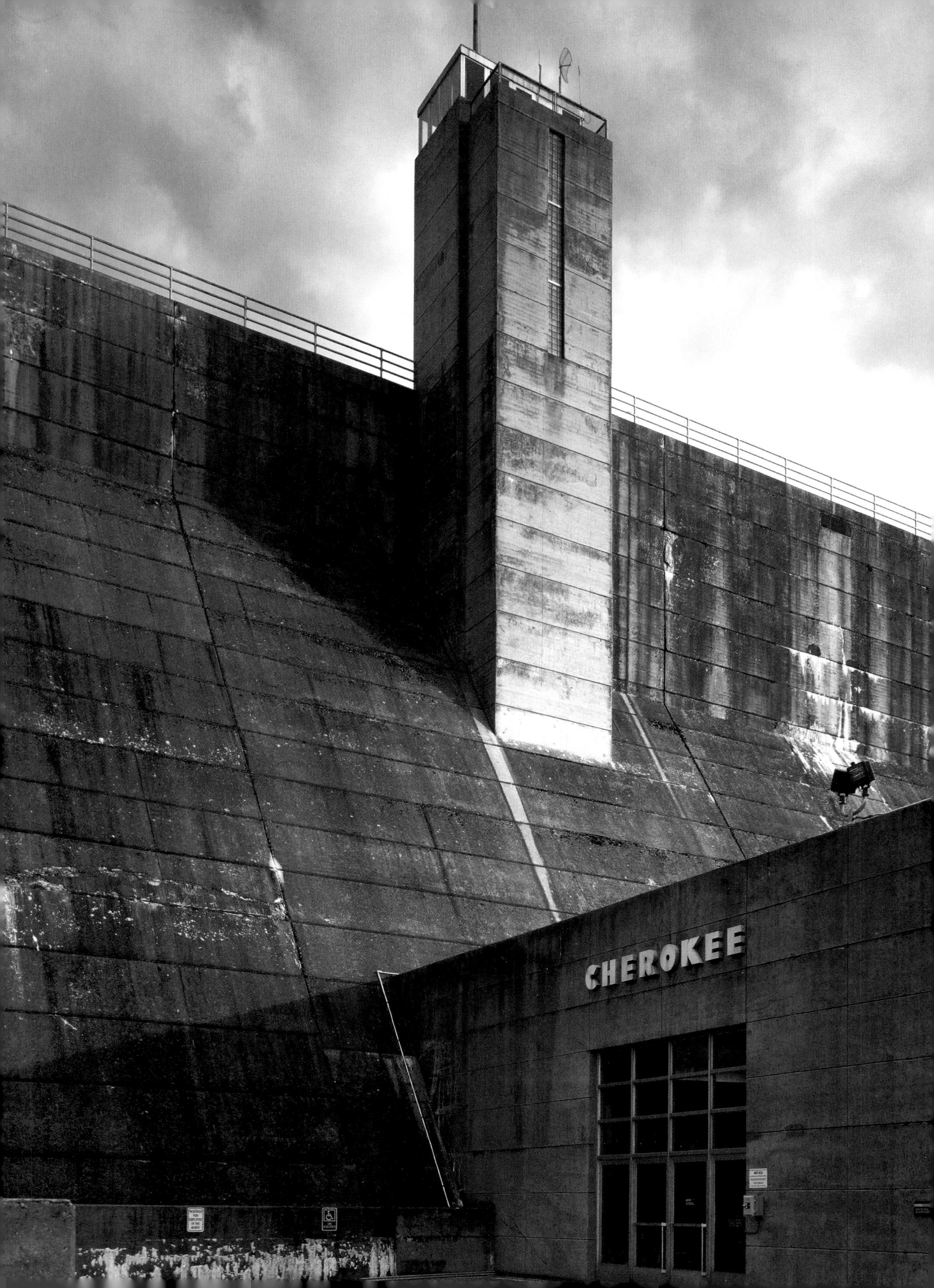
CHEROKEE

The Tennessee Valley Authority: Design and Persuasion

Tim Culvahouse, editor
Photographs by Richard Barnes

Afterword by former Senator Howard H. Baker, Jr.

Princeton Architectural Press, New York

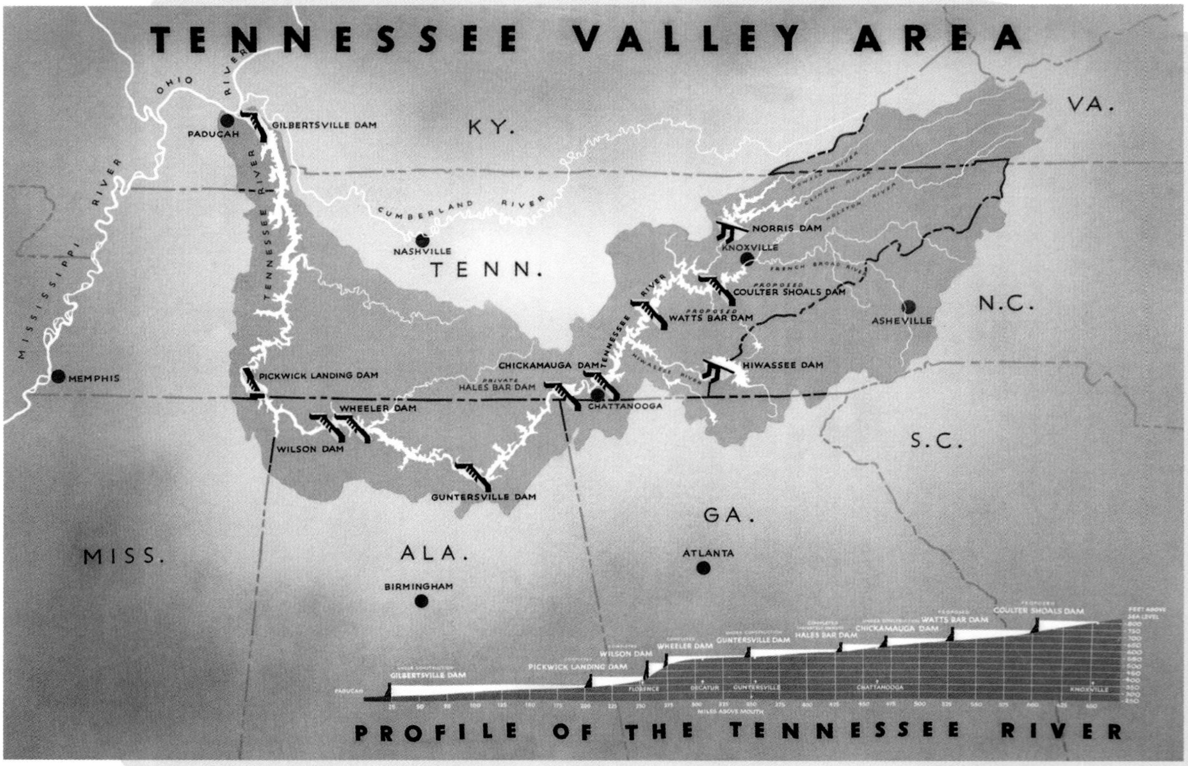
TENNESSEE VALLEY AREA
OHIO RIVER
MISSISSIPPI RIVER
TENNESSEE RIVER
CUMBERLAND RIVER
HIWASSEE RIVER
FRENCH BROAD RIVER
KY.
VA.
TENN.
N.C.
S.C.
GA.
ALA.
MISS.
PADUCAH
GILBERTSVILLE DAM
NASHVILLE
NORRIS DAM
KNOXVILLE
PROPOSED COULTER SHOALS DAM
PROPOSED WATTS BAR DAM
ASHEVILLE
HIWASSEE DAM
MEMPHIS
PICKWICK LANDING DAM
CHICKAMAUGA DAM
PRIVATE HALES BAR DAM
CHATTANOOGA
WHEELER DAM
WILSON DAM
GUNTERSVILLE DAM
ATLANTA
BIRMINGHAM
GILBERTSVILLE DAM
PICKWICK LANDING DAM
WILSON DAM
WHEELER DAM
GUNTERSVILLE DAM
HALES BAR DAM
CHICKAMAUGA DAM
WATTS BAR DAM
COULTER SHOALS DAM
FLORENCE
DECATUR
GUNTERSVILLE
CHATTANOOGA
KNOXVILLE
PROFILE OF THE TENNESSEE RIVER

The Tennessee Valley is the first place in America where we can sit down and design a civilization.

—Arthur E. Morgan

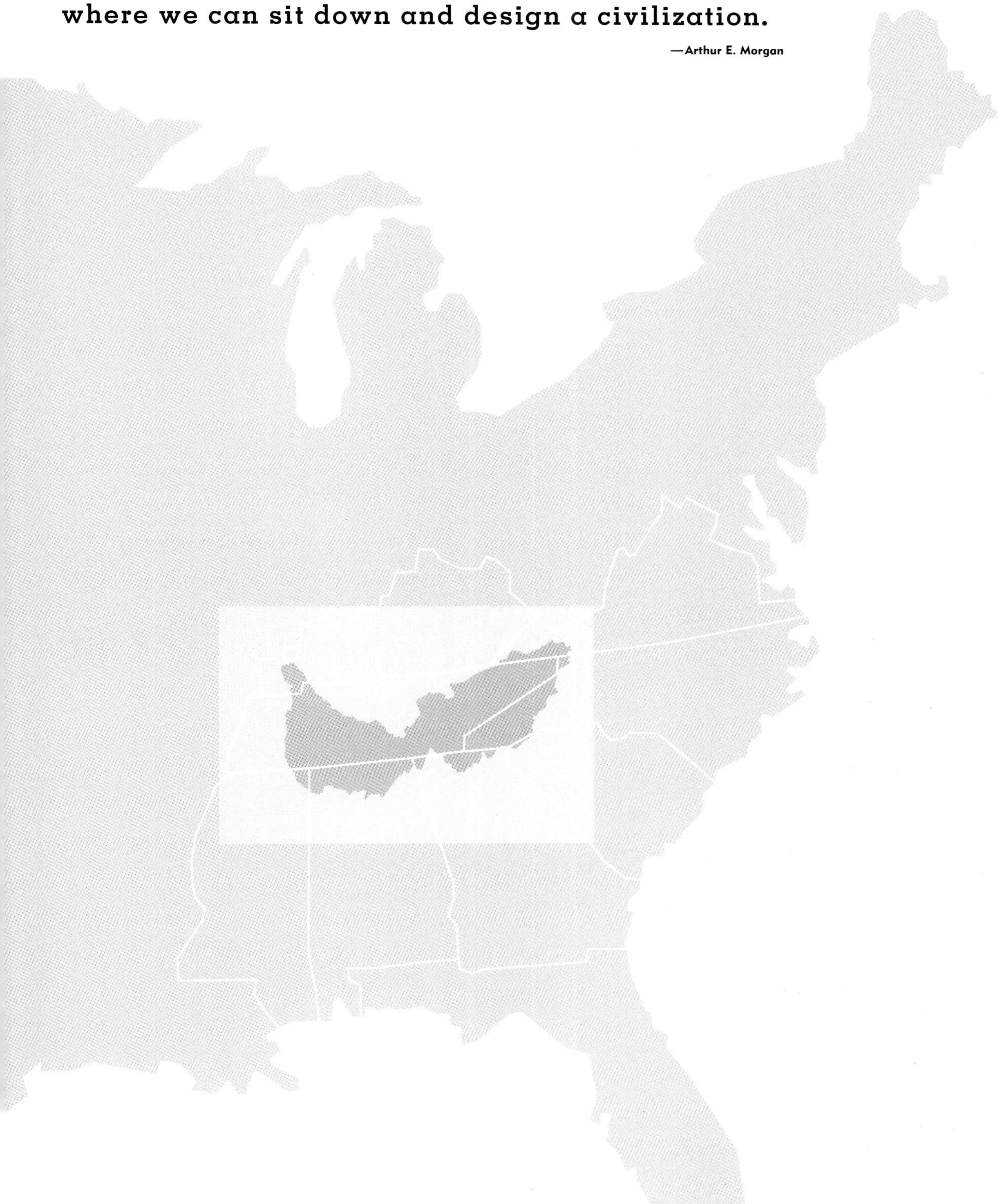

Published by
Princeton Architectural Press
37 East Seventh Street
New York, New York 10003

For a free catalog of books, call
1.800.722.6657.
Visit our Web site at
www.papress.com.

Printed and bound in China
10 09 08 07 4 3 2 1
First edition

Editing: Linda Lee
Design: Bob Aufuldish, Michael Thompson, Aufuldish & Warinner

Special thanks to: Nettie Aljian, Sara Bader, Dorothy Ball, Nicola Bednarek, Janet Behning, Becca Casbon, Penny (Yuen Pik) Chu, Russell Fernandez, Pete Fitzpatrick, Jan Haux, Clare Jacobson, John King, Nancy Eklund Later, Katharine Myers, Lauren Nelson Packard, Scott Tennent, Jennifer Thompson, Paul Wagner, Joseph Weston, and Deb Wood of Princeton Architectural Press —Kevin C. Lippert, publisher

Library of Congress Cataloging-in-Publication Data
The Tennessee Valley Authority : design and persuasion / Tim Culvahouse, editor ; photographs by Richard Barnes ; afterword by Senator Howard H. Baker, Jr. —1st ed.
p. cm.
Includes bibliographical references.
ISBN 978-1-56898-684-5 (hardcover : alk. paper)
1. Tennessee Valley Authority. 2. Design, Industrial—United States—History—20th century. 3. Architecture and state—United States—History—20th century. 4. Modern movement (Architecture)—United States. I. Culvahouse, Tim, 1957–
TK1425.M8T3517 2007
627'.80973—dc22
2007000115

Image Credits

Courtesy of the Amalgamated Housing Corporation: 31; Bob Aufuldish, Aufuldish & Warinner: 4–5, 138; Atlantic Mapping, Inc., Marietta, Georgia: 63; Howard H. Baker, Jr.: 135; Richard Barnes: front cover, back cover, 2, 18R, 27, 53, 57, 61R, 64–79, 81, 84, 87L, 88R, 97, 109, 121, 123, 125R; Bruno Bischofberger: 84L; CB&Q Photo-BRHS Archives: 87R; Cincinnati Museum Center–Cincinnati Historical Society Library: 33; City of Vienna, Austria: 39; Bob Culvahouse: 21; Tim Culvahouse: 11, 13, 14, 17L, 22L, 24L, 93; Dallas Museum of Art: 85R; *Knoxville News-Sentinel*: 132L; Library of Congress: 32, 40, 62; The Liliane and David M. Stewart Program for Modern Design, Gift of Eric Brill: 85L; Steven Heller: 99–101; Mildred Lane Kemper Art Museum, Washington University in St. Louis: 114L; MPTV.net: 115; National Gallery of Art: 111R; Courtesy of the Tennessee Valley Authority: 4 inset, 41, 42, 44, 45, 54R, 60, 91R, 112, 113, 125L; Courtesy of the Tennessee Valley Authority, photograph by Charles Krutch: 17R, 20, 22R, 24R, 30, 35, 43, 46, 54L, 55, 56, 58, 59, 61L, 86, 88L, 91L, 103–6, 111L, 130, 132R; Courtesy of the Tennessee Valley Authority, photograph by Cletus Mitchell: 114R, 116–17; Jane Wolff: 18L, 22C

Table of Contents

Acknowledgments

TIM CULVAHOUSE

As editor I am privileged to thank the brilliant team of writers—Jennifer Bloomer, Steven Heller, Barry Katz, Christine Macy, Todd Smith, and Jane Wolff—along with photographer Richard Barnes and designer Bob Aufuldish, who have made the construction of this volume an unforgettable pleasure.

The development of such a long-gestating project has depended on the generosity of innumerable people. Foremost is the staff of the Tennessee Valley Authority, which, without exception, has been unfailingly helpful, tolerant of the peskiness of a mob of disorganized investigators, and graciously welcoming, even in the days following September 11, 2001, when the TVA sites, important large-scale infrastructure, were officially closed to the public. Our guides throughout this process have been members of TVA Client Communications: Barbara Martocci, its director; Dick Salisbury (now retired), guide for our kick-off group field trip; and the indefatigable Terry Johnson, who guided Richard Barnes and me on several photographic tours. To Terry, the far-flung sites of the TVA are all part of a day's work, and it seemed nothing to him to meet us at eight o'clock in the morning after a three-hour drive from his home.

At the TVA headquarters, we enjoyed the hospitality and insight of Nancy Proctor, TVA librarian; Mike Dobrogosz, formerly curator of the TVA Artifact Collection and now its Watershed Team manager; the late architect Bob Cole; and Pat Bernard Ezzell, TVA historian and our guide to the archival photographs, whose *TVA Photography: Thirty Years of Life in the Tennessee Valley* (University Press of Mississippi, 2003) is a handsome recent addition to the TVA literature. We also received archival assistance from Arlene Royer of the U.S. National Archives and Record Administration, Southeast Region, Atlanta, Georgia.

We enjoyed equally gracious hospitality at every TVA site we visited. At Guntersville Dam, we thank technicians Lewis Frederick, Robert M. "Micky" Hunt, and Lynwood "Woodie" McCormick; at Kentucky Dam, laborer Steve Fiessinger, technician Lucas Newhouse, and foreman Lawrence Wooten; at Wheeler Dam, lead technician Jason Trousdale, technician Larry Green, electrician Byron Smith, and laborer Michelle Nichols Trousdale; and at Wilson Dam, retired hydro plant safety coordinators Mike Horton and Jimmie Richardson. Other TVA employees, at these and other dams, as well as at the TVA offices in Knoxville and Chattanooga, Tennessee, were unfailingly friendly and helpful.

The TVA is blessed by an unusually loyal following of former employees, who refer to themselves as "alumni." In addition to those alumni who staff—on a volunteer basis—the visitor centers at Norris, Fontana, and Kentucky dams, we benefited from the insight of alumni Robin Ellerthorpe, FAIA, and Dennis McCarthy, PhD, editor in chief of *Forum for Applied Research and Public Policy*.

The way to our initial contact with TVA Client Communications was paved by the office of Congressman Zach Wamp of Chattanooga, whose district director, Sarah Bryan, brought us up-to-date on current issues affecting the TVA system. While in Chattanooga, we enjoyed the kindness and insight of Congressman Wamp's father, architect Don Wamp, and of Spencer McCallie III.

Several individuals assisted Richard Barnes in locating the few remaining structures—silos and whatnot—emerging from the waters of the TVA lakes. These include Stephanie L. Palm of the Tennessee Wildlife Resources Agency, Tony Hale of Ft. Loudon Marina, Sabrina Kennedy Brown of Painter Creek Marina, and fishing guide Carl Boaz.

Christine Macy's chapter relies in part on *Architecture and Nature: Creating the American Landscape* (Routledge, 2003), which she wrote in collaboration with Sarah Bonnemaison. Macy thanks Kay Potts Bianculli, Earle S. Draper Jr., Peter Wank, and Marian Moffett for their guidance, recollections, and loan of documents; and Ed Frank, curator of special collections at the University of Memphis libraries, for his curatorial and archival assistance.

Jennifer Bloomer's daughter Sarah Cox and good friend Dera Weaver offered close readings and helpful critiques of "Watauga" as it was being developed. Her friend and fellow native East-Tennessean Damon Denton ("Thunderrumble") served as host, driver, servant, entertainer, and confidant. Much appreciation goes to her mother's cousin John Rice Irwin, founder and director of the Museum of Appalachia in Norris, Tennessee, who opened the museum's private holdings to her perusal.

We are especially grateful to former Senator Howard H. Baker, Jr., for taking time out of his demanding schedule to contribute the afterword to this volume. For introduction to Senator Baker, we thank Arthur B. Culvahouse, Jr., and in Baker's Huntsville, Tennessee, office, we thank Fred Marcum and Pat Butler for their assistance.

Funding for this volume has been generously provided by the Graham Foundation for Advanced Studies in the Fine Arts, where we especially thank Patricia M. Snyder, Stephanie Whitlock, and the late director, Richard Solomon,

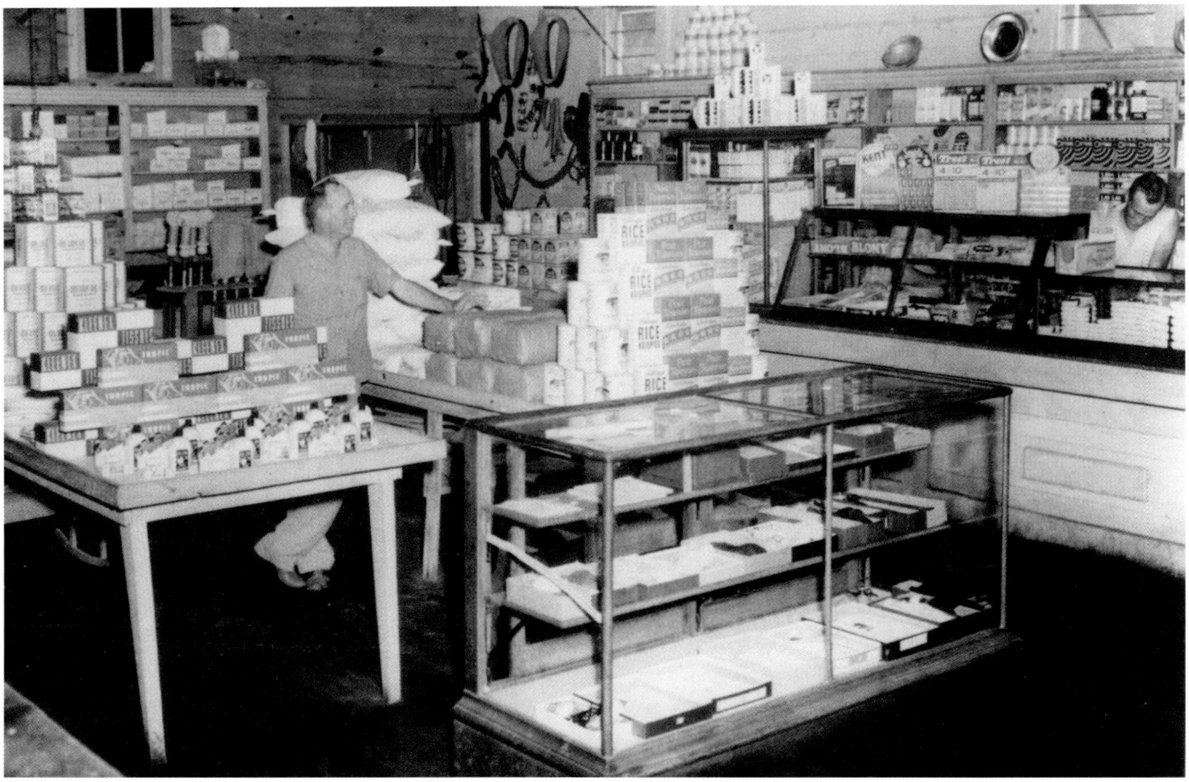

Interior of Chet Culvahouse's store, ca. 1940

FAIA. Additional financial support was provided by the AIA New York Chapter, through their Arnold W. Brunner Grant, and by California College of the Arts. For support in our fundraising efforts, we gratefully acknowledge Carol Burns, Todd Dalland, FAIA, William Littman, Robert W. Rindler, and William Saunders.

In Knoxville, we are grateful for the support of the College of Architecture and Design at the University of Tennessee, particularly Dean John McRae, FAIA, former dean Marleen K. Davis, FAIA, and faculty member Tom K. Davis. Faculty member Marian Moffett, a recognized expert on the TVA, is the author of the exhibition catalog *"Built for the People of the United States": Fifty Years of TVA Architecture* (Knoxville: Art and Architecture Gallery of the University of Tennessee, 1983), which has served as a guide for our efforts. We are grateful for the support of Dana Self, the Barbara W. and Bernard E. Bernstein Curator of Collections and Exhibitions at the Knoxville Museum of Art.

I am personally grateful to many members of the Culvahouse clan, both for factual information and for insight into the cultural impact of the TVA. With apologies to those I forget to mention (there are so damned many of them!), I especially thank my cousins Cynthia Roy, Martha Culvahouse, Wear Culvahouse, David Evans, Houston Gordon, Melinda Hardy, and Jann Howell; sometime cousin-in-law John Sharp Fox; aunt Mary V. Culvahouse; and my late, beloved aunts, Edna Evans, Rachel Culvahouse, and Ruth Culvahouse.

To the staff of Princeton Architectural Press, especially Kevin Lippert, publisher; Clare Jacobson, editorial director; Nancy Levinson, former acquisitions editor; and Linda Lee, the insightful editor of this volume—thank you for your faithful support and brilliant assistance.

Closer to home are those who have helped actively in the organization of this project: Billy Feuerman, who helped arrange the original group research trip, and my able assistant at Culvahouse Consulting Group, Laura Schatzkin.

My deepest thanks go to my family—my most cherished partner, Katie Snyder; my daughter, Sasha; son, Theo; my mother, Louisa Johnston Culvahouse; and my late father, Robert E. "Bob" Culvahouse, to whom this volume is dedicated.

Introduction

TIM CULVAHOUSE

Childhood Memories

Saturday mornings, when I was a child, after *Sergeant Preston of the Yukon* and *Mighty Mouse* on the big, black-and-white television in the wood-toned metal case, we would climb into the car and head for "The Country." The Country was where my cousins and my aunts and uncles lived. It was where my grandfather "Mr. Chet" Culvahouse lived, in a big, white, clapboard house on a point, surrounded on three sides by Watts Bar Lake. My father had grown up in this house, one of ten children—five boys, five girls.

We drove south out of Rockwood, Tennessee, on US 27, a two-lane highway snaking gently down the broad valley toward Chattanooga. The windows of the green-and-white Galaxie were down, and the warm air, softer than cotton, tumbled in. At Spring City, fifteen miles down the way, we turned left and wound through scrubby woods. A railroad track flanked us on the right. Wherever the road cut into the side of a hill, the dirt was deep orange. Roots of the southern yellow pines balancing on the edge of the cuts stuck out of crumbling banks.

Around one bend—the one I looked for, my signal—the ragged cuts gave way to gentle, carefully tended grass slopes, slipping smoothly into the dark pine woods. The road rose to the left, curved back to the right, over and down the hill, then up and down again in long sweeps through the tidy forest.

Rounding the final hill, we dropped down between concrete retaining walls, through the face of a bluff, and out into the open. That was my favorite moment, as the road passed from the wooded hills onto the top of Watts Bar Dam. To the left below us was the lake, to the right, much farther down, the river. On the far side of the dam, we passed over the lock, in which barges might be lowering on their way downriver from Knoxville, Tennessee. Beyond the lock a small road forked off to the left. We took it and, after a short distance, turned left again at a crossroad with a little store with a gas pump, onto the River Road. We were in The Country.

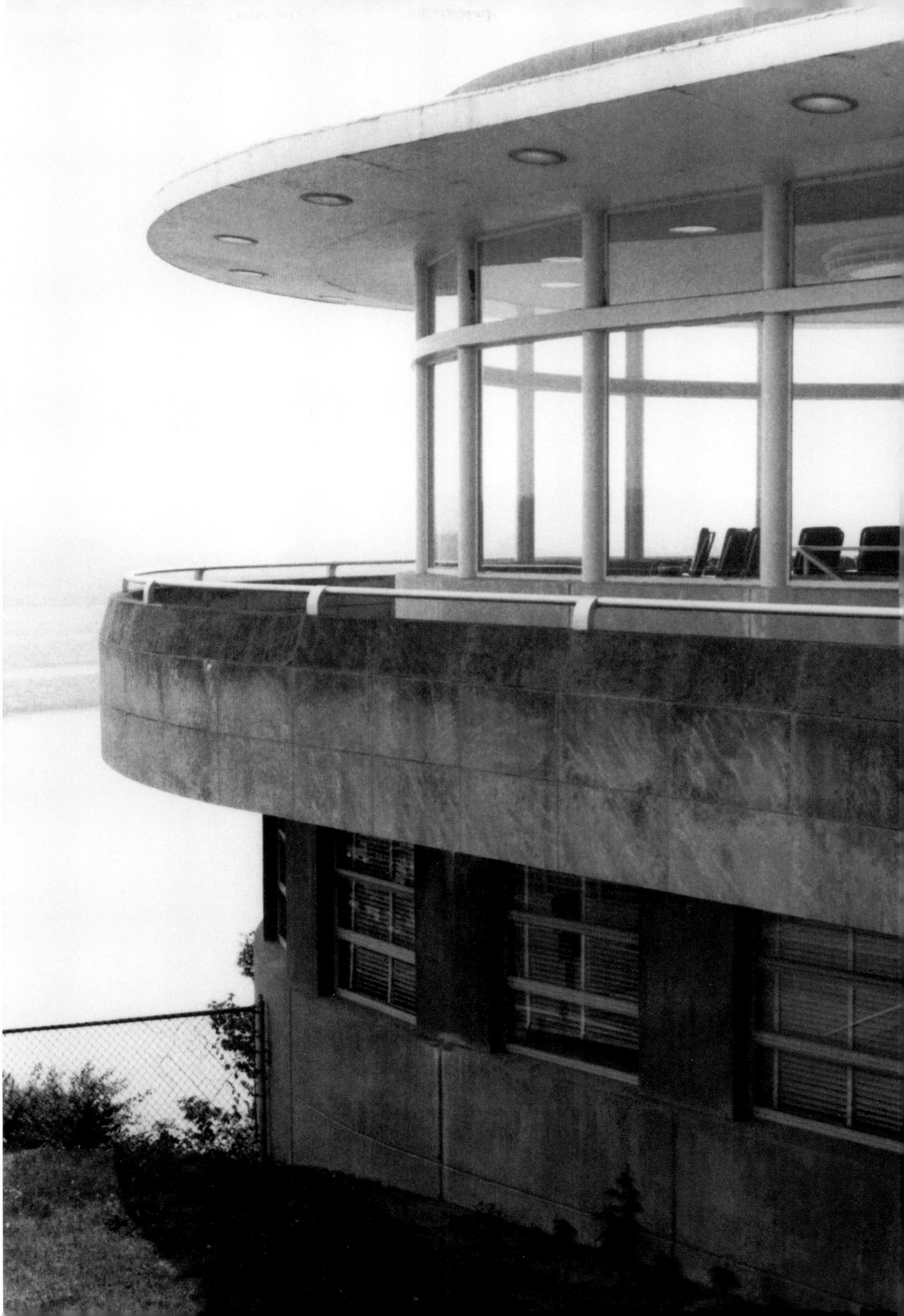

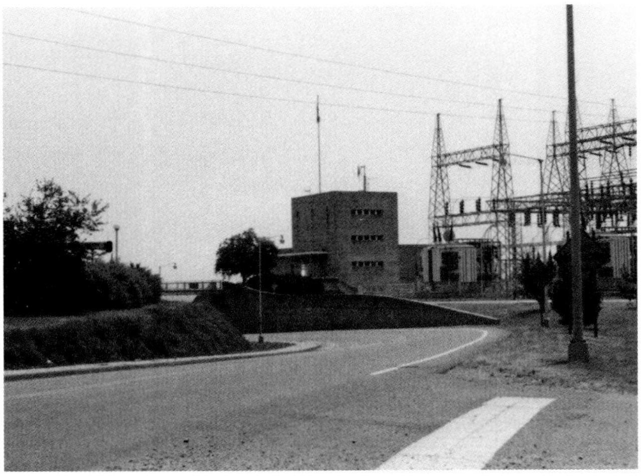

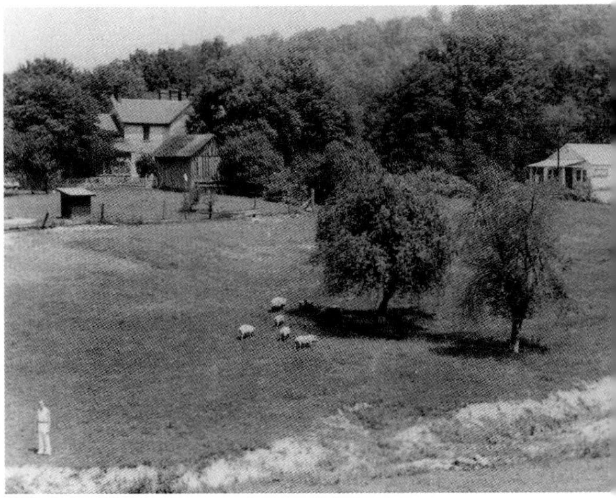

OVERLEAF Visitor center overlook at Watts Bar Dam, 1986

LEFT The approach to Watts Bar Dam, 1986

RIGHT The Culvahouse homeplace before the closing of Watts Bar Dam, with the house upper left and the store to the right, ca. 1940. The current level of Watts Bar Lake would be in the midst of the group of hogs.

Every so often we caught a glimpse of the lake off to the left, and as we drove along, my father pointed out the landmarks: the road to the Holloman Place, where there was a spring full of watercress; Erma and Hatsie Ewing's white house on the hill; and just beyond it Glamour Manor, a log house with a screen porch across the long front, where my parents had lived when they were first married. Somewhere just along there, the Culvahouse homestead began, along the right-hand side of the road where the ground rises quickly up the side of Looney Ridge. Once, the left-hand side of the road had been a part of the farm as well, but now it is dotted with lakeside cabins and mobile homes.

We turned left off River Road onto the long gravel drive up to the homeplace, and just before the house we passed Mr. Chet's store. The store faced the front of the house across a stretch of dirt road that came up out of the lake on one side of the point, ran straight across its quarter-mile width, and dropped back below the surface of the lake.

(My grandfather died when I was three. I barely remember him. My clearest memory—a mixture, perhaps, of recollection and the story that was frequently repeated to me—is of Mr. Chet taking me across to the store for the Coke forbidden by my parents. Coca-Cola came in heavy, green glass, returnable ten-ounce bottles, the perfect size for a toddler.)

The distance between the line marked by the mostly submerged dirt road in front of Mr. Chet's store to the natural bank of the Tennessee River had been exactly a mile. This had been the Culvahouse farm, productive land, where Mr. Chet raised cattle and hogs and corn. Then the TVA closed Watts Bar Dam.

The Authority

First conceived by former Senator George Norris of Nebraska in 1926,[1] the Tennessee Valley Authority (TVA) was chartered by Congress in 1933 at the urging of President Franklin Roosevelt to create "a corporation clothed with the power of government but possessed of the flexibility and initiative of a private enterprise."[2] Its purpose was

> to improve the navigability and to provide for the flood control of the Tennessee River; to provide for reforestation and the proper use of marginal lands in the Tennessee Valley; to provide for the agricultural and industrial development of said valley; to provide for the national defense by the creation of a corporation for the operation of Government properties at and near Muscle Shoals in the State of Alabama, and for other purposes.[3]

The TVA region, defined as the watershed of the Tennessee River and its tributaries, encompasses all of Tennessee and parts of six other states: Virginia, North Carolina, Georgia, Alabama, Mississippi, and Kentucky. In 1933, this area was unusually impoverished, even by Depression-era standards. Deforestation and poor farming practices, leading to soil erosion and exhaustion, had undermined both timbering and farming, mainstays of an agrarian economy. Other river-related problems restricted economic growth: flooding beset urbanized centers along the river and its tributaries with increasing frequency and severity, and swift currents and rocky shoals inhibited commercial navigation.

The TVA addressed these and other issues with unprecedented comprehensiveness—what the Authority refers to today as "integrated resource management." In the service of agriculture, it developed fertilizers and promoted improved farming methods. It reforested and worked to improve wildlife habitat. The hydroelectric dams—its most iconic structures—served triple duty: the regulation of water levels in the Tennessee river, to control both seasonal flooding and the malaria-carrying mosquito population; improved navigability; and provision of electricity, which not only increased the productivity of existing farms and businesses but also drew new industry to the region.[4]

With the United States' entry into World War II, the TVA was immediately enlisted into the war effort. Its electrical-generation facilities were put to work first for the production of ammonium nitrate for explosives and aluminum for aircraft, then for the refinement of plutonium for the atomic bomb. The town of Oak Ridge, Tennessee, was built twenty miles southwest of the TVA's first dam, Norris (1933–36) (named after the senator), to become, along with the University of Chicago's Stagg Field, Hanford Engineer Works in Washington State, and the Los Alamos National Laboratories, one of the four legs of the Manhattan Project. The urgency of the atomic weapons program accelerated the TVA's construction—to save time, for example, Cherokee and Douglas dams were built from the same plans—and reinforced its already powerful mandate. Fortunately, this urgency did not distract from, but rather helped focus, the Authority's design agenda.

Today the TVA is the nation's largest producer of electric power. It continues to serve its seven-state region as an independent agency of the federal government, self-financed through the sale of electricity. In addition to its thirty-four flood-control dams, twenty-nine of which provide hydroelectric generation, it operates eleven coal-fired, six combustion-turbine, and three nuclear power plants, seventeen solar-power sites, one wind-power site, and one methane-gas site, as well as the Raccoon Mountain Pumped Storage Plant, near Chattanooga, where electricity is consumed during off-peak hours to lift water to a mountaintop reservoir from which it is then released to generate power during peak hours.

Annually, 38,000 barges carry over fifty million tons of goods on the Tennessee River. A series of thirteen locks, integral to the main river dams but operated by the Army Corps of Engineers, permit navigation upriver as far as Knoxville, 650 river miles from the confluence of Tennessee and Ohio rivers at Paducah, Kentucky.[5]

The TVA reservoirs and the 290,000 acres of land associated with them provide recreation, including swimming, boating, fishing, camping, and picnicking. The Ocoee River Gorge, with its three hydroelectric dams managed by the TVA, was the site of the whitewater competitions of the 1996 Olympic Games.

The Necessity for Persuasion

In the published accounts of the TVA projects during the war years (including those in the architectural press), the landscape of eastern Tennessee was portrayed as an erosion-scarred wasteland. The portrayal was partly true. Like much of the United States, Tennessee had been largely deforested by the 1920s and '30s, and cultivation of steep hillside fields had devastated portions of the landscape. Runoff from the denuded hills produced increasingly frequent and damaging floods. In particular, Chattanooga, at the time a city of over 200,000 people, located where the river passes through a narrow mountain pass, was prone to devastating floods.

Protection of Chattanooga and other flood-prone cities in Tennessee, northern Alabama, and western Kentucky was one of the chief goals of the TVA, a goal it has largely achieved. The regulation of water levels in the tributary reservoirs provides catchment for spring runoff, and the introduction of more responsible agricultural practices, such as contour plowing, has controlled erosion on small upland farms.

In the bottomland of the Tennessee River itself, however, the control of urban flooding was accomplished by the regulated—and permanent—flooding of the countryside. A series of eight main river dams (of the twenty-nine dams ultimately built on the Tennessee River and its tributaries) inundated thousands of acres of rich, alluvial land along the floor of the valley.

Close to 1,000 of those acres had been part of the Culvahouse farm. Photographs, taken for court proceedings to contest the amount of compensation

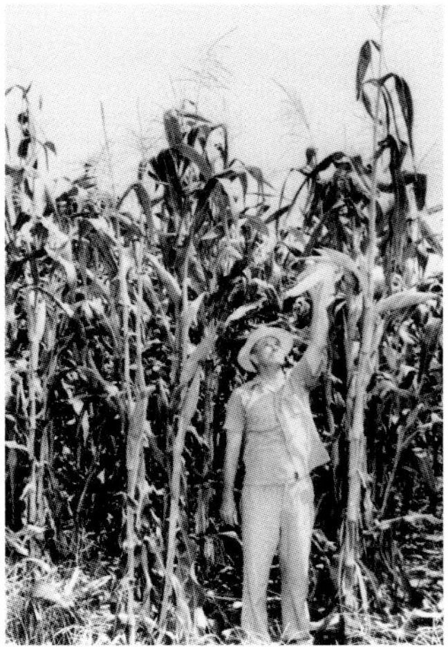

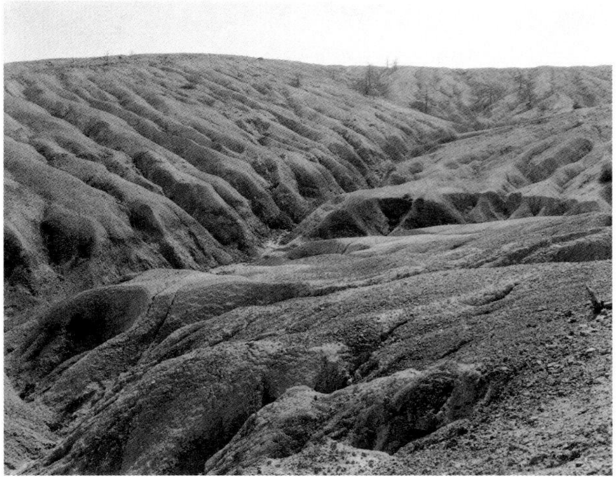

LEFT Chet Culvahouse in field of corn, ca. 1940

RIGHT Eroded landscape near Copper Hill, Tennessee, 1942. Here, fumes from copper smelting destroyed vegetation within a fifty-square-mile area. Such extreme conditions were at times treated by the press as if they were representative.

the government offered for the property, show fields of corn twice the height of my grandfather. Such images of fecundity are largely absent from the published record, which reflects a well-coordinated effort to persuade the public of the benefits of the TVA agenda. Persuasion was required, and not only because of the costs to bottomland farmers like Mr. Chet. Even with the benefits it would bring to the region, the sheer novelty of the project demanded explanation. It was novel in at least three ways: it was modern, it was international, and it was—literally—electrifying.

The Shape of Power

Electric power had been generated from the waters of the Tennessee and its tributaries for more than twenty years before the founding of the TVA. The Aluminum Company of America had built hydroelectric dams, beginning with Cheoah Dam in 1915, to power its plant at Alcoa, outside Knoxville.[6] Two privately built dams (built between 1910 and 1913) on the Ocoee River and the original Hales Bar Dam (ca. 1905, also privately developed) on the Tennessee provided electricity for, among other things, Chattanooga's street railway.[7] Between 1918 and 1924, the Army Corps of Engineers built Wilson Dam to fuel the production of wartime munitions and, later, fertilizer.[8] Wilson also provided power for distribution to individual households in the nearby town of Florence, Alabama. (To power Florence—a town of 36,000 people—today requires only the smallest of the turbines at Wilson. This "house generator," in its beautiful cast-iron case, is the only generator in the TVA system that is self-starting. Because it does not require current to already be flowing in the TVA grid, if the entire grid ever shut down, this would be the first generator to bring the grid back up.[9])

For rural households electricity was not, however, the obvious benefit we now take for granted. People were accustomed to other ways of doing things and

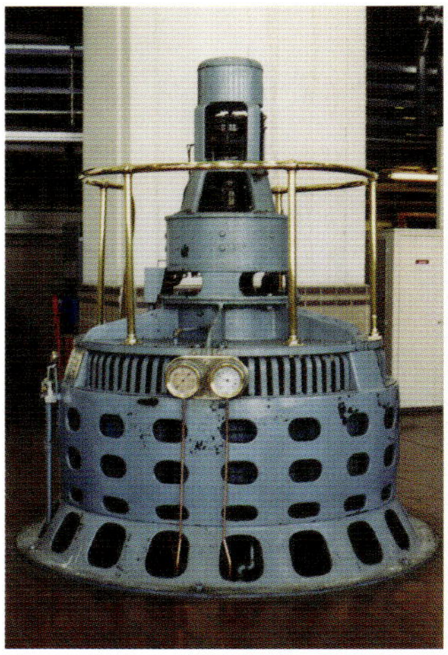

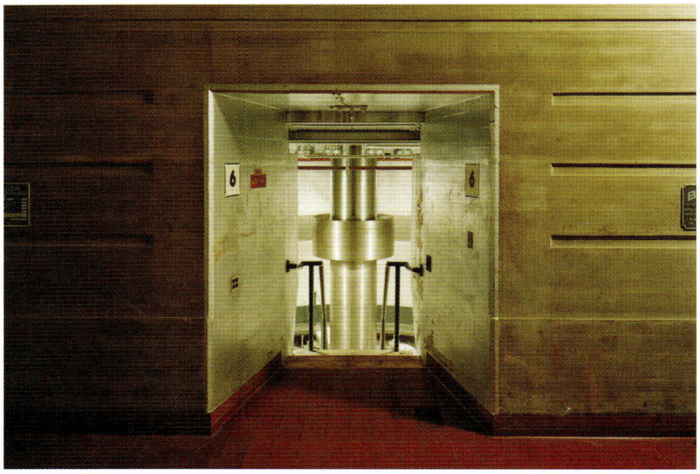

LEFT The "house generator" at Wilson Dam, 2004

RIGHT Entrance to turbine shaft chamber at Wheeler Dam, 2004. Note the abstraction of rusticated masonry joints in the reinforced concrete wall.

skeptical of dependence on large-scale infrastructure. The concept required selling. As Barry Katz describes in "Ideology and Engineering in the Tennessee Valley" (Chapter 4), the Authority not only provided electricity, it also sponsored the development of compact, efficient home appliances and promoted their sales. Beyond the home, it promoted the application of electric power to the evolution of regional craft industries such as ceramics.

Functionally, electricity was the most obviously modern element of the TVA. Formally, it was an enigma. Except in the jagged arcs of lightning or the miniature lightning of the Van de Graaff generator, electricity has no visible shape. The paraphernalia of its generation and distribution had shapes—many shapes, some suggestive, perhaps, of a new aesthetic, but an aesthetic not yet fully coalesced. The physical boundaries of water containment made more powerful formal suggestions: the great bulk and breadth of the dams raised novel questions of scale and articulation.

These questions were particularly novel for the rural South, but they arose amidst an international discussion that had been developing for some time. At least two of the emerging principles of modern design had their roots in the North American landscape. The first of these, the idea that the lines of a building should echo the forms of the landscape in which it resides, came out of the Prairie Style architecture of Frank Lloyd Wright. The second, a faith in the aesthetic virtue of strict engineering calculation, derived from an appreciation of the spare beauty of Canadian and American grain elevators. Both of these influences had traveled to Europe, the former through the publication of Wright's work in Germany, the latter through *Vers une Architecture (Towards a New Architecture)* (1923), the manifesto of the Swiss architect Le Corbusier. In it Le Corbusier published photographs of

American grain elevators alongside other new forms derived from engineering decisions: airplanes and steamships.

TVA's work itself continued this exchange of ideas between the United States and Europe. The use of rough, board-formed concrete at Norris Dam made an impression on Le Corbusier when he visited the TVA in 1946, as he copied the motif in his Unité d'Habitation in Marseilles (1947–52), managing at the same time to be credited as the "inventor" of *beton brut* ("raw concrete," showing the impression of its formwork).[10]

A third principle was developing in Europe in which the formal ideas of modernism were conjoined with a political idea (suggested as well by Wright) that dissolving the physical hierarchies of space into more continuous organizations of buildings and landscapes would lead to a more egalitarian, democratic society.

Each of these three principles—continuity with the landscape, forms derived from engineering function, and architectural form as a tool for social equality—complemented perfectly the ambitions of the TVA. This match may, in itself, have been enough to determine the thrust of TVA design, but the importation (and re-importation) of formal ideas from Europe arrived with an influx of European émigrés fleeing economic hardship and the fascist regimes of Germany and Italy and strongly affected the design agenda of the TVA. Two of these émigrés—Hungarian architect and engineer Roland Wank and Italian architect Mario Bianculli—joined the TVA Architect's Office as principal designers, bringing with them firsthand experience with, and commitment to, the emerging ideals of modern architecture. Wank played a seminal role in internal debates at the Authority over the proper expression of modernity in a traditional, agrarian context. Christine Macy, in "The Architect's Office of the Tennessee Valley Authority" (Chapter 1), explores Wank's role more deeply. As she relates, persuasion was as necessary within the TVA as it was outside of it.

The application of European or international ideas to the rural landscape of the Southern highlands was not, by any means, a foregone conclusion. Earle Draper, director of the Authority's Land Planning and Housing Division, advocated respect for and replication of the familiar forms of regional building, an attitude shared by TVA director Arthur Morgan. Wank, as chief architect, countered with an argument for modern methods to meet the need for housing production. He argued further for an economy of expression based on the necessities of construction, unembellished by ornament. The housing produced by the TVA illustrates the debate between regionalism and modernism, with some dwellings, such as those in the town of Norris, retaining the gabled forms of traditional dwellings, while others, including the modular cabins premanufactured for Fontana, North Carolina, are explicitly modern.

The tension between modernity and tradition is less apparent in the large-scale work of the TVA: the dams, powerhouses, and steam plants and the land-

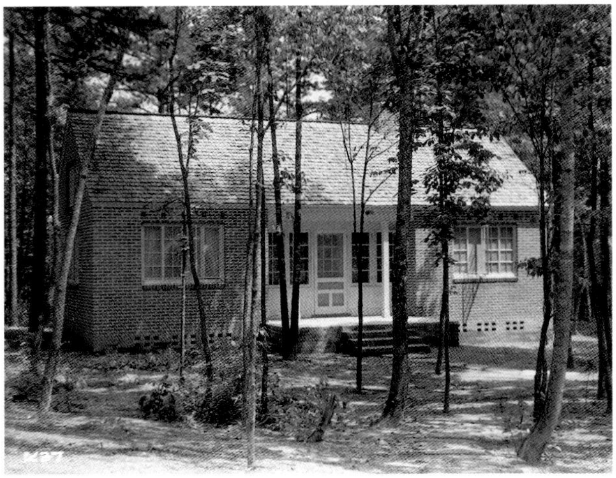

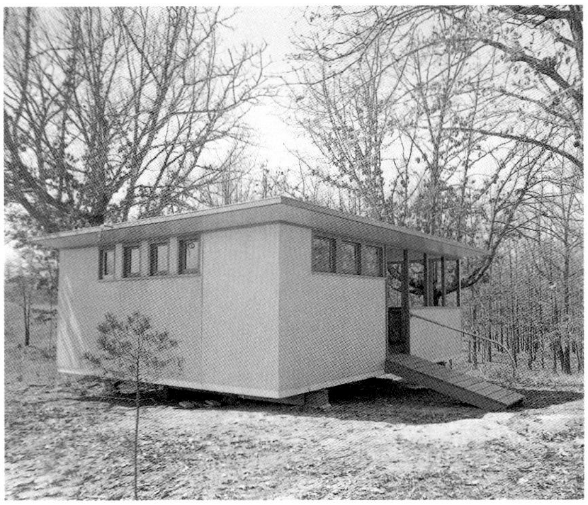

LEFT Typical house at Norris, Tennessee, 1934
RIGHT Prefabricated house at Pickwick Dam, 1941

scapes they inhabit. The Authority inherited one completed neoclassical dam, Wilson (1918–24), and a neoclassical design for its upriver neighbor, Wheeler (1933–36), as well as for Norris. But Wank successfully argued for a reconsideration of their appearance, and the only obvious trace of neoclassical thinking in either is a pared-down interpretation of rustication in the concrete walls around Wheeler's turbine shafts. Otherwise, the large projects are thoroughly modern, their persuasive appeal deriving not from familiar forms but from a consistency of treatment—both in style and quality. Because every detail fits seamlessly into the whole, there is a sense of rightness, even inevitability, to the projects.

From Ten Mile to Guadalcanal

Just as unfamiliar, international forms were being imported into rural Tennessee, via the TVA dams, rural Tennesseans were shipping off to unfamiliar places—Normandy, Anzio, the South Pacific. The experience of my father, Bob Culvahouse, was typical. On July 14, 1943, he boarded a train at Chattanooga's Terminal Station, bound for Camp Barkeley, Texas. At every station stop that long day—in Vicksburg, Mississippi; Delhi and Monroe, Louisiana—he sent my mother a postcard. After several weeks of basic training, he left Camp Barkeley, again by train. He boarded a troop ship in San Diego and spent the next two-and-a-half years in New Caledonia, Fiji, Guadalcanal, and Okinawa.

On January 19, 1946, he arrived back in the United States, at Vancouver Barracks, Washington, and eight days later he was discharged at Camp Chafee, Arkansas. From there he took a train back to Chattanooga, and he was home. During those years he had spent more time than he would have liked on transport ships, but he died, more than fifty years later, without ever having flown in an airplane. How typical that was of his peers in rural East Tennessee, I cannot say. But

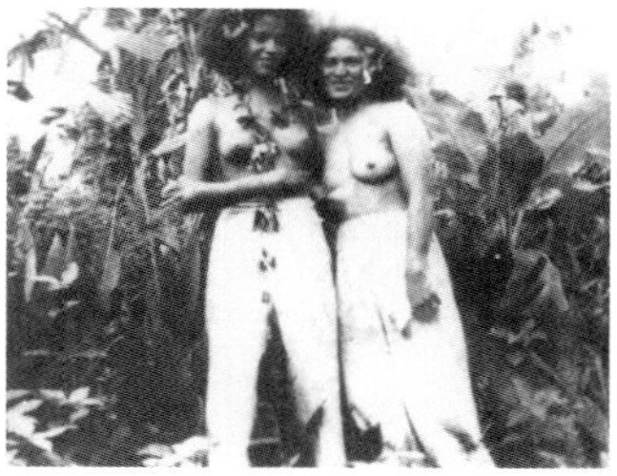

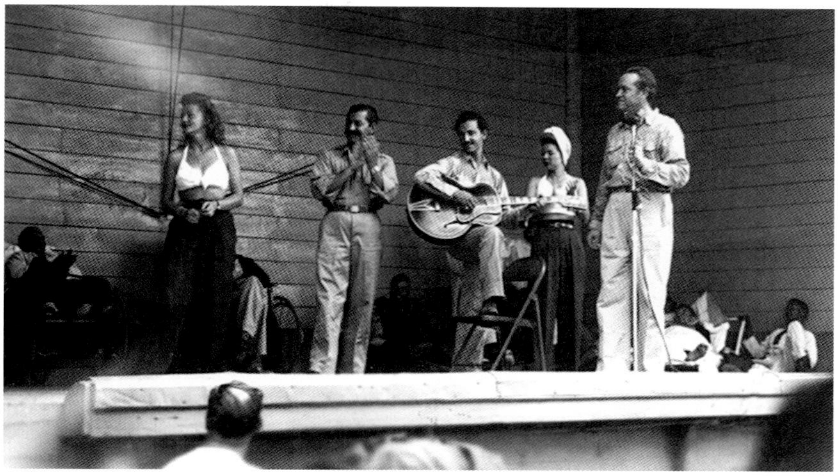

LEFT Photograph of inhabitants of Fiji, ca. 1944

RIGHT Bob Hope's USO review, with, left to right, Patty Thomas, Jerry Colonna, Tony Romano, Frances Langford, and Hope, unidentified Pacific island, ca. 1944

he was not, generally speaking, a Luddite: a high-school math teacher, he studied COBOL computer programming in the summer of 1962. What *was* typical was the experience of picking up, going to a foreign, faraway place, and then returning to the small, rural settlement where he had been born and raised, as if nothing had changed. But it had.

On the first day of January 1942—three weeks after the bombing of Pearl Harbor—Watts Bar Dam closed. The reservoir was filled before the events of the war sent my father to the Pacific, but there had hardly been time to get used to it. The Culvahouse homeplace was no longer on a hill—it was on a peninsula.

Continuities

Riding in the back of that 1959 Ford, unharnessed on the wide bench seat, I enjoyed the gentle roll and curve of the road into Watts Bar Dam. It did not occur to me then, and not for thirty years after, that the curves and the ups and downs of that road were *designed*. I thought roads were placed as they are as a matter of convenience; that, following old cow paths or Indian trails, they wound around the hills because it was the easiest way to go. If I had stopped to think about it, however, I would have noticed that the roads outside the TVA reservation cut the curves short, seeking a straighter line. That is where the orange clay banks emerged. The TVA roads betray a different attitude, gentler and less abrupt. Their designers did not merely defer to the hills, they choreographed a partnership of automobile and landscape. Long before artist Michael Heizer employed a bulldozer to draw his *Double Negative* (1969)—the pioneering minimalist earthwork near Overton, Nevada—TVA engineers applied grading equipment to the land as a sculptor would apply a chisel to marble.

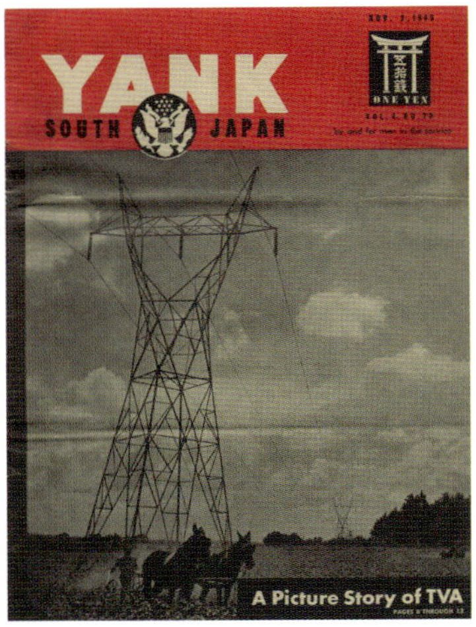

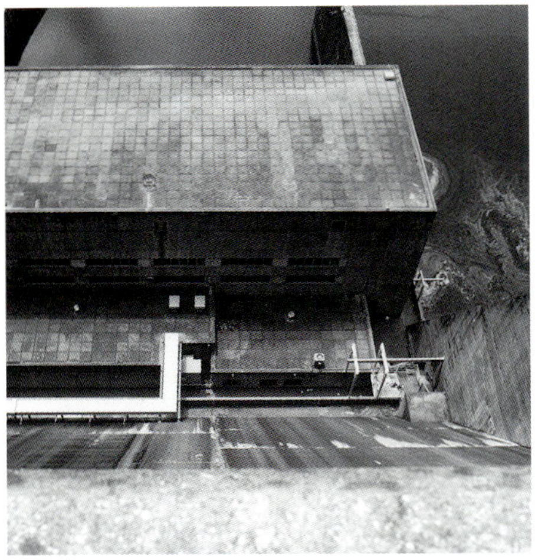

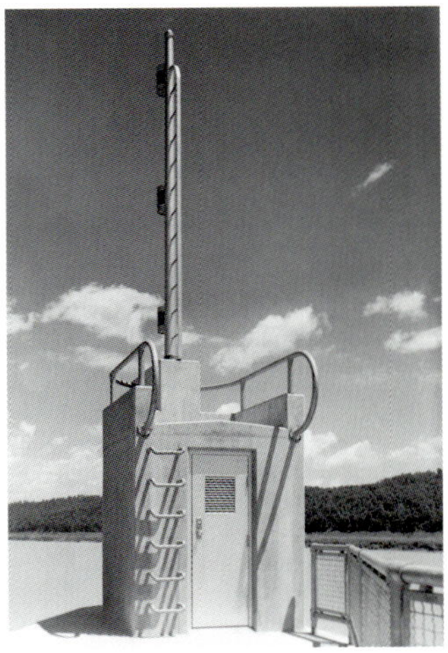

LEFT Cover of *Yank: South Japan*, a weekly newspaper published by the enlisted men of the U.S. Army, November 2, 1945. "This Week's Cover: This scene shows a high-power TVA transmission line running through a Tennessee Valley rural area—symbolic of the benefits that have come from the world's first attempt to develop an entire region."

CENTER Roof of Norris Dam powerhouse, from the top of the dam, 2002

RIGHT Combined gauge house and navigation light pole, Guntersville Lock at Guntersville Dam, 1938

Today that equipment has grown to such gargantuan proportions that the highway engineer has little incentive even to acknowledge a small hill, much less engage it artistically. Here, as in other areas, the TVA offers compelling lessons in the value of design for human experience.

But these lessons require careful observation. Unlike Heizer's cut in the edge of Mormon Mesa, which depends on contrast for its effect, the roadways of the TVA reservations form a seamless continuity with the ground they traverse. You can usually tell when you have entered a TVA reservation—the shoulders of the road are more neatly mowed than elsewhere—but there is nothing abrupt about the transition. As Jane Wolff describes in "Redefining Landscape" (Chapter 2), the continuities of the designed landscape obscure innumerable dislocations in the preexisting landscape—of dwellings, commercial and agricultural buildings, fields, even cemeteries—but these dislocations were themselves assiduously coordinated. The visible choreography of designed elements holds throughout the reservation, from the scale of the landscape, through the scale of the dam itself, down to the detail of a light fixture or a door handle.

The novelist Henry James writes, "Really, universally, relations stop nowhere, and it is the exquisite problem of the artist to draw, through a geometry of his own, the circle within which they shall happily appear to do so."[11] Though James was referring to novels and the obligation the novelist has to invent a fictional world without loose ends, his words are applicable to the designers of the TVA. For them the goal was to bring the abrupt forms of modern engineering design into continuity with the natural landscape and then to develop a connection among the built forms themselves, making of the whole a new nature.

As I experienced the Watts Bar reservation as a child, the cohesiveness of the TVA landscapes began with the roads. "The road goes ever on and on," sings

Bilbo Baggins, and of things manmade, the road is the one that most literally connects distant parts of the landscape. The TVA designers took care to bring their roads into continuity with the immediate landscape as well, choreographing a tableau of built structures unfolding before the moving automobile. The structures themselves are marked by a similar relationship. This continuity can be literal and physical, as in the increasingly streamlined skins of turbine gantries that Barry Katz describes in "Ideology and Engineering in the Tennessee Valley" (Chapter 4), in which he explores the Authority's industrial and product design. It can also be idiomatic, as seen in the design of building elements conceived so that each belongs to the whole.[12]

Two examples may suggest the thoroughness of the TVA Architect's Office in creating a seamless architectural idiom. One is the application of concrete panels to the roofs of the powerhouses in the awareness that these roofs would be prominent visual elements as seen from above. While serving to protect the roofing material from ultraviolet radiation, the formal purpose of the concrete panels is to complete the visible form—to leave no element undesigned. The second is a typical navigation light at a lock entrance, in which the location of the lighting mast and the ladder used to replace the bulb also become the delicate and graceful termination of the massive concrete wall of the lock. The ladder on the lighting mast, oriented to reinforce the prow-shaped form of the wall as it meets the river's current, ends in a radial return matching the semicircular ends of the guardrail. The same descending curve is seen in the down-turned profile of the lower ladder rungs set into the concrete wall below. Together, these elements form a common language.

Words and Pictures

In addition to the three-dimensional elements of landscape, building, and details, the Authority also mustered two-dimensional design in the service of its persuasive program. In "TVA Graphics: A Language of Power" (Chapter 5), Steven Heller illuminates the commercial modernism present in American graphic design that informed the graphic work of the TVA; in "Almost Fully Modern: The TVA's Visual Art Campaign" (Chapter 6), Todd Smith focuses on a single representative mural at Daniel Boone Dam, tracing the interplay of progressive and traditional elements in the Authority's visual rendition of its story of technological and social progress. Here, as in the TVA's housing program, progressive ideology meets popular effectiveness in a well-tempered compromise.

The landscapes, buildings, details, graphic elements, and murals of the TVA form a unified ensemble, a completeness in the classical sense, in which nothing may be added or taken away without diminishing the whole. The comprehensiveness of this vision is perhaps as important as any of its explicit messages in asserting the value of the TVA's unprecedented transformation of a region. In the work of the TVA's first decade, design *is* persuasion.

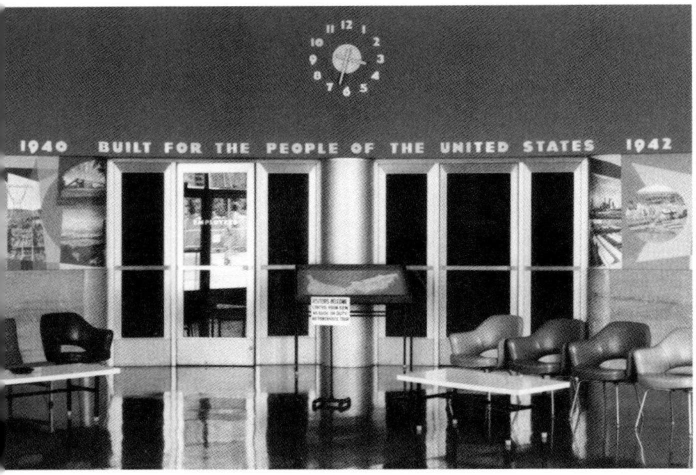

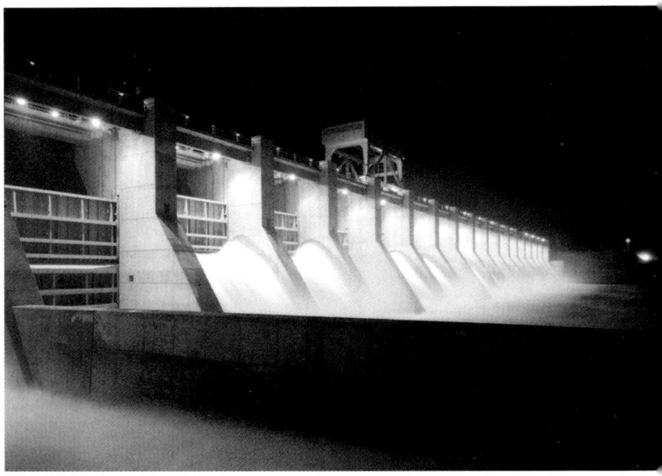

LEFT TVA visitor center of Cherokee Dam, showing the Built for the People of the United States motto, with the dates of construction, 1986

RIGHT Chickamauga Dam, spillway at night, 1940

But Nobody's Perfect

Of course, not everyone was convinced. Certainly Mr. Chet and his five sons and five daughters were not. The intricate weave of people's lives in the landscape does not readily admit comprehensive visions or earthly utopias. Resentment of the TVA's reengineering of the region lingers there. But just as certain are the benefits to the region, rich in new ways of intertwining our lives with the land.

Richard Barnes's photographs deepen this account of the TVA in many ways. Those that appear as chapter illustrations provide the first widely published color images of the original TVA work, otherwise known only in black-and-white photographs that, beautiful as they are, cannot convey the insightful color palettes that shape the experience of the TVA facilities. But perhaps more important are the images that form Barnes's photo essay (Chapter 3). These pictures bring to light the poignant disruptions that the TVA has made in a regional landscape—disruptions that can never be wholly mended. At the same time, they portray the everyday pleasures of the new landscape.

Jennifer Bloomer's closing essay, "Watauga" (Chapter 7), draws together the pleasures and sorrows of our nation's most ambitious planning effort in the terms that matter: those of the lives of people living through and in the designed landscape. As architects and other designers contemplate our role in the world, in its political, economic, and social life, the work of the TVA offers lessons, both encouraging and cautionary, for the persuasive power of design.

Notes

1. Jack Neely, "Clash of the Titans," Tennessee Valley Authority, http://www.tva.gov/heritage/titans/index.htm.

2. "From the New Deal to a New Century: A Short History of TVA," Tennessee Valley Authority, http://www.tva.gov/abouttva/history.htm.

3. Tennessee Valley Authority Act, U.S. Code, vol. 16, sec. 831 (1933).

4. "From the New Deal to a New Century."

5. "TVA at a Glance" (TVA fact sheet), Tennessee Valley Authority, http://www.tva.gov/abouttva/index.htm.

6. Alberta and Carson Brewer, *Valley So Wild: A Folk History* (Knoxville: East Tennessee Historical Society, 1975), 239–44.

7. David H. Steinberg, *And to Think It Only Cost a Nickel!: the Development of Public Transportation in the Chattanooga Area,* (Chattanooga: privately published, 1975), 41.

8. *Wilson* (Tennessee Valley Authority, 1996).

9. Terry Johnson, TVA News Bureau, in conversation with author, October 2002.

10. Christine Macy provides the following account: During Le Corbusier's 1946 tour of the United States, his first stop was New York City, where he met with Albert Einstein and Henry Kaiser.

> My second visit was to Knoxville to see Mr. Lilienthal, the Director-General of the Tennessee Valley Authority [and] the guiding spirit of that harmonious plan, sponsored by President Roosevelt, which built the dams on the Tennessee River and the new towns, rescued American agriculture, and gave it new life.

He was particularly interested in seeing the TVA's use of concrete and its experiments with town planning in Norris and Fontana Village. He discussed both with Lilienthal. Le Corbusier reported,

> Our conversation was a friendly one indeed, for my golden rule speaks of harmony, and harmony is the aim of all Mr. Lilienthal's work. His face lit up at the delightful thought of establishing a reign of harmony... by undertaking the most gigantic works and coordinating the most immense projects: water, motive power, fertilizers, agriculture, transport, industry.... The end result: a territory as large as France snatched from the grip of erosion, which, with a terrifying speed, was laying waste wide stretches of arable land. Now, victorious life was regaining possession of the salvaged land, performing upon it one of the greatest syntheses of modern organization.

Le Corbusier, *Le Modulor* (Paris, 1947).

11. Henry James, *Literary Criticism: French Writers, Other European Writers, the Prefaces to the New York Edition* (New York: Literary Classics of the United States, Inc., 1984), 1041.

12. Edward Said defines "authority" in a way particularly apt to the TVA's design work:

> Every sort of writing establishes explicit and implicit rules of pertinence for itself: certain things are admissible, certain others not. I call these rules of pertinence *authority*—both in the sense of explicit law and guiding force (what we usually mean by the term) and in the sense of that implicit power to generate another word that will *belong* to the writing as a whole.

Edward Said, *Beginnings: Intention and Method* (Baltimore: Johns Hopkins University Press, 1975), 16.

The Architect's Office of the Tennessee Valley Authority

CHRISTINE MACY

When the Tennessee Valley Authority's first dams were opened to the public, they drew hundreds of thousands of people who came to see an extraordinary achievement in the remote back hills of Tennessee. Although the TVA dams were not the earliest, biggest, or most spectacular dams of the twentieth century, they captured the imagination of everyone who saw them. In an artificial landscape of extraordinary elegance and power, they communicated the promise of social and economic renewal. They were glimpses of utopia. Even before the buildings and structures began to rise in the Tennessee Valley, merely the promise of things to come had journalist Lorena Hickok describing her 1934 visit as "a promised land, bathed in golden sunlight... rising out of the grey shadows of want and squalor and wretchedness down here in the Tennessee Valley these days."[1]

The scope of the project was vast, eventually extending across seven states and encompassing the entire watershed of the river. It involved eleven main river dams and numerous tributary dams, public power generation and distribution, resettlement of long-established residents, model towns, construction camps, experimental farms, parklands on reservoirs, a freeway, and much more.

In the TVA, design, and particularly architectural design, played a central role in the public's perception of its success. And the success of the young agency was by no means certain, in spite of having the full weight of presidential authority behind it—President Franklin Roosevelt saw it as the flagship project of his New Deal. It may have been even more embattled for that reason: as evidence of creeping socialism, as un-American, as a dangerous assault on the idea that electricity and other utilities should be left to market forces. We might say that in its early years, from 1933 to 1936, the TVA was more of an "architecture of public relations" than an agency able to deliver any concrete benefits. Director David

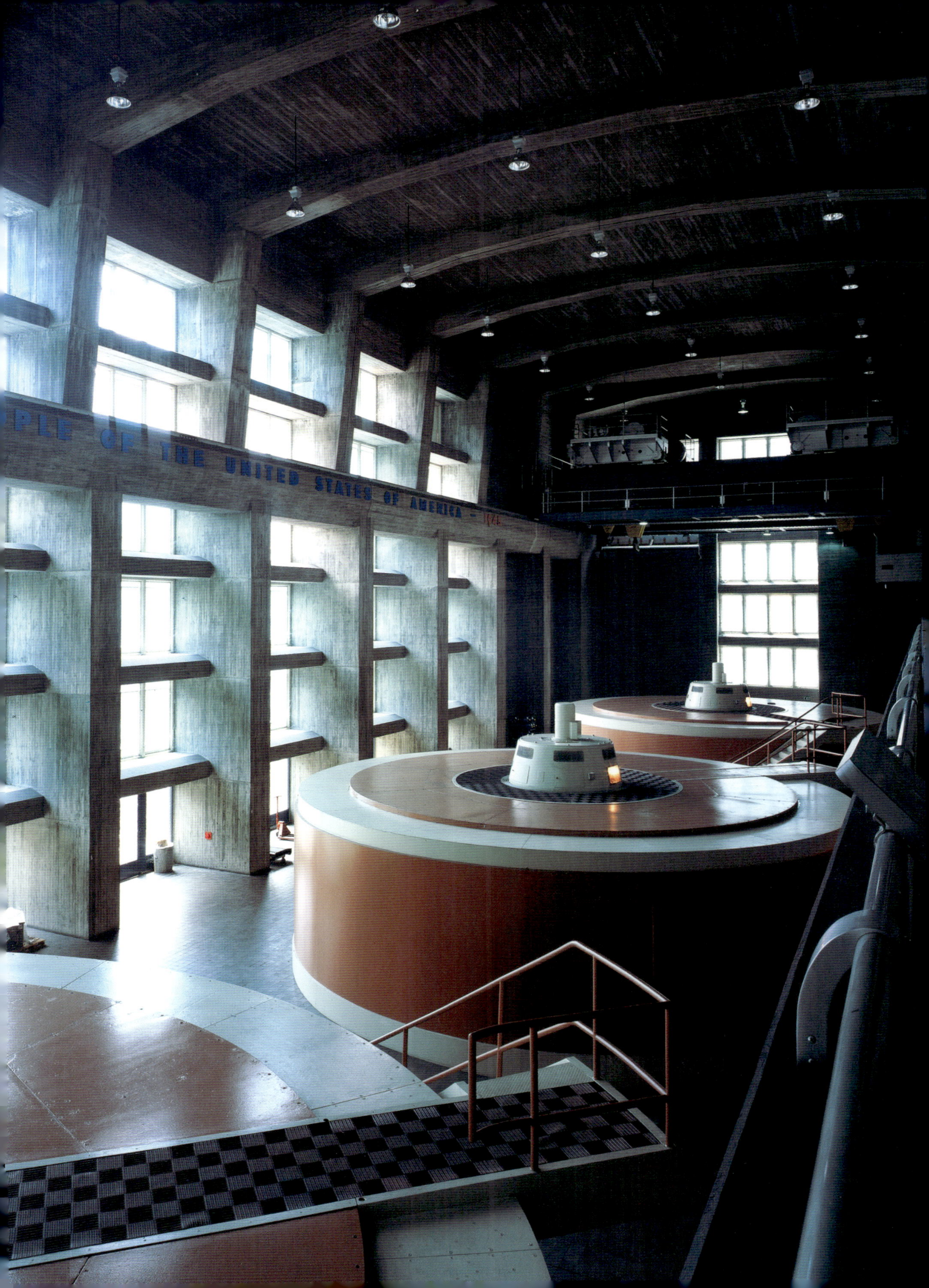
PLE OF THE UNITED STATES OF AMERICA

OVERLEAF Interior of Fontana Dam powerhouse, 2005

Lilienthal, for example, succeeded "in giving the TVA power program a substantial image when, in reality, it was no more than a Potemkin village."[2] Similarly, fellow director Arthur E. Morgan, who was responsible for the engineering works, recognized the strategic role that design would play in selling the TVA to the public when he gave to the TVA architects an unusual degree of responsibility for designing the look of what was essentially an engineering project.

If this project were to usher in a new age, its look had to be modern. The TVA had some of the most forward-thinking young architects of the era. If the chief of them, Roland Wank, remains little known today, it is because the TVA's policy was to stress teamwork and shy away from recognizing individual contributions. Yet the design work spoke for itself. Historian Lewis Mumford writing in the *New Yorker* called them "breathtaking... as close to perfection as our age has come."[3] Writer Frederick Gutheim observed: "From the conception of the scheme to its final execution you feel that each decision has been made in the light of the fact that the public would come, look, and judge by what it saw."[4] And architectural historian and critic Talbot Hamlin observed that "the designers have somehow, through subtle design and human planning, set human beings as the center of the whole scheme."[5]

The design of the TVA holds an important lesson for architects and planners today. Its architects eagerly embraced the larger implications of their designs for social renewal, and they seized the opportunity to create a new world in the image of a better place. Its sophistication is as startling today as its clarity of purpose—a grand design project that recognized the complex interdependence among people, place, nature, technology, region, and nation and won the hearts of millions in the period between 1933 and 1939.

Why Look at the TVA Architect's Office?

When the TVA was first established, its architectural activities were seen as a subset of its town and regional planning. Under the initiative of Wank and his team of modernist architects, they became powerful instruments for promoting the Authority and winning public support for its projects. The TVA was, in fact, an early platform for the development of modern architecture in the United States. Established barely a year after Alfred Barr, Henry-Russell Hitchcock, and Philip Johnson opened their exhibit on modern architecture at the Museum of Modern Art (MoMA) in New York in 1932, the Authority drew young talent from across the country, who leapt at the opportunity to put their own visions into practice. The TVA architects included all types of idealistic and progressively minded individuals: Americans trained in the Beaux-Arts tradition and European émigrés who brought with them a sense that social transformation was somehow aligned to modernist aesthetics.[6] They came from design offices and public agencies in New York, Philadelphia, and the Midwest, from private practice, industry, and academic settings. Although they differed in their aesthetic sensibilities, they all shared a social vision, a commitment to industrialization, an attraction to modern materials, and a sense of mission.

The TVA extended equally deep fingers into the most progressive town-planning circles in the country, recruiting faculty from Ivy League schools, activists from the Regional Planning Association of America and the American Institute of Planners, and planners from private practice. The list of architects and planners who served as consultants and advisors to the Authority is broad, including such luminaries as Albert Kahn, Gordon Kaufmann, Eliel Saarinen, and Benton MacKaye.[7]

Given its contradictory and even paradoxical character, the TVA's process of architectural design decision-making is itself a study in the persuasive representation of ideas. It was a large hierarchical government agency but one created under the aegis of "collective cooperation." The TVA also was a nimble organization that was able to build its designs by "force account," moving its expert workforce from one dam to the next without having to tender work out for competitive bids. And so the TVA's young architects and planners, who were creating visions of a new world, could see them take shape very rapidly and at an unprecedented scale. Beginning with Norris Dam and the site of its town, its freeway, and its reservoir parklands, one project soon followed another—main river dams, remote hill-country dams, high-head dams, dams in cities, and dams flung across several states.

The sensation must have been heady. We know, from archival records and people's recollections, that there were plenty of personal tensions regarding the contradictions of the agency—between its goals of public welfare and collective undertaking and the possibilities it offered for enhancing professional reputations and consolidating power in the hands of a few individuals.

The Man with a Modernist Mission—Roland Wank

We enter this story through the person of Roland Anthony Wank (1898–1970), a key figure in TVA architecture. Praised as an "architectural genius" and derided as a "cocktail-glass holder,"[8] Wank is an enigmatic figure with few historical studies devoted to him.[9] The chief architect responsible for the visual appearance of all TVA projects from 1933 until his departure eleven years later, Wank went on to work with Albert Kahn Associates in Detroit and eventually returned to become a partner with his former employers at Fellheimer and Wagner in New York, which he later restructured under his own name as Wank Adams Slavin Associates (WASA). From 1946 to 1947, he served as an architectural consultant to the United Nations Headquarters Commission. He continued to serve as consulting architect to the TVA and other federal agencies for decades, until his death in 1970.

The formative moment in Wank's architectural education did not likely occur during his studies in his native Budapest, at the Academy of Fine Arts, which he attended from 1916 to 1918, or the Royal Technical University, where he studied

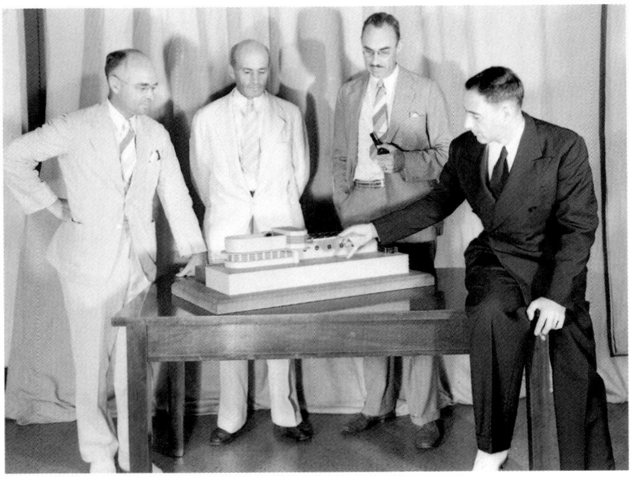

Roland A. Wank, in dark suit, with other members of the TVA design team, 1939

from 1918 to 1919, but rather during his time at the Technical University of Brno, just established in 1919, the year he began his studies there. A hotbed for ideas related to the "new" architecture, particularly with respect to cubism, functionalism, and nationalism, the school operated within the political context of Czechoslovakia's First Republic and Brno's progressive municipal administration. Wank resided in Brno from 1919 to 1921, during which time the Bauhaus was established in Weimar, Germany, and the VKhUTEMAS in Moscow, Russia, both alternative schools of architecture that looked to industry as a model for design and argued for the transformative social potential of modern design. This was also a time for the explosive proliferation of new journals, newspaper editorials, and manifestoes about the new architecture and the role it could play in the new nations created at the end of the First World War.

The juncture of a new school in a new nation was attractive enough to entice Wank to leave his native city and language to continue his studies in this exciting setting—still in the shadow of the Austro-Hungarian empire but recast in the mold of an emerging world. In this context, Wank was exposed to the idea that modern architecture could express a new and democratic society—not only rhetorically, as a break with the historicism of a failed empire, but instrumentally, promising, through social engineering, to actually bring about modernity in the form of social housing and new industrial infrastructure. This vision, enthusiastically endorsed by Wank's generation of young architects from Weimar to Vienna to Moscow, figured prominently in the atmosphere of this school in the capital of industrial Moravia, an eastern region of Czechoslovakia.

The year Wank began his studies in Brno was also the year Walter Gropius reorganized several schools into the Bauhaus, an institution dedicated to modern architecture. The Bauhaus was only a short distance away from the new school in

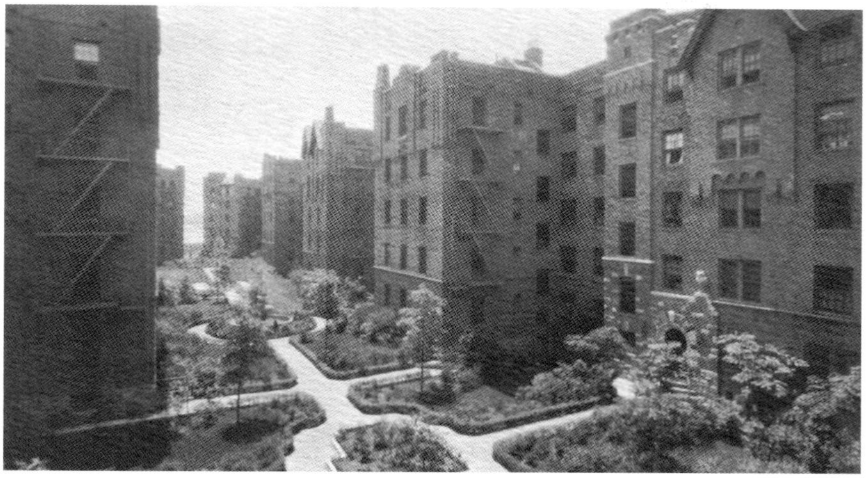

Amalgamated Housing Corporation's first project in the Arts and Crafts style, the Bronx, New York, 1927. Springsteen and Goldhammer, architects.

Brno, uniting Czechoslovakia and Germany linguistically, culturally, and intellectually. Barbara Miller Lane sums up the hopes of this era:

> Throughout Europe, "radical" architects came to share with other intellectuals the belief that the Great War spelled the end of an outworn system of values, and [the new architecture] which they created was consciously intended to express their violent rejection of the past. . . . The new architecture achieved its success in Germany primarily through government patronage. The Bauhaus, the architectural school which Gropius set up in Weimar in 1919, was the first product of this patronage; a few years later the radical architects received as their largest commissions the great new mass-housing projects built in many major German cities. The new style came to be identified with the liberal and left-wing municipal governments which constructed these housing developments.[10]

After World War I, radical architects throughout Europe came to share a belief that the turn to industry was a methodological and aesthetic exemplar that could lead to a modern world that lay just beyond the horizon. They also acknowledged housing as the proper focus for architectural efforts if one was to bring about a new society. What was new was the application of the techniques of industry to housing.

Wank was one of the young architects who fervently believed in the possibilities for this new architecture and who helped give it shape during these years. From 1921 to 1922, he worked in an engineering and construction firm designing and building factories, workers' housing, utilities, harbors, and bridges in central and southern Europe. He then returned to Budapest and entered a partnership, designing

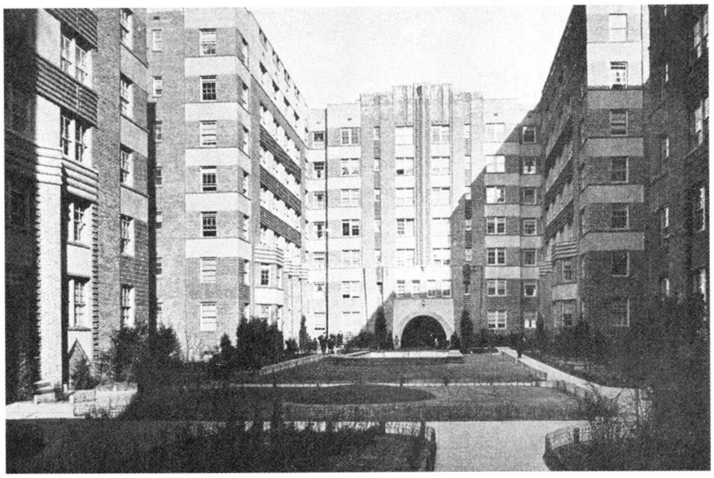

The modernist Amalgamated Dwellings, Grand Street, Lower East Side, New York, New York, 1929. Springsteen and Goldhammer, architect, with Roland A. Wank, project architect.

mills, industrial houses, apartment houses, and residences until 1924 when, growing frustrated with the financial instabilities brought on by currency devaluation, he decided at the age of twenty-six to emigrate to the United States.[11]

Wank worked on a number of projects after arriving in the United States that revealed the interests formed at Brno. He joined Fellheimer and Wagner in 1927. During the late twenties he briefly worked with Springsteen & Goldhammer for the design of the Consumer's Cooperative Association housing (1929) and the Amalgamated Dwellings on Grand Street (1929). The latter was commissioned by the Amalgamated Housing Corporation, a cooperative society established by a garment-workers union, which had built its first cooperative housing project in the Bronx in 1927.

The project was a resounding success, marrying modernist aesthetics to a socially progressive program of cooperative housing. It was awarded an American Institute of Architects (AIA) New York Chapter Gold Medal in 1930, and Wank was reaffirmed in his vision of modern architecture's role in social reform. He soon returned to Fellheimer and Wagner to work on two transportation infrastructure projects, well-matched to his interest in industrial aesthetics: a railway station (1932) in Hamilton, Ontario, and the magnificent Union Station (1929–33) in Cincinnati, Ohio, for which he was project architect, in collaboration with principal design consultant, Paul Cret. The Union Station earned an AIA Gold Medal, this time for Fellheimer and Wagner. In 1933, Wank was recruited by the TVA.

Land Planning and Housing at the TVA

Immediately upon the TVA's establishment in 1933, President Roosevelt appointed the engineer and educator Arthur Morgan as chairman of the new authority, largely because of his pioneering work on flood-control dams in the populated

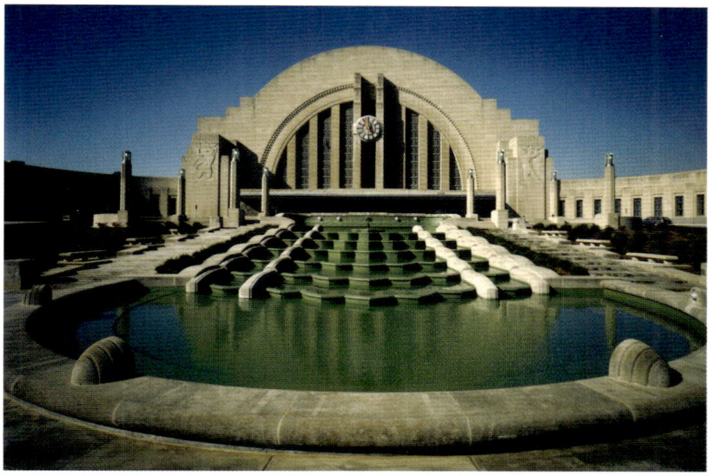

Union Terminal, Cincinnati, Ohio, 1930. Fellheimer and Wagner, architect, with Roland A. Wank, project architect.

Ohio River Valley. Morgan in turn identified two codirectors: the agriculturalist Harcourt Morgan, a Canadian expatriate who had lived in the Tennessee region for many years, and the young lawyer and public-power advocate Lilienthal, a protégé of the progressives Felix Frankfurter and Robert La Follette. Although Arthur Morgan was the chairman of the TVA board, his particular focus was its engineering and planning works. Wank was one of the early hires, joining the TVA in August 1933, two months after the board of directors met for the first time. He was recruited by Earle Sumner Draper, director of the Land Planning and Housing Division, who was responsible for assembling a team of planners and architects to work on the new town of Norris.[12]

The center of TVA operations was the Sprankle Building, a six-story office block in downtown Knoxville. Between the ground-floor entrance, filled with hundreds of job-seekers, and the fourth-floor offices of the board of directors were the offices of the TVA's planners and architects, on the third floor, with Draper's planning team in one office, J. W. Bradner working on Norris Freeway next door, and Wank's architectural designers across the hall.[13] Planning and architectural work was under the supervision of Draper, a professionally trained city planner and landscape architect from Massachusetts, who had worked with John Nolen, perhaps the best-known planner of Draper's day.[14] During his tenure at Nolen's office, Draper moved to the South to supervise one of Nolen's projects. He decided to stay, setting up his own office in Charlotte, North Carolina, in 1917. He rapidly built a reputation, designing over a hundred mill towns in the Carolinas and Georgia, his projects lauded for their civic amenities, sensitive siting, and parks.[15] Morgan chose Draper over better-known planners such as Lewis Mumford or Clarence Stein because of this experience, saying, "I think [Draper is] the kind of man who knows the South, has lived in the South, who can understand local conditions and won't be dominated by a clique [with] preconceived... notions of what has to be done down there."[16]

As chief of the TVA's Land Planning and Housing Division, Draper hired planners, landscape architects, and architects to work on the layout of Norris. All architectural work in the Authority ran through his division because, as he said, "we had the best personnel to handle it."[17] In addition to Wank, Draper brought in Tracy Augur and Carroll Towne for town planning, the Knoxville architect Charles Barber, Louis Grandgent for housing design, and Robert Cerney and Mel Dill for site planning. Eliel Saarinen was also retained as a consultant for town and regional planning on an advisory basis.

The pace of the work was intense, running nonstop day and night. Draper's operation was divided into sections: one for planning the town and its utilities, another for planning the housing ("We had, I think, thirty different types of houses to place on the sites."), another group for siting the housing, and another for carrying on the construction of the town, utilities, and the houses. "And I'll tell you," he said, "that moved very fast."[18]

It was also a tight-knit group, with a sense of mission and idealism that manifested itself in both the planning and architectural work. One of the most visionary planners was Benton MacKaye, the cofounder of the Regional Planning Association, whom Draper hired in 1934 to write a comprehensive plan for the Tennessee Valley region.[19] Draper resigned himself to MacKaye's focus on general goals and frameworks at the expense of specific plans or proposals:

> Ben[ton] was given an office upstairs; about once a week he would come down to a staff meeting with fresh diagrams showing the flows of waters, men and goods in a region, pep the others up with fresh imagination and then disappear upstairs again.[20]

Yet among the work force, the younger planners were drawn to the fifty-five-year-old MacKaye because of his reputation, his progressive ideals, and the national connections he had established through the Regional Planning Association, and they met frequently with him—often in the evenings or for weekend trips—to discuss these broader visionary issues. This group, which adopted the name "Philosopher's Club," debated the region's future and discussed policies beyond the TVA's agenda.[21] They saw the valley's natural resources as its most precious commodity and criticized what they saw as the exploitation of these resources for economic development as shortsighted and ultimately counterproductive. According to the park planner Bob Howes, who kept in touch with MacKaye after his departure from the TVA,

> MacKaye's *tour de force* during his Knoxville years was his influence on other people and ideas. In the office or the field, MacKaye was available to any

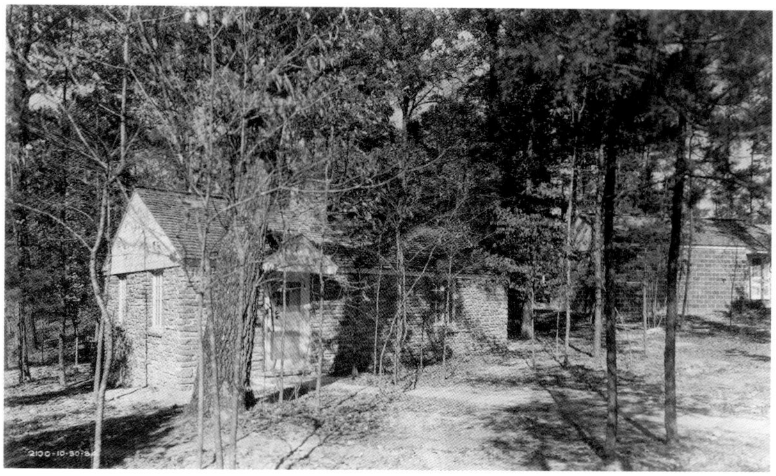

A house in Norris, 1933–36

of us who elected to drop by for an exchange of ideas, comment, or opinion—for a pow-wow, as Benton used to say. In such pow-wows, Benton left his imprint on TVA's pioneering work in land classification, forestry, erosion control, recreation, town planning and transportation.[22]

In his planning for the town of Norris, Draper insisted that houses fit the environment so they would not differ from the surrounding communities.[23] He coordinated the research and outreach efforts that were necessary to ensure that the designs "fit into" local ways of life.[24] He followed garden-city ideals, separating pedestrian paths from vehicular roads and incorporating numerous public amenities, as he had done in his industrial town plans of the 1920s. He also appointed a team (Dill and Howes) to work on planning the parklands that would be developed on the margins of the rising reservoirs.[25] Fifty years later, still proud of Norris, he declared that "the siting of the houses on the lots [in Norris] is the best of any development I have ever seen."[26] For Draper, good town planning married livable communities with natural settings.

> I am not in touch with the present generation of landscape architects but I know that the older ones were aware and gave full consideration to ecological and environmental conditions. It was so much a part of our approach to landscape problems...that we did not feel it necessary to give it special status. Whenever I examined the topo[graphic maps] for subdivisions, I always looked out for special areas suitable for parks and recreational areas and noted such features as woods, specimen trees, wet areas, etc. It was a consistent policy to avoid heavy grading or upsetting native flora. You have seen Norris which is a good example of such an approach....this has always

been part of the landscape approach and . . . ecology has developed nothing new in our profession![27]

Draper's goals for Norris Town were very much in tune with those of Arthur Morgan. Morgan was more than an innovative engineer, he was a social reformer influenced by his Quaker faith and the utopian socialist ideas of nineteenth-century progressives like Edward Bellamy, whose novel *Looking Backward* (1888) spawned many hundreds of Bellamy Clubs across the country at the turn of the century. These clubs promoted Bellamy's utopian ideal of a perfectly planned society in which economic competition and conflict are replaced by expert planning and cooperation. Morgan saw the design of the town at Norris as an opportunity to create such a model planned community from scratch, a community that would represent everything the TVA could be in terms of renewing a region and re-empowering a disenfranchised and downtrodden people. Morgan wanted the scientific planning and management he exercised in his flood control and land-reclamation projects to extend to the design of human settlements.[28] In this he had an ally in Roosevelt, who expected "all forms of human concerns" to be touched by the TVA.

While eager to experiment with many aspects of the new community, Morgan stressed in his public speeches that the innovations applied at Norris were pragmatic and "common sense." He affirmed the TVA's opposition to Soviet-style social and economic planning and insisted that there was no five- or ten-year plan for the valley, claiming an American lineage for his communal ideals, a sort of home-grown and cooperative socialism that was reinforced in the folksy, home-spun appearance of the houses in Norris.[29]

He was actively involved in bringing expert planning and cooperation to "his" town of Norris. For example, he mandated a single dispensary to avoid commercial competition and one house of worship to prevent conflicts of faith that might fracture the young community's solidarity. Bringing his experience as an educator (as the former head of Antioch College) to his new appointment at the TVA, Morgan stressed the importance of education for both children and adults—in fact, the children's school in Norris was renowned for its innovative programming.

For Morgan, women's work was to be structured quite differently from that of men. He shied away from any hint of collective enterprise in traditional women's roles—childcare, cooking, cleaning, and other domestic work.[30] In rejecting any idea of collective households, Morgan followed in the footsteps of fellow Quaker Herbert Hoover, who had advocated the single-family house as the "natural" model for American domestic life and thus the only one deserving of governmental mortgage assistance and tax relief.[31]

For men, however, Norris offered unique access to community activities. Morgan was eager to experiment with collective farming and cooperative industry for the men employed in dam construction, and he actively promoted inventive or experimental cooperative enterprises, such as demonstration farms that used new fertilizers and contour farming techniques espoused by TVA agronomists, porcelain pottery manufactures that employed a local source of kaolin clay, and a dairy that experimented with new refrigeration techniques. Adult education focused on the kind of practical skills that would contribute to effective home maintenance or small farming: carpentry, blacksmithing, automobile repair, and operation of small-farm machinery.[32] While the dam was still under construction, these activities were meant to fill the hours remaining to workers after a five-and-a-half-hour day at the job site. Once the dam was completed, these small industries were to become the basis for an independent economy. Looking back on the marriage of community infrastructure and town planning fifty years after the completion of Norris, Draper reflected:

> I must have been born and practiced fifty years too soon. . . . In the '20s when I was laying out new industrial towns in the South, "they" called it *industrial autocracy* (to be deplored); in the '30s when I was laying out and building TVA towns, they called it *socialism;* and in the '40s during the war, when I was trying to get suburban towns under FHA Title VI—war housing—erected, the field TVA directors and the mortgage bankers held back claiming it was too risky. Now, [developers trying to do the same thing] are "the toast of the town."[33]

Wank's Modern Architecture Encounters Draper's Community Plan

The possibility of designing workers' housing in this new experimental community was tremendously exciting to Wank. That enthusiasm is evident in an interview he gave four months after he was hired:

> I could never become interested in designing grand homes for the few who can afford them. I always wanted to feel that my work was of some public interest and that it will add to the comfort and enjoyment of many. We have a great many architects who are doing an excellent job of housing the well-to-do individuals [yet] the unsolved problem, large enough to appeal to all lovers of good fights, lies the other way. Private enterprise has made a sorry mess of housing but it is becoming increasingly a matter of public concern, and there are indications that it may become a field of semi-government activity. . . . It seems that only well-organized mass production will bring the "model" house within the means of the "forgotten man," and mass production can only exist when balanced by mass purchasing power.[34]

Wank was taken with the idea that he was designing for the society of the future. In a passionate fourteen-page letter to Morgan, Wank declares, "The social revolution is going on at an accelerated pace. If we do not lead it somebody else will." He envisioned a socialist transformation of the United States in which the TVA would be the first step toward establishing a nationwide "army" to produce all kinds of goods, offer better wages, and abolish profiteering. All that was lacking was good leadership, so the TVA needed to be "ready for their duty and anticipate events by having the work all laid out when the call sounds"—an avant-garde, he implies, in the military as well as the cultural sense, in the struggle against capitalism: "The battle lines will be drawn soon anyway and the power and glory will not go to those who are tardy in joining the ranks. Men all over the country are aching for leadership." He laments the lack of unified purpose in the architectural staff working on Norris, resulting in "backtracking, wasting of time and effort; [and] the most important, the possibility of half-decisions, affecting the value of our entire work." A solution, he suggests, is to begin a number of designs for cooperative enterprises—collective farms with all the necessary infrastructure of schools, community houses, recreation fields, and hospitals. Then Wank expands at some length on the thorny issue of housing, which to him posed an insoluble problem under the existing system. What is needed, he writes, is total government control of prefabricated housing production—not just in Norris, but nationwide. And because this is a de facto army, bunkhouses will be good enough for the year or so it will take to get such a large-scale housing program underway. Wank signs off the letter reassuring Morgan that "quite a few members of the force are thinking along the same lines—an illustration of the fact that advanced thought is more prevalent than generally suspected."[35] There is no record of Morgan's response, but considering that his social utopianism was in the mold of Bellamy, one might imagine a shrinking retreat from the militant Marxism of Wank's letter.

Draper did not appreciate Wank raising his ideas directly with the board. He viewed it as a circumvention of the proper lines of communication and repeatedly reminded Wank that it was unacceptable:

> It was Wank's nature to assert himself...he had very strong ideas about things....farfetched ideas sometimes—yes he had them, but I was glad to have his originality and his presentation of ideas whether we accepted them or not. By and large, we did. We didn't in the case of Norris; I don't think he ever felt happy about the housing in Norris for that reason. But I think it's true of geniuses in any field that they go haywire (if I might use the common phrase) at times, with respect to [their] ideas and they have to be reined in a little bit. And that didn't affect his activities or his ability in the slightest. He'd come right back for a next time.[36]

It was perhaps inevitable that Wank would compare the houses of Norris—laid out along garden-city lines—to the garden *Siedlungen* (literally, "settlements") built on the peripheries of Vienna, Berlin, Rotterdam, and Brussels in the 1920s.[37]

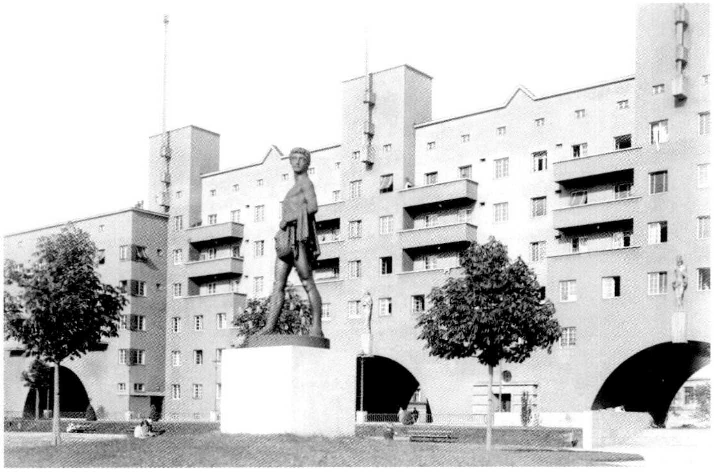

Karl-Marx-Hof, settlement housing project, Vienna, Austria, ca. 1931. J. Bittner, Hubert Gessner, A. Stockl, architects.

The difference, of course, is that the European examples of these new communities employed a modernist imagery that was polemically aligned to the new, emerging mass society. The American version, by contrast, employed vernacular traditions to ease the tensions of modernization.[38] Speaking to the *Knoxville News-Sentinel* in 1933, Wank revealed his impatience with this situation:

> [Moldings, cornices, and ornaments] are not justified until we have attained utopia. Then, when we are all comfortably fixed, we shall sit down and wonder about the comparative merits of artistic detail. In the meantime, these ornaments express a desire to imitate what the financially able could afford in the more leisurely days of the past, and in that sense they are untruthful and needless when the problem under consideration calls for the utmost efficiency in disposing of available funds.... Until mass production puts the materials of the twentieth century—steel, glass, cork, rubber, resin compositions, etc.—within our reach, we are confined to much the same materials as our forefathers used, and they have already made a pretty thorough job of exploring all the possibilities of lumber, brick, stone, and mortar. The only task left for us in this direction is stripping off all unnecessary detail.[39]

Regarding the dispensability of ornaments, Wank recalled Adolf Loos's assertion that the evolution of culture proceeds with the removal of ornament from useful objects.[40] Wank also seemed to have adopted Mumford's position that modern architects should use materials appropriate to the electric, or "neotechnic," age, such as new alloys, synthetic resins, or aluminum.[41]

Wank did not limit his "advanced" ideas to housing design but applied them equally to the engineering work. In time, his energies were almost exclusively

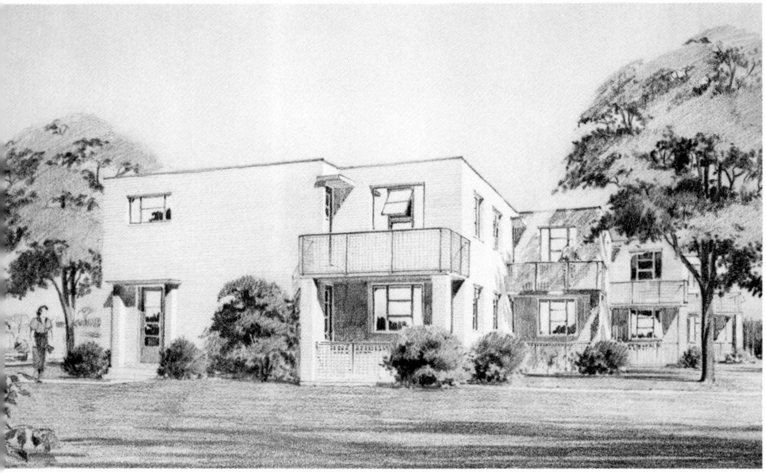

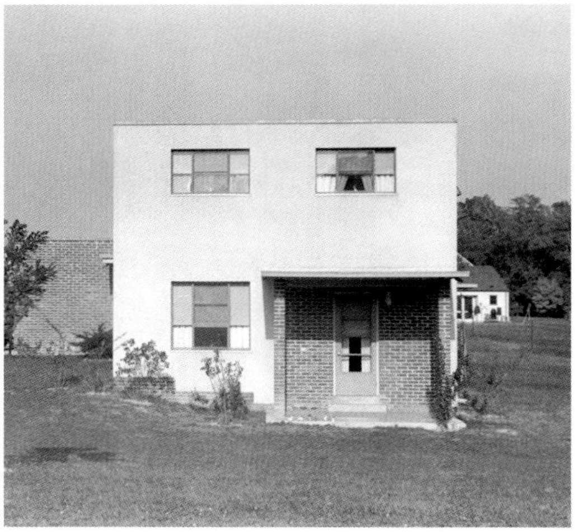

LEFT AND RIGHT Modernist housing in Resettlement Administration's green-belt town of Greenhills, Ohio, 1936–39. Roland Wank, chief architect.

OPPOSITE Prefabricated house design, 1940. Seth Harrison Gurnee, illustrator.

directed toward the architectural treatment of the powerhouses and dams. In 1934, he was replaced as chief architect of Norris by Charles Barber and became, in the words of Draper, a "floating architect in charge of special projects." Yet throughout his years at the TVA, Wank never lost his interest in housing. In the fall of 1935, a month after his architectural consulting team was transferred to the Engineering Design Division, Wank requested permission from Draper to be assigned to the Resettlement Administration for two thirds of his time, presumably so he could better implement his ideas for (modernist) housing.[42] Throughout his time with the TVA, he remained true to form as a modernist architect, believing, as Mumford stated in his curatorial text for the International Style show at the MoMA, "the construction of housing is the principle architectural task for all civilization. The greatest success of modern architecture is in its contribution to the problem of housing."[43]

With the advance of the war in the first years of the 1940s, Wank was able to pursue his interest in industrial housing production, as all of the TVA's housing efforts had moved to prefabrication—to facilitate the ease of relocation of workers' dwellings from one dam site to the next. Prefabricated houses were used to create the overnight city at Oak Ridge, Tennessee, built for the atomic program, and were sold to England for emergency relief under the Lend-Lease program. In awarding him a fellowship years later, the AIA cited his designs for

> six types of prefabricated unit housing, of which about 10,000 units were used at various TVA projects and at Oak Ridge. He designed the first prefabricated aluminum shower booths for use at the town of Norris. He worked with the TVA and the Royal British commission on three-dimensional sectional prefabrication of dwellings, libraries, schools and other buildings.[44]

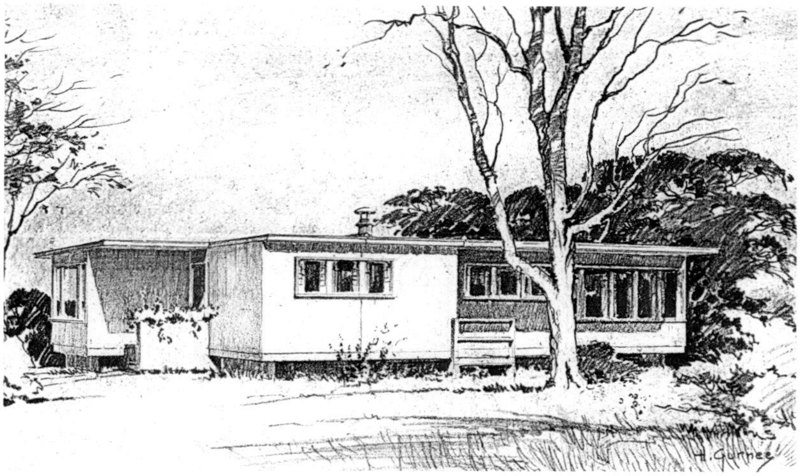

The Architectural Design of the Dams

From his first day on the job, Wank pushed for modernist design in TVA architecture—in its houses, public buildings, and engineering works alike. Although Draper remained firm in his conviction that the new town had to fit into the local culture, resisting Wank's agitation for modernistic designs for the housing, he was happy to raise the young architect's critical comments about the design of Norris Dam with Morgan.[45] The problem, according to Wank, was that the dam had not been considered as a compositional whole. The drawings, completed several years earlier by the Army Corps of Engineers, revealed, like most dams of its day, the employment of unnecessary decorative arches on the downstream face of the dam and a classically inspired language on the powerhouse. Neither element had any relation to the utilitarian structure.

Morgan responded by asking Wank to draw up his suggestions for the dam. Wank recomposed the elements of the downstream face of the dam, pulling the building volumes closer together, studying their proportional relationships, and removing all ornament. He rearranged the spillway so the water overflow would cascade down the steepest face of the dam rather than flow gradually down the adjacent hillside. The sheer wall of the dam was thereby emphasized, and its junction with the adjacent rock hillside was made more visible. The result was a composition sculpted as a whole ensemble, as if from a solid block of concrete.

When Theodore B. Parker, the chief engineer, objected to this stylistic interference, Morgan referred the dispute to an arbiter who was nationally respected by both engineers and architects—Albert Kahn, the designer of Henry Ford's new River Rouge Plant. Kahn decided in favor of Wank's modernist design, and Morgan, in turn, decided that future issues of composition, external appearances, and siting would be sketched by architects before being developed by the engineers.

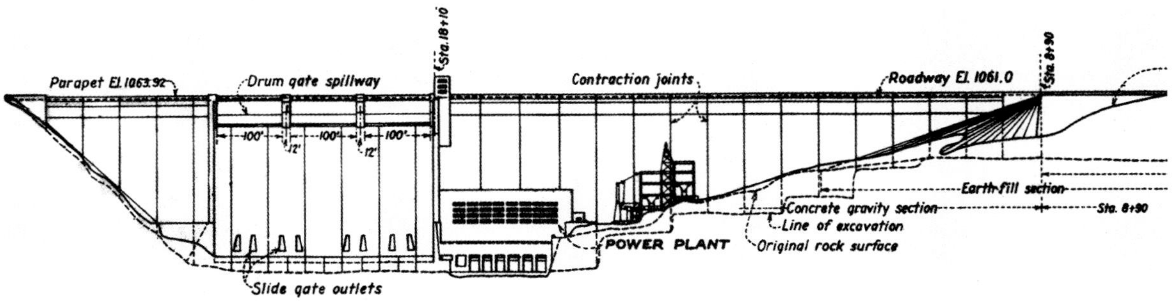

Redesigned downstream elevation, Norris Dam, 1936. From Tennessee Valley Authority, *The Norris Project* (Washington, D.C.: U.S. Government Printing Office, 1940), 72.

Draper recalled that it was this way from the outset because "we had the best personnel," but it is likely that Wank's energetic interference paved the way for an unprecedented approach to the design of large public works—giving their visual appearance and their public image primacy in the design process. The TVA placed importance on the artistic composition of these dams and on the centrality of architectural modernism to the public image of these structures.

In establishing this hierarchy in the design process, Morgan and the other directors recognized the strategic role that design would play in promoting the public profile of the project. Departing from the usual practice in which architects worked under the project engineer and were restricted to decorating and detailing ancillary buildings, Morgan set up an architectural design group answering directly to him and empowered to rearrange the project components, as long as their design did not interfere with its functionality. Headed by Wank, a group of architects was also given primary responsibility for designing the visible details of the project. Wank approached the directors—first Morgan and later Lilienthal—directly with architectural issues he felt strongly about, a practice that irritated his supervisor, Draper, to no end.[46] In short, as architectural critic Reyner Banham suggests, Wank's aggressive response to the original scheme for Norris Dam set a precedent for the primacy of design issues in the project.[47] The engineer George Palo recollects: "When Roland Wank had trouble selling an idea to the TVA engineers, he could and did go around [to] get his ideas approved."[48]

Wank's role as a consulting architect for the design of the dams and supporting structures evolved into a "consulting service" out of the Land Planning and Housing Division by 1934. There, he continuously supplied architectural drawings to the Bureau of Reclamation and to the TVA engineers involved in

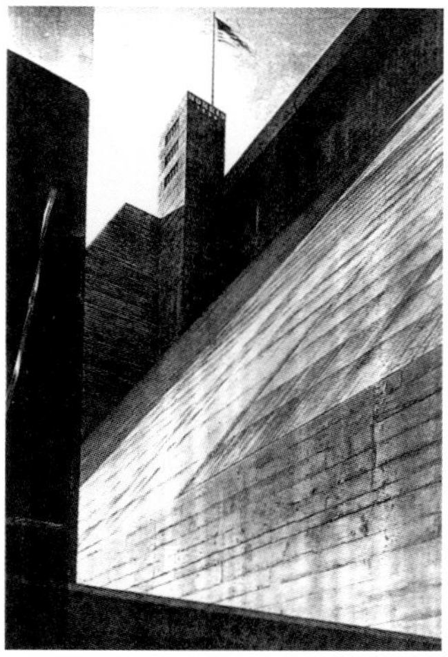

Norris Dam seen from entry to visitor's center, 1936

designs for the dams. Over time, his architectural consulting operation assumed complete responsibility for architectural detailing and interior design in these projects. By 1935, Land Planning and Housing was allocating a considerable sum to cover architectural consulting services for the dams and powerhouses.

That year, Wank described his activities as divided into two major areas: "architectural" investigations into the economics, materials, and management of housing activities carried out by Land Planning and Housing and special architectural design work that required "thorough familiarity with modern design, materials, and decoration and with large-scale engineering construction such as bridges, dams, and powerhouses."[49] He designed demonstration pavilions to promote electricity use and community buildings in Norris, but most of his work was devoted to the architectural design of the dams and their supporting structures and elements—spillways, bridges, and approaches at Norris, Wheeler, and Pickwick; nighttime illumination, air conditioning, and heating; and all interior design for these projects. The design team included the architects Henson, Robert Cerney, Seth Harrison Gurnee, W. G. Monning, two mechanical engineers, and other part-time staff. The architectural engineer Harry B. Tour was the principal liaison in the engineering division.[50] Between 1936 and 1937, with Norris, Wheeler, Pickwick, and Guntersville dams underway, Wank's operation was transferred to the Design Department of the engineering division, leaving only a small design consultancy service remaining in Land Planning and Housing.[51] At this time, the Italian architect Mario Bianculli joined his team.

Once the architectural design team was restructured as a part of the engineering division, the jockeying for ultimate control of design resumed. The dispute centered on the treatment of the powerhouse at Guntersville Dam—whether it was to be gray or yellow brick—but there is little doubt that what was at stake was who had the final control over the appearance of the projects. Once again, the matter was referred to Kahn, who again decided in favor of the architects.[52] A joint committee would oversee each project, under the control of a chief architectural designer, whose responsibility was to draft the initial sketches for the design and then collaborate with the engineers to develop it. Wank filled this role until his departure in 1944, when he was succeeded by his assistant, Bianculli, then later by Rudolf J. Mock and, subsequently, Frederick Roth.[53] According to Tour, the chief design architects "would stay for a few years [and] were probably the most important members of the staff" in the engineering division.[54]

The Visitor's Experience

The circulation of visitors within and through these structures was as important to the architects as the flow of water through the turbines was to the engineers. Wank's design for the crest of Norris Dam reflects this. Draper recalled that a road was planned to go across the dam from the outset—when in 1933 this decision

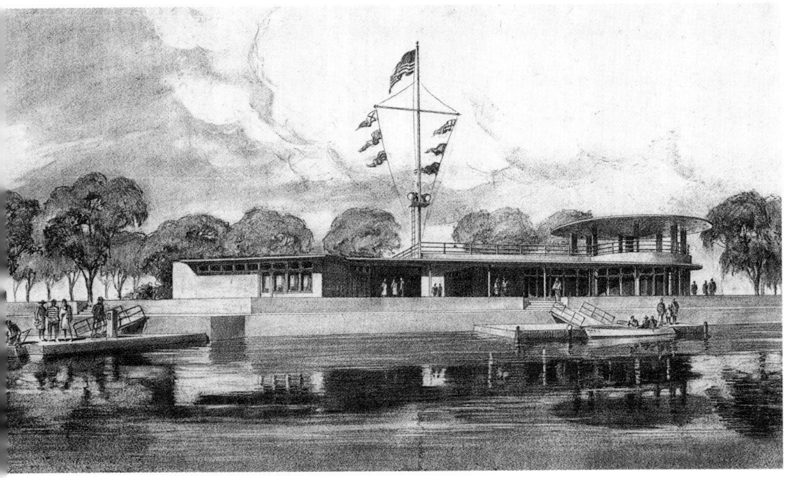

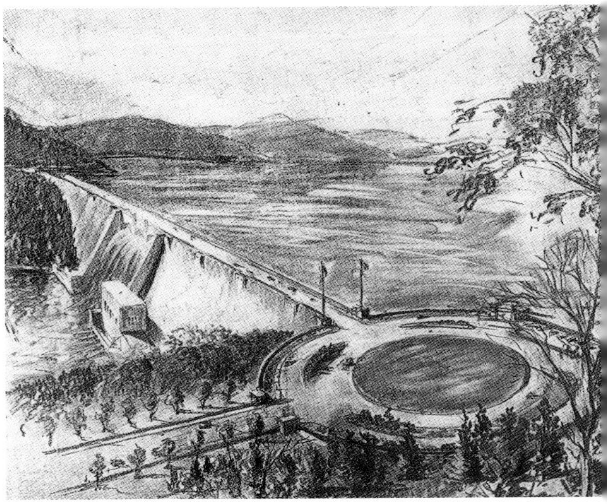

LEFT Proposal for a harbormaster's and concession building, Guntersville Dam, ca. 1945. Seth Harrison Gurnee, illustrator.
RIGHT Sketch of Norris Dam, showing highway over crest and powerhouse below, ca. 1935. Attributed to Roland Wank.

was made is not clear, but Wank did design a series of projecting balconies along the pedestrian promenade that paralleled the road so that visitors could sit right at the precipice of the structure, thrust out over the sheer downstream face of the dam. The experience of the dam was designed to thrill, and this sensation was magnified with careful attention to the nighttime lighting of the complex, with low, glare-free fixtures that softly lit the paths and roadways and highlighted the lines of the massive dam from a distance.

Wank included visitor centers, exhibition pavilions, picnic areas, outlook points, and overlooks at all the TVA's dams—although Norris Dam received the most attention in this regard, perhaps because it was the first project and continued to be augmented throughout the 1930s. At Norris there are carefully designed roundabouts to carry the freeway across the crest, a soda shop and retail store for local crafts, promenades at each abutment of the dam, and even an outdoor dance pavilion with a platform for an orchestra. It seems that Wank fully expected the dam at Norris to become the center of a future city.

In this careful orchestration of the viewer's experience, Wank's conception of civic design parallels that of Viennese architect Otto Wagner, best known for his concept of the *Großstadt*, or metropolis.[55] Gropius expressed it well when he introduced his Bauhaus exhibition of 1923.

> We want to create a clear organic architecture, whose inner logic will be radiant and naked, unencumbered by lying facades and trickeries; we want an architecture adapted to our world of machines, radios, and fast motor cars, an architecture whose function is clearly recognizable in the relation of its forms.[56]

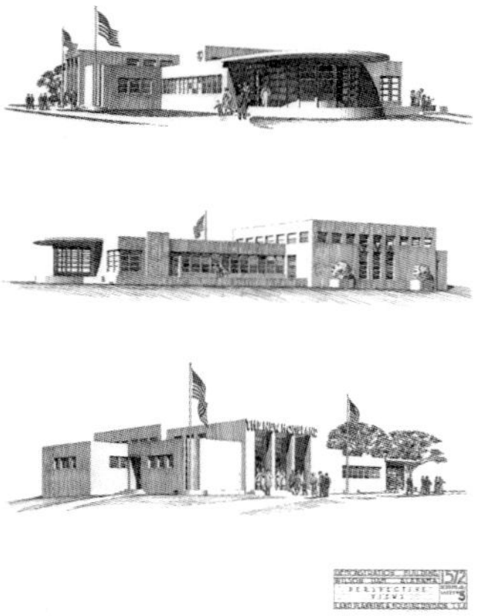

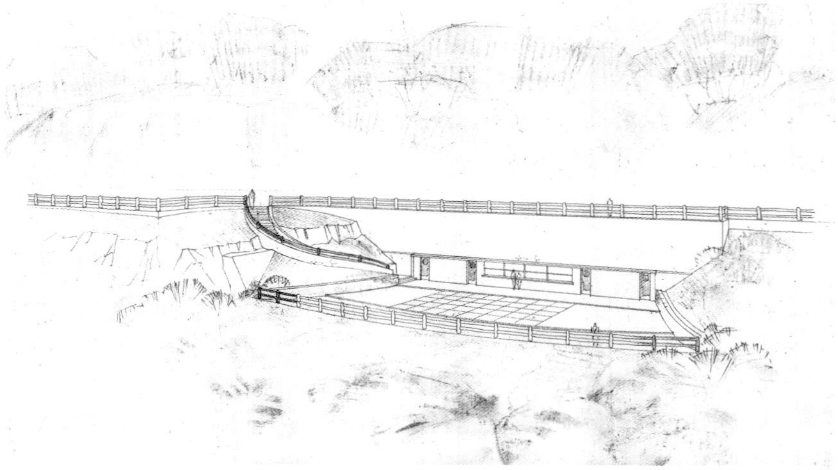

LEFT Demonstration building, Wilson Dam, ca. 1936. Mario Bianculli, illustrator.
RIGHT Proposal for a dance terrace at west abutment, Norris Dam, 1936. Mario Bianculli, illustrator.

The viewer's experience of the TVA dams was carefully orchestrated. In all the TVA projects, visitors circulated through a world of modern architecture, with open-air terraces, white-plastered exteriors, and richly polychromed interiors of tile, stone, and aluminum. They encountered backlit TVA exhibits that extolled the accomplishments of the Authority, and they reclined on upholstered banquettes overlooking dams and powerhouses, locks, and recreational facilities.

The Power of Architecture—The Machinery of Publicity

The early press coverage of TVA architecture focused on Norris Town, discussing its progressive layout, its sensitively designed, vernacular-looking houses full of technical innovations, and its community facilities. From 1933 to 1938, there was little coverage of the dams and virtually no discussion of modern styles being used by the TVA. This was not because of a lack of completed dams. Already by 1936, large numbers of visitors were pouring through Norris, Wheeler, and Wilson dams, and the TVA had massively photographed the dams both during construction and afterward. (Many of the images, by Lewis Hine, Charles Krutch, and other highly skilled TVA photographers were recognized as being extraordinarily beautiful.[57]) The design of the dams was overshadowed by the social agenda of the town of Norris—what people wished to read about at the time, and thus the topic offered to them. Norris Town, as a part of the overall project, was the example par excellence of Roosevelt's New Deal, providing the American people with the perfect antidote to the Depression—employment, community, health, education, and welfare.

A few years later, the focus shifted decisively to the dams. This shift may be attributed to the advent of the Second World War in Europe, an increased

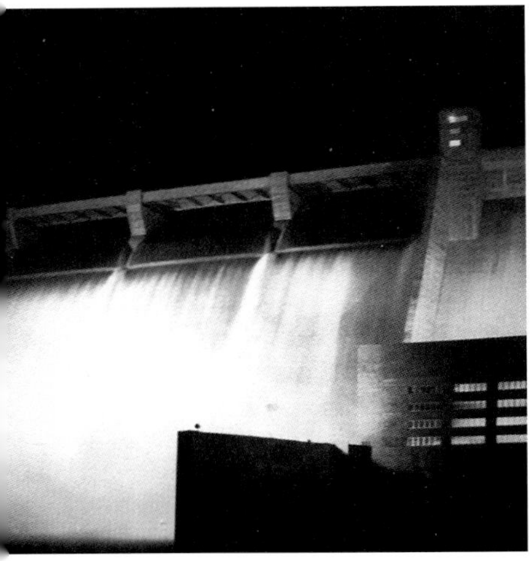

Downstream face of Norris Dam, showing night-lighting effects, ca. 1939

awareness of the importance of power for the nation, or the coverage of a number of major dams out West—from Fort Peck in Missouri to the Grand Coulee in Washington State. In the architectural press, the TVA's dams became more newsworthy than its town planning, once modern design had begun to be mainstreamed in universities, journals, competitions, and architectural commissions. In the United States, this sea change took place between 1938 and 1940, and the success of the TVA dams rode the wave.

Wank actively promoted the TVA's modern design in the architectural press. He was the TVA's principal liaison to architectural journals, competitions, and exhibitions. He worked with editors to frame the coverage and develop story lines; he chose the photographs and wrote the captions, even the articles in many cases. By 1939, the floodgates had broken loose and entire issues of *Architectural Forum* and *Pencil Points* were dedicated to the modern design of the dams and public works of the TVA. The photography is stunning, the imagery modern.[58] The *Magazine of Art* in the following year reinforced the arrival of modernism in architecture and the architectural press. The houses of Norris Town were now dismissed as "too romantic, too historical."[59] By 1941, as the MoMA opened its exhibit on TVA architecture, discussions of the modernist styling of the dams had extended to *Time* magazine, the *New Yorker*, and the *Nation*. The *Magazine of Art*, pleased to have been ahead of the game, even wrote a "TVA Postscript." Most of this coverage describes the dams as having "purely functional" designs or being a "fusion of architecture and engineering." The photographs accompanying the texts, however, belie these statements. What we see is a visual celebration of architectural modernism, with smooth surfaces, asymmetric and dynamic compositions, strong relief of shadow, sun-drenched surfaces, simple lines, and bold masses.[60]

In his review of the TVA show at the MoMA, Mumford asserts that the "largely unconscious" American precedents of grain elevators and coal bins that so inspired early European modernists were now being upstaged by a new American architecture of dams and power stations that showed "conscious aesthetic expression." He cites economist and engineer Stuart Chase's text that was placed at the entrance to exhibit: "A new architecture, bold as the engineering from which it springs, has risen in the valley... Look at it, and be proud that you are an American." Mumford here is wresting modernism from the Europeans. He wants the world to know that, in the TVA, America has produced "modern architecture at its mightiest and its best. The Pharaoh did not do any better."[61] For Mumford, the TVA dams were evidence that American architects had regained their aesthetic standing in the face of European avant-gardes. It did not matter that the principal design architect behind the look of these structures was a socialist-expatriate-Hungarian.

The TVA structures began to be seen as advertisements for American supremacy in political and economic spheres. When the scale of the TVA could be seen for the first time, it became clear that the project was more than just a representation of technological and aesthetic modernity. The British critic Julian Huxley describes the TVA as "an outstanding example of democratic planning...the first large-scale regional planning organization which operated...on the democratic principles of persuasion, consent, and participation."[62] In his review of the TVA in *Pencil Points* the following year, Talbot Hamlin concludes with a meditation on the relationship between design and democracy:

> It is the world's most striking contemporary example that planning—large-scale planning—is possible in a democracy; that no such false efficiency as that of a dictatorship is necessary to produce great national works, conceived and executed for the benefit of all the people. Perhaps one could go further and even say that, under a dictatorship, that controlling atmosphere which creates the humanity and charm of much of TVA would have been impossible. The designers have somehow, through subtle design and human planning, set human beings as the center of the whole scheme... perhaps this matter of democracy goes even deeper than the mere purpose of this enterprise; perhaps it is this ideal of democracy itself, permeating the entire TVA organization, which has made possible within it a type of enthusiastic, sympathetic, understanding cooperation that no other system could produce.[63]

This sentiment, perhaps, is what led Banham to comment more than thirty years later, that, as the child of lefties, he grew up loving the TVA. For throughout the twentieth century, the TVA was to remain the greatest project of modernist architecture, marrying an epic vision of social progress with beautifully realized buildings at a scale unparalleled before or since.

Notes

1. From Lorena Hickok's report of June 6, 1934, to Harry Hopkins about her visit to the Tennessee Valley. Hopkins, director of the Federal Emergency Relief Administration, assigned her to report as an "ordinary citizen" on relief work being carried out through the country. Erwin C. Hargrove and Paul K. Conklin, *TVA: Fifty Years of Grassroots Democracy* (Urbana: University of Illinois Press, 1983), 49. Hickok, here, picked up where Walter Davenport left off in "The Promised Land," *Collier's Magazine* 91 (June 3, 1933): 12–13, 36–38.

2. Steven M. Neuse, *David E. Lilienthal: The Journey of an American Liberal* (Knoxville: University of Tennessee Press, 1996), 83.

3. Lewis Mumford, "The Architecture of Power," *New Yorker*, June 7, 1941, 58.

4. Frederick A. Gutheim, "Tennessee Valley Authority: A New Phase in Architecture," *Magazine of Art* 33 (September 1940): 516–31. Reprinted as n.a., *TVA Architecture, as shown at the Museum of Modern Art* (Knoxville: Tennessee Valley Authory, 1941), 17.

5. Talbot Hamlin, "Architecture of the TVA," *Pencil Points* 20 (November 1939): 722, 731.

6. As architectural historian William Jordy points out, long before Walter Gropius, Mies van der Rohe, or the other Bauhaus émigrés arrived on American shores, TVA architects were at the forefront of modernism in the United States. William H. Jordy, *American Buildings and Their Architects: The Impact of European Modernism in the Mid-twentieth Century* (Garden City, NY: Anchor Press/Doubleday, 1976), 102. Outside of the TVA, the arrival of modern ideas to the United States was evidenced by changes like the 1927 redesign of *Architectural Record* and the focus on modern topics, such as "Modern Railway Passenger Terminals" and "Modern Designers influenced by Modern Materials," of *Architectural Forum* in 1930. That year, George Howe, Buckminster Fuller, Philip Johnson, and Matthew Nowicki founded the journal about modern architecture *T-Square*, which became *Shelter*. Margaret Kentgens-Craig, *The Bauhaus and America, First Contacts 1919–1936* (Cambridge, MA: MIT Press, 2001), 28.

7. Gordon Kaufmann's work on Hoover Dam so impressed the Bureau of Reclamation engineers that he was asked to advise the TVA on Norris and Wheeler dams in 1933. Richard Guy Wilson, "Gordon B. Kaufmann and Modernism," in *Johnson Kaufmann Coate, Partners in the California Style*, ed. Joseph N. Newland (Claremont, CA: Scripps College, 1992), 77.

8. The two characterizations are from Earle S. Draper, Wank's TVA supervisor, and Kay Bianculli, the wife of his co-worker Mario Bianculli. Interview of Earle S. Draper by Mr. Winter, 18, E. S. Draper personal file, TVA Archives, NARA-Southeast Region, Atlanta; Kay Bianculli, interview with the author, 1997.

9. A notable exception is Marian Moffett, "Looking to the Future: The Architecture of Roland Wank," *Arris: Journal of the Southeast Chapter of the Society of Architectural Historians* 1 (1989): 5–17. See also, Jane Karlin Feinberg, "The Architecture of the Tennessee Valley Authority Dams" (unpublished paper, Brown University, January 19, 1973), TVA Library, Knoxville.

10. Barbara Miller Lane, *Architecture and Politics in Germany, 1918–1945* (Cambridge, MA: Harvard University Press, 1968), 4, 41.

11. Moffett, "Looking to the Future: The Architecture of Roland Wank," 5.

12. Draper was one of the first four appointees of the TVA Board at its initial meeting on June 16, 1933.

> We spent six to eight weeks in Washington selecting personnel.... I knew the majority of the planners around the country, and I knew those that could do the job, so that selection was easy. I knew many of the architects. So that we gradually accumulated personnel.

From *Remarks of Earle S. Draper at the Norris, Tennessee 50th Anniversary Homecoming Celebration and Community Development Conference*, 1983, TVA Archives, NARA-Southeast Region, Atlanta.

13. "Opening Night at TVA Central," *Tennessee Valley Authority*, http://www.tva.gov/heritage/central/index.htm (accessed October 21, 2006).

14. Draper was a graduate of the Massachusetts Agricultural College at Amherst, a leading institution in landscape architecture. Upon graduating in 1915, Draper went to work for John Nolen, who

> oriented Draper towards town planning and after several months sent him to Charlotte, North Carolina, as his southern representative with major responsibilities for supervising the development of Myers Park subdivision in Charlotte and the new industrial city of Kingsport, Tennessee.

Kay Haire Huggins, "Town Planning in the New South: the Work of Earle S. Draper, 1915–1933" (conference paper, Citadel Conference, The New South, Charleston, South Carolina, April 20, 1978), 1.

15. Chicopee, Georgia, a mill town named after Chicopee Falls, Massachusetts, was planned as a model community—Draper's design was considered a great success,

contributing to the retention of workers in an industry with high turnover. This was a period of large-scale migration of New England textile industries into the Southeast for cheaper labor and power. Norman T. Newton, *Design on the Land: The Development of Landscape Architecture* (Cambridge, MA: The Belknap Press of Harvard University, 1971), 483.

16. Earle S. Draper interview, 30 December 1969, Oral History Collection, University of Memphis (Tennessee), 31.

17. Interview of Earle S. Draper by Mr. Winter, 19.

18. From *Remarks of Earle S. Draper at the Norris, Tennessee 50th Anniversary Homecoming*.

19. Daniel Schaffer, "Benton MacKaye: The TVA Years," *Planning Perspectives* 5 (1990): 9.

20. Ibid., 19.

21. Members of the Philosopher's Club included Robert M. Howes, G. Donald Hudson, Victor Roterus, Cal Towne, John Ferris, Bernard Frank, and Allen Twichell.

22. Schaffer, "Benton MacKaye," 17–18.

23. Draper interview, 30 December 1969, 18.

24. T. Levron Howard was chief of the research division in Land Planning and Housing, leading a team of sociologists and economists who investigated the social and economic impacts of the TVA dams on communities, populations, labor, housing, and industrial development. The team published their findings in numerous government reports and pamphlets and included Paul Carringer, Paul L. David, Lawrence L. Durisch, R. E. Lowry, Hershal L. Macon, Vernon G. Morrison, C. Hernan Pritchett, Harry M. Satterfield, Charles M. Stephenson, and Margaret Ambrose.

25. Draper considered the design of the land around the reservoirs to be one of the great accomplishments of his division at the TVA. He was also very proud of the Norris Freeway, the first limited-access road in the United States to use the term "free-way." Like the reservoirs, Norris Freeway had large easements to prevent development along its length, and it also forbade billboards, ensuring the "parkway" effect.

26. Earle S. Draper, letter to Kay H. Huggins, November 6, 1978.

27. Earle S. Draper, letter to Norman Newton, August 12, 1974.

28. Arthur E. Morgan's national reputation as an engineer was the result of his innovative schemes for dry earthen dams along the populated Miami River valley in the Ohio River system—the plans offered minimal disruption to agricultural activities while serving to restrain waters during floods.

29. Nancy L. Grant, *TVA and Black Americans: Planning for the Status Quo* (Philadelphia: Temple University Press, 1990), 10.

30. See Dolores Hayden's significant work on the centrality of feminism to early communitarian social planning in the United States. Dolores Hayden, *Seven American Utopias: The Architecture of Communitarian Socialism, 1790–1975* (Cambridge, MA: MIT Press, 1976).

31. While paid employment of women was not ruled out in TVA towns, it was discouraged in this project as in other New Deal resettlement programs. In Greenhills, Ohio, a Resettlement Administration greenbelt town designed by Wank, families in which the mother worked outside the home were denied eligibility for the houses.

32. Walter L. Creese, *TVA's Public Planning: The Vision, the Reality* (Knoxville: University of Tennessee Press, 1990), 259. Other crafts taught at Norris included pewter-pounding, weaving, and leatherwork. Michael J. McDonald and John Muldowny, *TVA and the Dispossessed: The Resettlement of Population in the Norris Dam Area* (Knoxville: University of Tennessee Press, 1982), 233.

33. Earle S. Draper, letter to Sumner Jr. and Lillian Draper, July 26, 1966.

34. John T. Moutoux, "R. A. Wank, TVA Architect, Sees Worker's Housing as Great Challenge of Tennessee Basin's New Deal," *Knoxville News-Sentinel*, December 2, 1933.

35. Letter from Roland A. Wank to Arthur E. Morgan, 4 December 1933, 2, 4, 6, 8, 10, 11, 14. TVA Archives, NARA-Southeast Region, Atlanta.

36. Interview of Earle S. Draper by Mr. Winter, 22, 31.

37. Compare the settlement communities designed by Adolf Loos on the outskirts of Vienna during his tenure as chief architect for the Settlement Office of Vienna (1920–24). Am Heuberg and Vienna West *Siedlungen* were make-work projects employing future residents as builders. Am Heuberg, which became a model for other later projects, consisted of two-story dwellings economically erected with cement-board ceilings and wood siding and small gardening plots for family sustenance in each yard.

38. Christine Macy and Sarah Bonnemaison, *Architecture and Nature: Creating the American*

Landscape (London: Routledge, 2003), 188–92.

39. Moutoux, "R. A. Wank, TVA Architect."

40. Adolf Loos, "Ornament and Crime," in *Programs and Manifestoes on 20th-century Architecture*, ed. Ulrich Conrads, trans. Michael Bullock (Cambridge, MA: MIT Press, 1975), 20.

41. Lewis Mumford, *Technics and Civilization* (New York: Harcourt, Brace and Company, 1934), 229. Aluminum—which Mumford called "the most distinctively neotechnic metal"—required enormous amounts of energy for its production.

42. "Summary of the writer's discussion with Mr. Blandford this morning," letter from Roland A. Wank to Earle S. Draper, September 27, 1935. TVA Archives, NARA-Southeast Region, Atlanta.

43. Lewis Mumford, "Housing," curatorial text for Modern Architecture International Exhibition, 1932, Museum of Modern Art, New York.

44. As stated on the American Institute of Architects citation awarding Roland Wank Fellowship in the AIA, 1951.

45. Interview of Earle S. Draper by Mr. Winter, 29–31. Wank refers to this exchange in a memorandum summarizing his architectural services from 1933 to 1938:

> Design consultation [on Norris] started in the late fall of 1933 when the then chairman [A.E. Morgan] sent to the Division of Land Planning and Housing two preliminary sketches showing the proposed design for Norris Dam and Powerhouse and asked for comments. Without specific appropriation, comments in the form of sketches and criticism were transmitted during the balance of the fiscal year. "

"Architectural Consultancy on Dams and Powerhouses," letter from Roland A. Wank to Carroll A. Towne, August 10, 1938, TVA Archives, NARA-Southeast Region, Atlanta.

46. Draper interview, 30 December 1969, 18.

47. Reyner Banham, "Tennessee Valley Authority: The Engineering of Utopia," *Casabella* 542–43 (January–February 1988): 74.

48. George Palo, "The Building of the TVA," 1977–78, George P. Palo Papers, MS-2674, box 6, folder 28, Special Collections Library, University of Tennessee, Knoxville.

49. "Reclassification of R. A. Wank," letter from Roland A. Wank to M. J. Rand, 6 August 1935, TVA Archives, NARA-Southeast Region, Atlanta.

50. Harry B. Tour "quite often opposed Wank's design concepts." Earle S. Draper, letter to Sumner Jr., February 23, 1971.

51. On August 15, 1936, the Land Planning Division handed over detailed construction drawings for the powerhouses and dams to the Dams Design Division, retaining only the "architectural supervision of the work in a consulting capacity." Design work was already advanced on Norris, Wheeler, Pickwick, and Guntersville. Earle S. Draper, *Annual Report of the Land Planning and Housing Division for the Fiscal Year Ended June 30, 1937* (Knoxville: Tennessee Valley Authority, 1937), 8.

52. Mario Bianculli interview, 25 March 1970, Oral History Collection, University of Memphis, 36–37.

53. Mario Bianculli came to the United States in 1924 on a fellowship after completing his studies in architecture and engineering at the University of Naples. He designed power plants, housing, and hospitals before being hired by the TVA in January 1936. During his tenure at the TVA, he became Wank's principal assistant, ultimately replacing him as chief architect in 1944.

Rudolf Mock was a German émigré who had worked with Frank Lloyd Wright at Taliesen and with Louis Kahn and Oscar Stonorov on the Arts Centre competition of 1938, sponsored by the MoMA and *Architectural Forum*. He joined the TVA's Design Department in 1948 as chief architect. His work was published in Elizabeth Mock, *If You Want to Build a House* (New York: MoMA, 1946); Thomas Creighton, Frank Lopez, Charles Magruder, and George Sanderson, eds., *Homes: Small, Medium, Large* (New York: Reinhold, 1947).

Frederick Roth was a native of Milwaukee, Wisconsin, who had studied architecture at Minnesota and MIT before joining the TVA in 1946. After his departure in 1952, he moved to Philadelphia to the office of his MIT classmate Vincent Kling.

54. Harry B. Tour interview, cited in Creese, *TVA's Public Planning*, 172.

55. As principal architect for the modernization of Vienna's urban railway and inner-city canals, Wagner reconciled the technical demands of modernization with a contemporary visual language that included prefabricated components. Between 1892 and 1898, Wagner designed over thirty urban railway stations, bridges, tunnels, and viaducts, along with floodgates, locks, and other structures to regulate the Danube Canal and the Vienna River. It would likely be difficult to overstate the impact of Wagner's work on the young Wank, fascinated both with modernity and with technically demanding projects.

56. Walter Gropius, "Die Mitarbeit des Künstlers in Wirtschaft und

Technik" [The Collaboration of the Artist in Economy and Technology], cited in Lane, *Architecture and Politics in Germany*, 67.

57. Reviews of the 1941 MoMA show: "U.S. Monument," *Time* 37, no.19 (May 12, 1941): 46; Mumford, "The Architecture of Power," 58.

58. "TVA Program," a pictorial essay, *Architectural Forum* 71, no. 7 (August 1939): 73–114; Hamlin, "Architecture of the TVA"; Kenneth Reid, "Design in TVA Structures," *Pencil Points* 20 (November 1939): 691–744.

59. Gutheim, "Tennessee Valley Authority." Thirty years later, architectural modernism was so dominant that Gutheim, writing Wank's obituary, admired that he "did not allow himself to be diverted from the main job, the construction of dams and engineering works, to such trifles as the design of the town of Norris and its housing." Frederick A. Gutheim, "Roland Wank: 1898–1970," *Architectural Forum* 133, no. 2 (September 1970): 59. Wank, of course, was not only initially hired to design houses in Norris, but he continued to consider both house design and town planning as important, if not central, parts of his work.

60. Wayne Gard, "The Farmer's Rebellion," *the Nation*, September 7, 1932. Benton MacKaye, "Challenge of Muscle Shoals," *the Nation*, April 19, 1933, 445–46; K. H. Amend, "Government Builds Houses," *The Nation*, December 6, 1933, 644–45; Stuart Chase, "TVA: The New Deal's Best Asset," *Nation*, June 3–24, 1936, 702–5, 738–41, 775–77, 804–5; Douglas Haskell, "Architecture of the TVA," *The Nation*, May 17, 1941, 592–93; "TVA Postscript," *Magazine of Art* 34 (May 1941): 260–63.

61. Mumford, "The Architecture of Power," 58.

62. Julian Huxley, "TVA: an Achievement of Democratic Planning," special issue of *Architectural Review* 93, no. 558 (June 1943): 139–66. Published in book form as *TVA—Adventure in Planning* (Cheam, England: The Architectural Press, 1943), 139.

63. Hamlin, "Architecture of the TVA," 731.

Redefining Landscape

JANE WOLFF

You might say of the Tennessee Valley Authority that the landscape was both its medium and its message. In the space of a dozen years, the agency completely remade the physical, social, and technological terrain of a seven-state region roughly the size of Ohio. Its immediate impact was huge, but the ripple effects of its efforts were even greater: the TVA radically redefined contemporary ideas about what a landscape is and what it can mean.

The agency's work began with the design of infrastructure along the Tennessee River and its tributaries, and the water control system became the catalyst for a wide range of forward-looking and unconventional physical and social programs. One of the first agencies chartered by the New Deal, the TVA was conceived as an activist undertaking. It reached into every corner of the Tennessee Valley, and it transformed the notion of what a landscape comprised. It developed a series of new programs, and it reinvented the Tennessee Valley as a collection of idealized scenes—rustic, pastoral, and monumental.

The places that the TVA created argued for its agenda. Meant to look as if they had always existed, they declared that progress was not at odds with tradition, that old images and new technologies could be integrated, and that history and geography were continuous and coherent. The agency's terms for the landscape were so internally consistent and so convincing that its rhetoric was barely questioned. But seen from half a century away, the TVA's work seems deeply ironic: its message that the future could grow out of the past was achieved by the destruction and reinvention of much of what had actually existed.

The Context of the Project

The 1930s was a period of enormous public interest in the American landscape, and the TVA was only one of a number of federal agencies that played an active

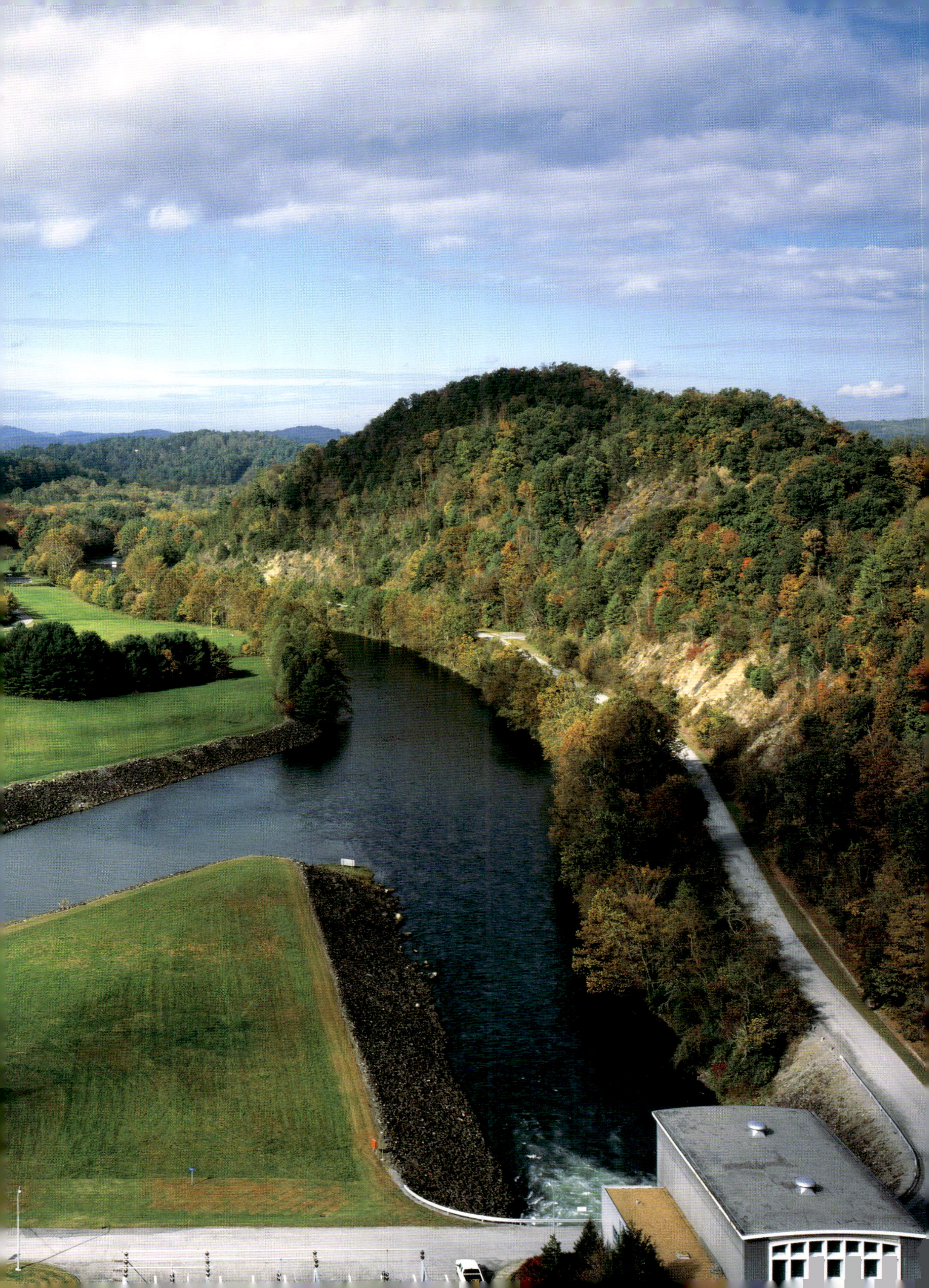

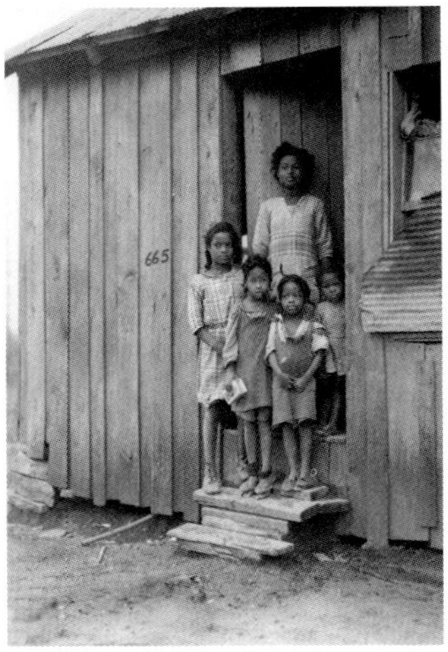

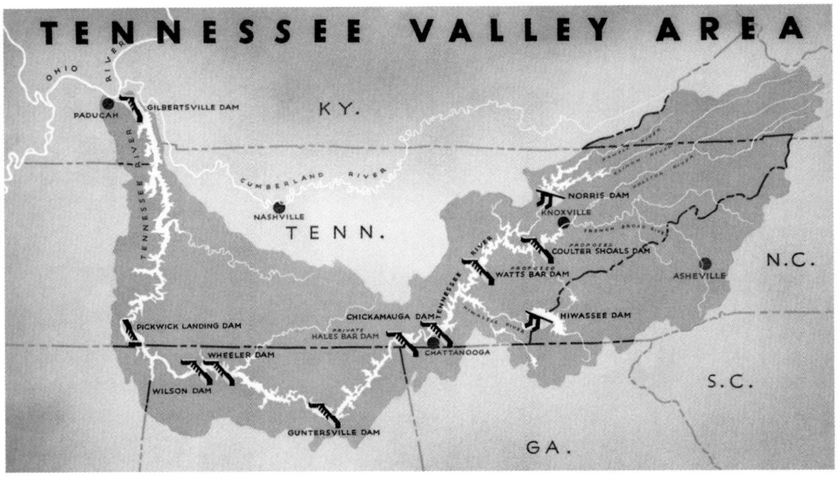

OVERLEAF The downstream view from Watuaga Dam, 2004

LEFT The TVA documented conditions in the Tennessee Valley as a precursor to design work.

RIGHT Map of the Tennessee River system

role in the documentation and transformation of the country's social and physical geography. The American Guide series, Films of Merit, and the work of Roy Stryker's photographers at the Farm Security Administration created a comprehensive picture of the American scene: they described the landscape as a compendium of inhabitants, practices, artifacts, and places. The Civilian Conservation Corps, the Works Progress Administration, the Resettlement Administration and its descendent, the Farm Security Administration, and the Rural Electrification Administration were all involved in both describing the country and reinventing it.

The federal agencies' double agenda—recording what existed and projecting what could be—produced a powerful argument for change. Their documentary work—in numerous reports as well as books such as the WPA guides published for popular consumption—composed an image of the landscape that was simultaneously idiosyncratic, impoverished, untidy, and heroic. It made the particular monumental.[1] As a counterpoint to noble and tragic images of the then present, the TVA offered an equally monumental image of the future: it described the Tennessee Valley of the early 1930s as a lost Eden and proposed to rebuild the region as a new Utopia.

E Pluribus Unum

The TVA's idea of the landscape was radical from its earliest conception: It defined a series of disparate and far-flung places as a *region*. The agency's purview was determined not by political boundaries or local identities but by a geomorphological condition—the watershed of the Tennessee River and its tributaries. Before the TVA, physical geography had never been used to specify the powers and limits of an American agency. Even the national parks, which were instituted to protect special geographic features, had politically determined boundaries: for example, Yellowstone's edge was determined not by the geomorphology of the geysers it was intended to protect but by the Wyoming state line.

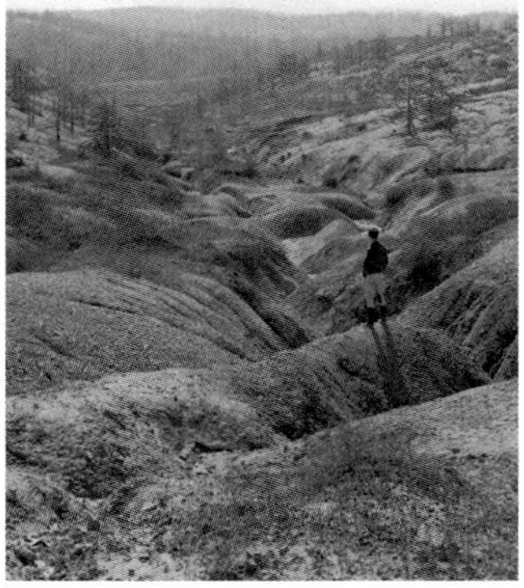

Example of severe erosion of overworked land

The Tennessee River lay at the literal and metaphorical center of all of the TVA's work. It was used as a legal mechanism, an electrical generator, a planning tool, and a rhetorical figure. The agency's mandate rested on the federal government's jurisdiction over interstate waterways. Its objectives, strictly interpreted, were to improve navigation and stop flooding along the Tennessee and its tributaries. The river began to create a popular image for the agency well before any of its work was realized. In a 1933 article for *Fortune*, written just after the TVA's inception, James Agee opens with a description of the Tennessee River:

> The Tennessee River system begins on the worn magnificent crests of the southern Appalachians, among the earth's older mountains, and the Tennessee River shapes its valley into the form of a boomerang, bowing it to its sweep through seven states. Near Knoxville the streams still fresh from the mountains are linked and thence the master stream spreads the valley most richly southward, swims past Chattanooga and bends down into Alabama to roar like blown smoke through the floodgates of Wilson Dam, to slide becalmed along the crop-cleansed fields of Shiloh, to march due north across the high diminished plains of Tennessee and through Kentucky spreading marshes toward the valley's end where finally, at the toes of Paducah, in one wide glassy golden swarm the water stoops forward and continuously dies into the Ohio.[2]

Agee's description juxtaposes two powerful themes: the continuity of the river and the diversity of the 44,000 square miles it traversed. The linear course of the Tennessee and its tributaries was approximately 900 miles, and the landscapes within the TVA's jurisdiction ranged from the steep, remote valleys of the Great Smoky Mountains to the flat, open regions of western Tennessee and northern Alabama. Different areas of the valley were extremely isolated from each other: roads were poor and telephone and electrical service limited, and many places were difficult to reach. The valley's population was as heterogeneous as its terrain. Agee's account of the region describes cities and farms, blacks and whites, rich and poor, mountaineers, miners, lumber camps, mills—two million people without much in common.[3]

What the people did share, besides a drainage basin, was a history of poverty and bad land management—something the TVA used as a rallying point. In 1933, the Tennessee Valley was the poorest part of the United States and the least likely to have electrical service. The average precipitation in the drainage basin was fifty inches a year, and some places received as much as sixty-three inches. With its forests cleared to create farmland and its soil exposed to wind and rain,

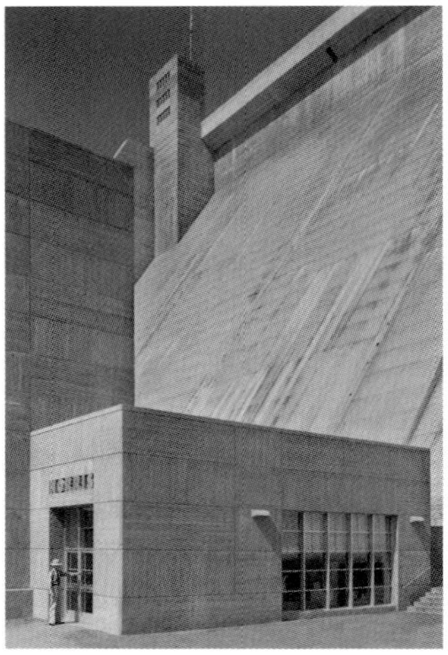

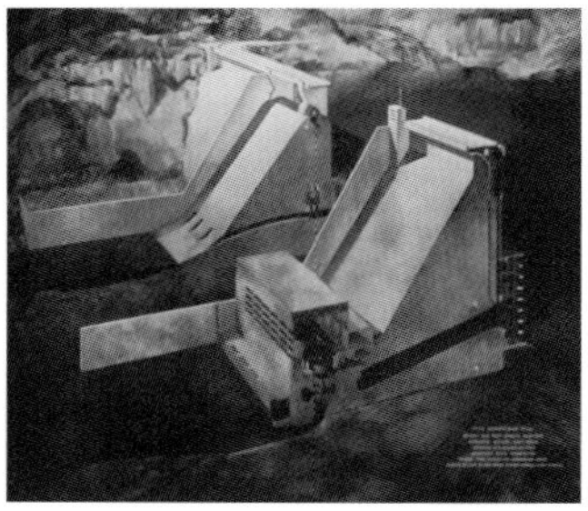

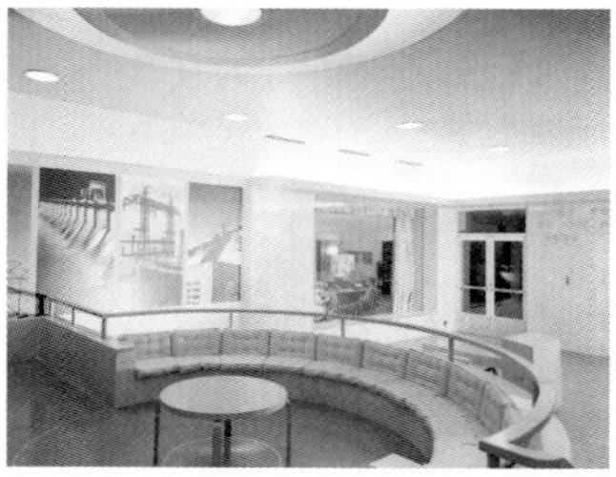

TOP Norris Dam, 1938

CENTER Mural at Norris Dam visitor center, showing section through the dam, 1939

BOTTOM Visitor center at Watts Bar Dam, 1943

the valley was washing away, water quality was disastrous, and flooding caused enormous damage almost every year.

Methods and Means

One of the TVA's first projects was to present the valley's situation in a way that would mobilize public support for an agenda of change. The agency's version of the region's story had the clarity, structure, and consistent language of a fable. English biologist and science popularizer Julian Huxley summarized the TVA's position in his 1940s chronicle of the agency's work, *TVA: Adventure in Planning*. In a segment titled "The Soil Wasted and Regenerated," Huxley writes:

> These bare hills were at one time—and that within the memory of men still alive—rich, virgin forests. Lumbermen came and as long as the forest lasted, there was work in the woods and sawmills for many men. When the timber was gone, they had to turn to agriculture for a living.... When the timber was first cleared the hillside produced rich yields of corn. Soon, however, the method of row cropping allowed the topsoil to be washed away...because there seemed to be so much land, it became general practice to abandon fields ruined by corn and clear new ones.... Overgrazing followed, and now the land is completely useless.[4]

The written descriptions were accompanied by equally vivid images—hillsides wasted by erosion, old men driving donkey carts, toothless women on windswept porches, decrepit cabins sitting below washed-out gullies.

Having described the landscape's fall, the TVA proposed a strategy hinged on the Tennessee River for its redemption. An artifact of the sublime and ancient forces of geology, the river had the capacity to generate the powerful and futuristic forces of electricity. The agency's mandate to control flooding and improve navigation demanded the building of dams: the dams had the ability to generate power, and power was a means to remake the valley in the image of progress. The river was reconceived as a heroic piece of infrastructure, a monument to new technologies. It became the armature that prompted, unified, and supported the landscape's phoenixlike revival.

The design of the dams insisted that their character be an essential part of the valley: they were tied to their surroundings by scale, image, material, and movement. Norris Dam, for instance, had the mass, solidity, and vastness of a geological feature, and its lack of traditional ornament made it seem even larger.

The dams' monumental quality was amplified in photographs. Subsidiary spaces and components were documented for publication at angles that emphasized their size, and many of the TVA's most iconic images—the gantry crane at Kentucky Dam, the entry to the powerhouse at Norris, and the turbines at Pickwick—include a person dwarfed by the scale of the machinery.

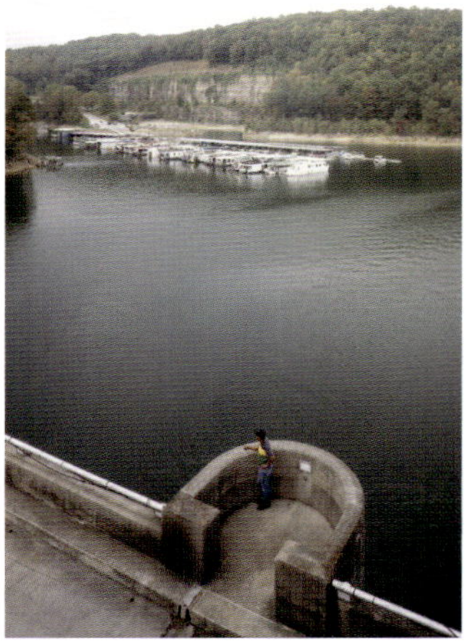

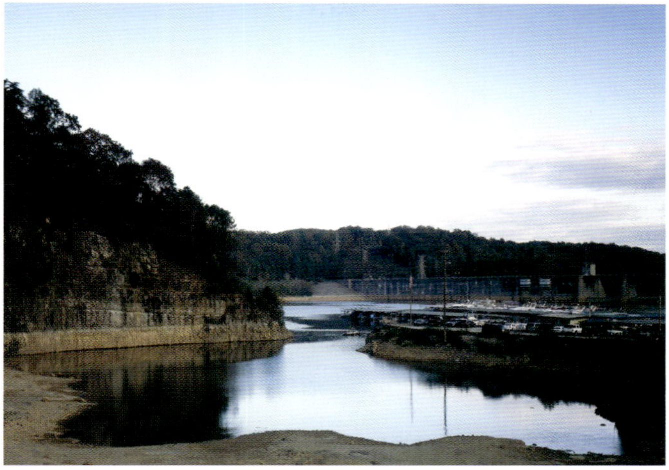

LEFT The quarry seen from the roadway of Norris Dam, 2005

RIGHT Quarry at Norris Dam, 2006

The abstract, high-modern imagery of the dams did not preclude the use of didactic, narrative images and words in interior spaces. Each powerhouse was inscribed with "Built for the People of the United States," and the agency's projects were understood as public attractions—the people in the photographs were stand-ins for the thousands who actually came to see the dams. The mural on the wall of the reception room at Norris explained to visitors how water flowed in and through the turbines to generate power. At Chickamauga Dam, the mezzanine overlooking the turbines was painted with a giant map of the Tennessee Valley and the dams along the rivers. Each dam had a visitor center that recapitulated the TVA's story of the valley. Inside, these pavilions displayed photographs, murals, models, and text that described the agency's territory, purview, and projects. Picture windows and balconies framed views of the dams and their surroundings, which had been reconfigured so subtly and so gracefully that the pouring of hundreds of thousands of tons of concrete did not seem to have entailed any disruption. Foreign visitors were heard to comment on the fortunate location of so many dams in such beautiful parks.

Each dam was connected to its visitor center and the landscape beyond by a road designed to reveal and accentuate this relationship. The roads created sequences of images—dam from afar, wooded hillsides, visitor center, dam from nearby, view of dam and visitor center from middle distance, for instance—and juxtaposed related scenes. From the road at Norris, which ran along the top of the dam, it was possible to see the face of the quarry that had produced the aggregate for the concrete in the structure. The two sheer faces—the rock wall and the dam—were the raw and cooked version of the same phenomenon: ancient surface had produced the rock that comprised the futuristic one. Geology had made electricity.

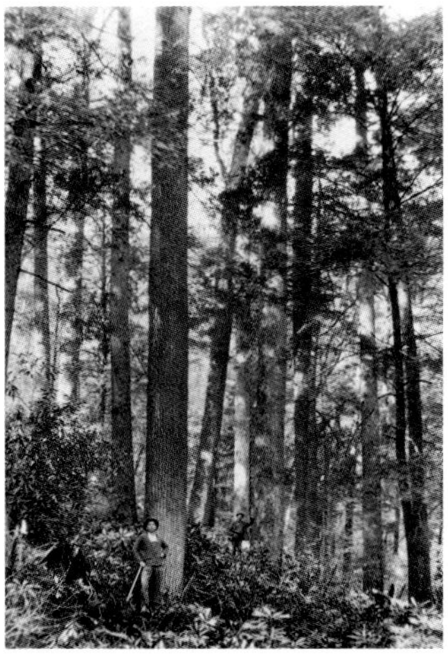

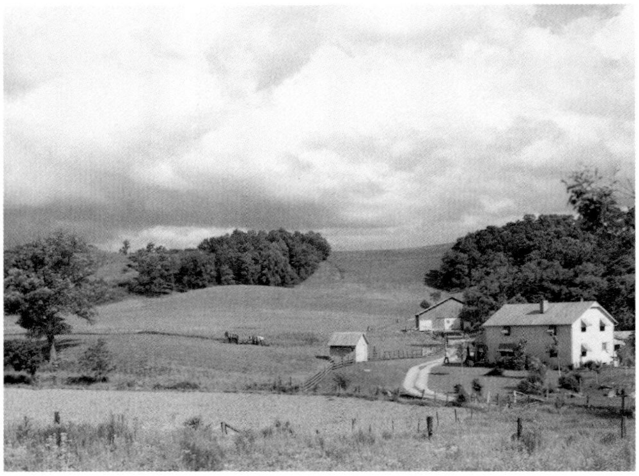

LEFT An unidentified forest setting similar in character to the Joyce Kilmer Forest, 1937
RIGHT Farming landscape along Dandridge Pike, eastern Tennessee, 1939

The Range of the Possible

The dams did more than produce electricity, they were used to extend the range of land uses in the Tennessee Valley. These ancillary uses were related to the construction, maintenance, and exploitation of this new infrastructure. Roads were built to provide access, towns and villages were developed to house workers, forests were replanted and new farming techniques were developed to control erosion, and recreational facilities were built on the dammed lakes to encourage and accommodate tourism. Expanding the uses of the landscape entailed the remaking of the whole Tennessee Valley, but the image of the places the TVA created was remarkably familiar. The agency situated its work in a series of set pieces, scenes that evoked and idealized the region's vernacular landscapes.

The TVA insisted, verbally and through the selection and framing of views, on the similarity of its new landscapes to the Edenic past it had construed for the valley. Its commentators agreed. Huxley's photo captions in *TVA: Adventure in Planning* all emphasize the historical validity of the new landscapes. For instance, his caption for a photograph of the TVA's replanted Joyce Kilmer Memorial Forest (established 1936) reads: "Originally the vegetal cover of the Valley was like that in [this forest] on the headwaters of the Tennessee River."[5] In some cases a real historical artifact was placed in the new landscape to lend authenticity. Norris had an old mill and farm equipment near its demonstration orchards, and Fontana Village featured a salvaged farmhouse at its center.

Large parts of the valley were again fertile enough to be used for agriculture, and the TVA worked with farmers to develop scientific-farming techniques. Scientific farming, which used repeatable experiments to develop methods for increasing agricultural productivity, had emerged at the turn of the nineteenth century, but its strategies were not widely adopted in the Tennessee Valley before

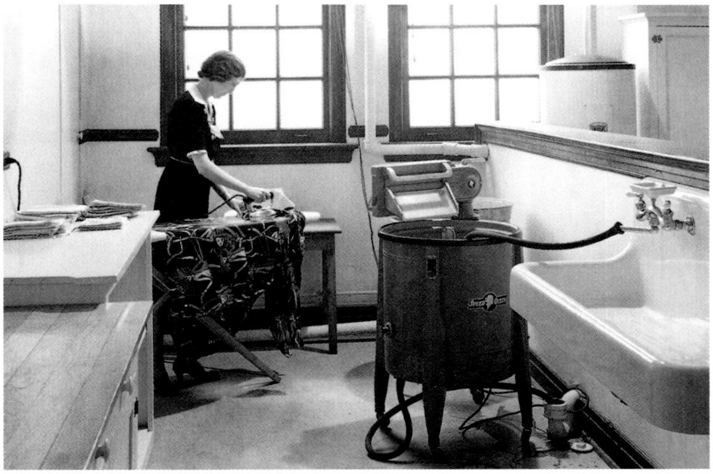

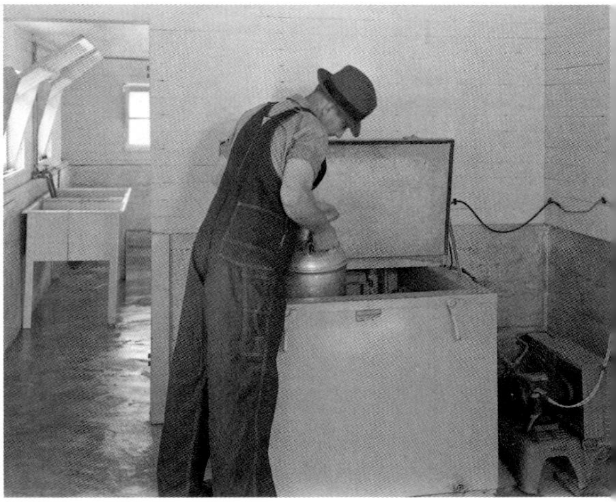

LEFT Laundry facilities at Mississippi State College, 1940

RIGHT Milk cooler at J. A. Locker farm, Lauderdale County, Alabama, 1939

the New Deal. These scientific farms and the dams benefited each other. The new farming methods reduced soil erosion and prevented the deposition of silt in the reservoirs. At the same time, they created markets for the fertilizers and electricity that the TVA produced. In his discussion of the TVA and its agricultural reforms, Huxley offers the case of one farmer, who had worked with TVA advisors and acquired machinery to improve his yields:

> [Farmer Cox] owns a typical Tennessee Valley demonstration farm. He has been chosen by a group of farmers to carry out, over a period of years, the new methods of cropping and fertilizing which are recommended by his county agent. The other members of his group act as a supervisory committee and decide which crops shall be grown...and other details of management...Farmer Cox receives fertilizers free of charge from the TVA....The prize sow...which Farmer Cox is admiring owes much of its excellence to the improved breeding and feeding which the demonstration group is trying....The huge power dams of the TVA provide electricity at cheap rates for rural areas and make it possible for farmers to use scientific methods unheard of in the region before. Farmer Cox can now use an electric incubator...for hatching his chicks, while in the farmhouse itself, Mrs. Cox is able to speed her work by using appliances like the electric ironing machine.[6]

In addition to the pastoral scenery produced by scientific farming, the TVA also created a series of rustic landscapes: parks, lakeshores, forests, and settlements like Norris Town and Fontana Village. The new forests, like the farms, were important for erosion control. Parks and marinas made the newly formed lakes into public attractions, and they offered revenue from this new tourist industry.

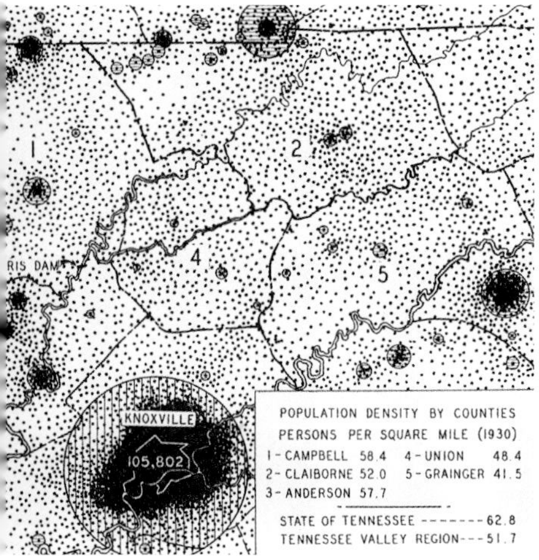

Population density map, with Knoxville at lower center, 1930. From Tennessee Valley Authority, *The Norris Project*, 60.

The housing that the TVA built for workers also helped to create a romantic representation of the past: much of it recalled wood cabins of the pre-TVA era, and the buildings were situated along small lanes bordered by open water channels instead of gutters. The image was quaint, but the reality was modern: Like the scientific farms, the new housing used vernacular idioms to package new technologies. Even the most modest cottages were equipped with electrical appliances, and many of the structures took advantage of new construction materials and methods. A number of the houses at Norris were built of concrete block, which was just coming into use, and the cabins at Fontana included prefabricated and demountable plywood structures. Also like the scientific farming, the new housing had multiple agendas: it provided clean, decent, comfortable accommodation for TVA workers, it created a market of consumers for TVA electricity, and it broadcast the message that the TVA and its work belonged to the history of the valley.

The TVA's programs were broad because its conception of the landscape was vast. The agency treated the Tennessee Valley as a series of layered, integrated systems. Its investigation and management of the valley ranged from geology to social practices, and it considered natural and cultural processes as reciprocal and equally significant forces in the shaping of the landscape. One of the TVA's first undertakings was the production of a comprehensive map showing the region at, above, and below the ground level. In the 1960s, the work of landscape architects and regional planners Ian McHarg, Carl Steinitz, and their colleagues made the idea of the landscape as a set of layered systems commonplace. That understanding has become more pervasive—it forms the basis of contemporary geographic information systems. In the 1930s, however, the synthetic research and interventions of the TVA were radical.

For each of its dams the TVA produced what came to be known as a "Brown Book," an encyclopedic report of initial conditions, plans, and work carried out. The Brown Book for Norris Dam, its first and farthest-reaching project, includes a wide range of topics surveyed before the dam was undertaken: geology (including locations and elevations of surrounding caves), river history, the Clinch River Basin, past floods, rainfall patterns, soil conditions, existing infrastructure, population density, settlement patterns, tax base and revenue sources, and a survey of people living in the area to be flooded, with questions about household size, income, and composition, education, religious preferences, newspaper subscriptions, rooms per dwelling, distances from public facilities, and farm production.[7] The agency's interests brought together subjects from professions as far ranging as geology and public health. Its expenditures were not limited to infrastructure: the TVA was the largest spender on malaria research in the years before World War II, and it managed—and still manages—lake levels to control the breeding of mosquitoes that carry the disease.

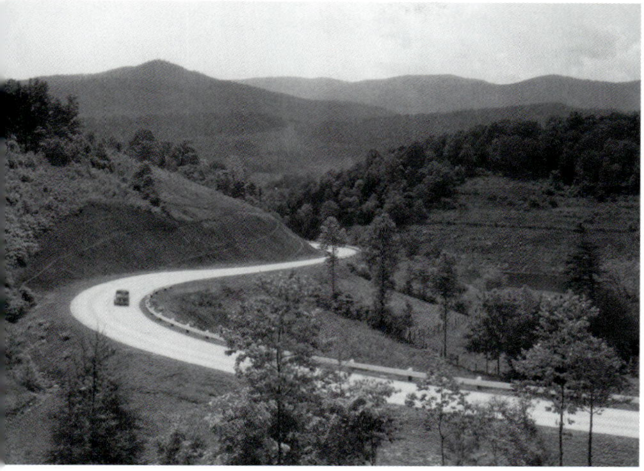

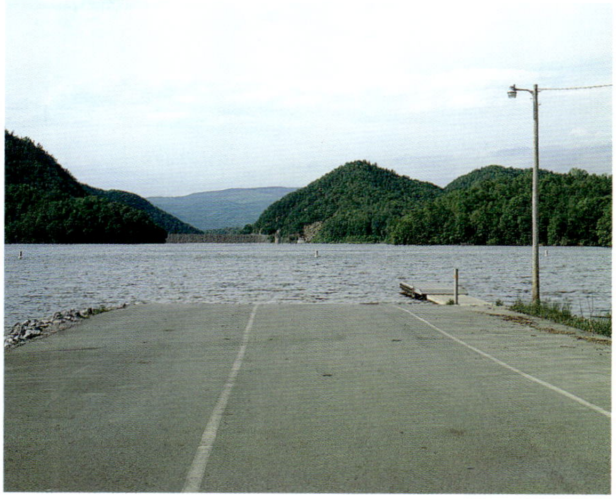

LEFT Part of completed permanent highway between Coal Creek and Norris Dam, 1934
RIGHT A road ends at a TVA lake, 2004

Eggs and Omelettes

The Tennessee River and its tributaries were the TVA's means for effecting change, and the image of the system's continuous waters became a symbol of the agency's programs. The TVA's accomplishments in the landscape were enormous: it created a unified region from disparate places; it developed cultural practices that stabilized and sustained the region's physical geography; it provided technology to an impoverished population; and it created idealized scenery that argued for a progressive agenda. But there was a cost. The story that the agency's landscapes tell is compelling, but the seamlessness of its presentation hides a wrinkle in time. The physical power that the dams generated came from the discontinuity they created in the river, and one might say that their rhetorical power came from the discontinuity they created in time, interrupting and even erasing history.

The TVA made a landscape that is extraordinarily coherent. It conceived of the valley as a series of linked systems and scenes; it made ways to see those places as continuous. The Norris Freeway, for instance, took travelers through the idealized places that Norris Dam had made possible and then took them to the dam itself. It created poetic and legible relationships between geology and electricity, between land and water, between past and future. Places like the one in Richard Barnes's photograph of the vanishing road—where the discontinuity created by flooding becomes apparent—are scarce. But once a person becomes aware of one of these strange gaps, the rest of the scenery seems like a photograph of the Russian Revolution from which Trotsky has been airbrushed out.

What was lost in the flooding of the valleys and the production of a new, standardized, more prosperous landscape? The TVA left the evidence out of its built landscapes but not out of its written records. The Brown Books that describe

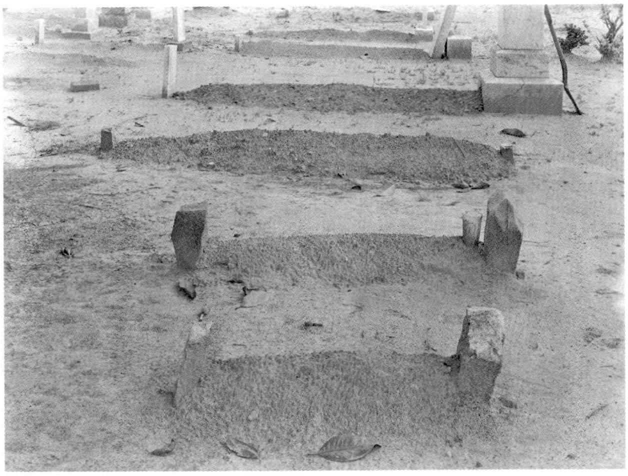

Walker Evans "Country Graveyard," 1936. Photograph of a graveyard in Southeastern United States.

the construction of the new projects also contain meticulous inventories of what was flooded or moved: farmhouses, boat landings, granaries, villages, and cemeteries. Norris Dam alone effected the disposition of more than 5,000 graves in several hundred small family cemeteries and numerous church and community cemeteries. Many of the graves were unmarked, and many were very old. The Norris Brown Book details the process of surveying graves that would be flooded or isolated (12,000 were surveyed in total); the options offered to families of the buried; the process of location, inventory, removal, and reburial; the maintenance of records, including the identification and history of each grave; the agreements concluded for removal or retention of a grave; and records of original and reinterment locations, including cemetery plats, maps of graves that were moved, and costs per grave and in total.[7] What is strange is that, except for the Brown Book, there is almost no way to find these places or to mark this process in the landscape. The TVA's ghosts are buried in the back pages of its long-forgotten records, and sometimes, quite literally, under water.

There is one other source of clues besides the Brown Book: boaters' maps, which list underwater hazards. Someone who bothers to read the key of the map for Watts Bar Lake, for instance, will discover a whole world under water: the inundated Cemetery Island (shown by name), submerged stumps (shown as red dots), submerged building foundations (shown as black squares), and submerged roadbeds (shown as double lines). None of this is visible in the rhetorical landscapes that the TVA created. Comparing the valley as it exists now to these ghost documents complicates the message of the TVA; it makes the promise of continuity more fraught than it seems in the finely honed places that the agency created. The TVA's landscapes can be read as an essay on history, but if compared to the written record, they seem more like an essay on history's selective memory.

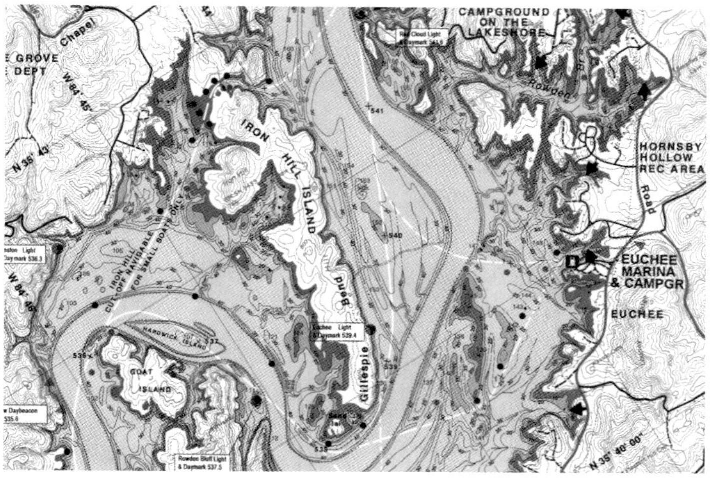

"Watts Bar Lake Recreation and Fishing Guide," produced by Atlantic Mapping, Inc., 1999

Why was the TVA so brutal in its erasures? It was an activist agency. It effected radical change, but to do so it had to present an unambiguous story about the benefits it brought. The single-minded character of what it left behind raises interesting questions for historians. To what extent can historical rhetoric be trusted? What are the implications of historical rhetoric that not only replaces artifacts but erases their memory from the landscape? It raises an even more interesting question for designers: Is it possible to effect change without writing over the past? Can you make an omelette without breaking quite so many eggs?

Notes

1. In addition to working for the Farm Security Administration, photographer Walker Evans and his sometime partner, author James Agee, also received a commission from *Fortune* to document life in the rural South. This work, never published by *Fortune*, formed the basis for their book, *Let Us Now Praise Famous Men* (Boston: Houghton, Mifflin and Company, 1941).

2. James Agee, "Tennessee Valley Authority," *Fortune*, October 1933, 81.

3. Agee was a native of Knoxville, so he was familiar with the region. He also knew his audience—the article "Tennessee Valley Authority" offers discussion not only of the TVA's socially progressive agenda but also of the opportunities for industry and commerce that their project entailed.

4. Julian Huxley, *TVA: Adventure in Planning* (Surrey, U.K.: The Architectural Press, 1943), 33–35.

5. Huxley, *TVA: Adventure in Planning*, 58.

6. Ibid., 46–47.

7. *The Norris Project* (Washington, D.C.: United States Government Printing Office, 1940), 509–13.

Domesticity and Power: A Photo Essay

RICHARD BARNES

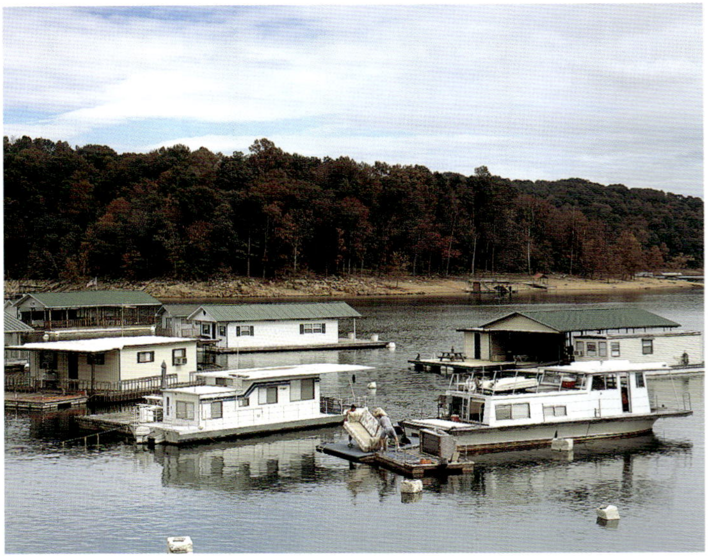

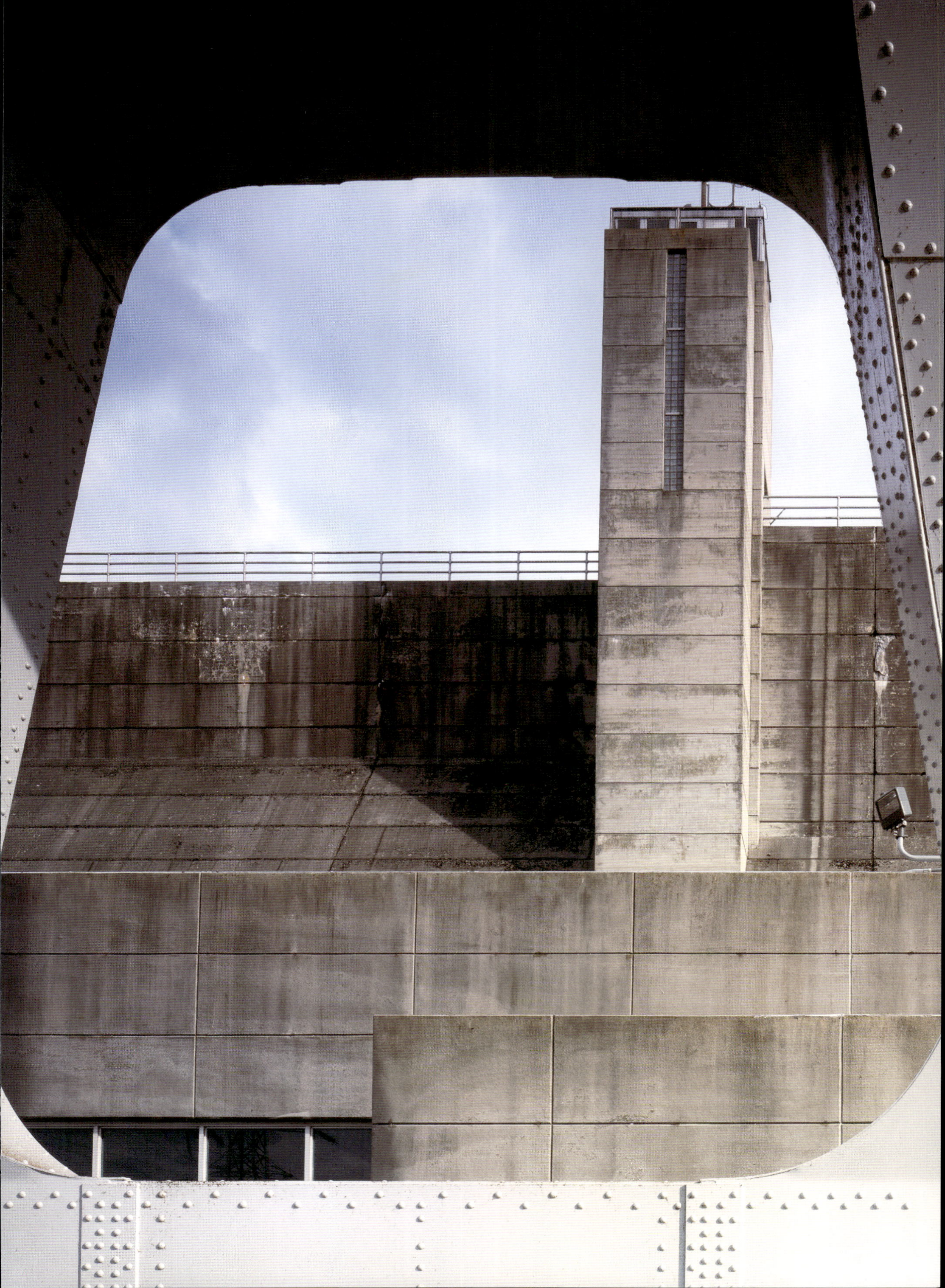

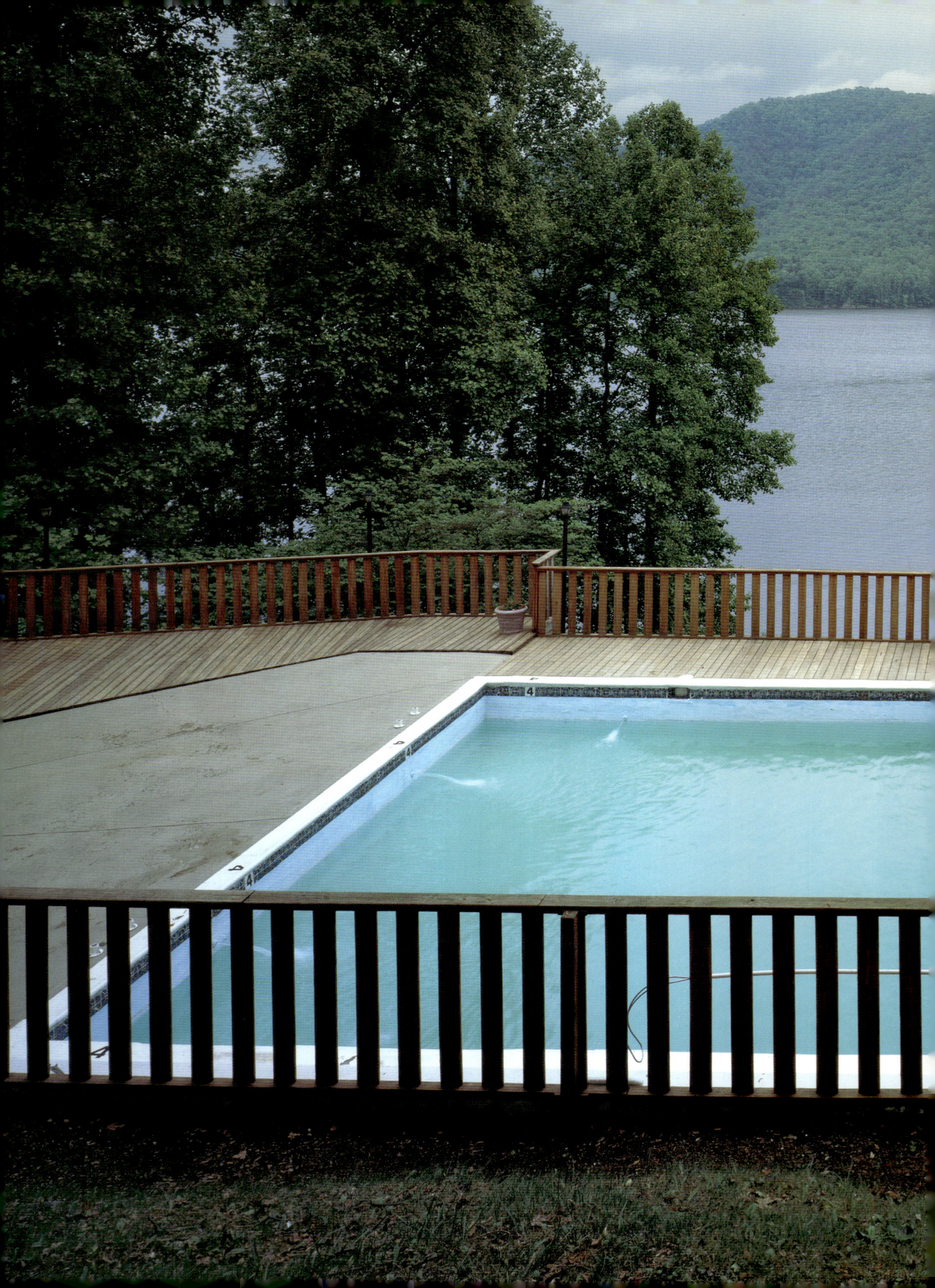

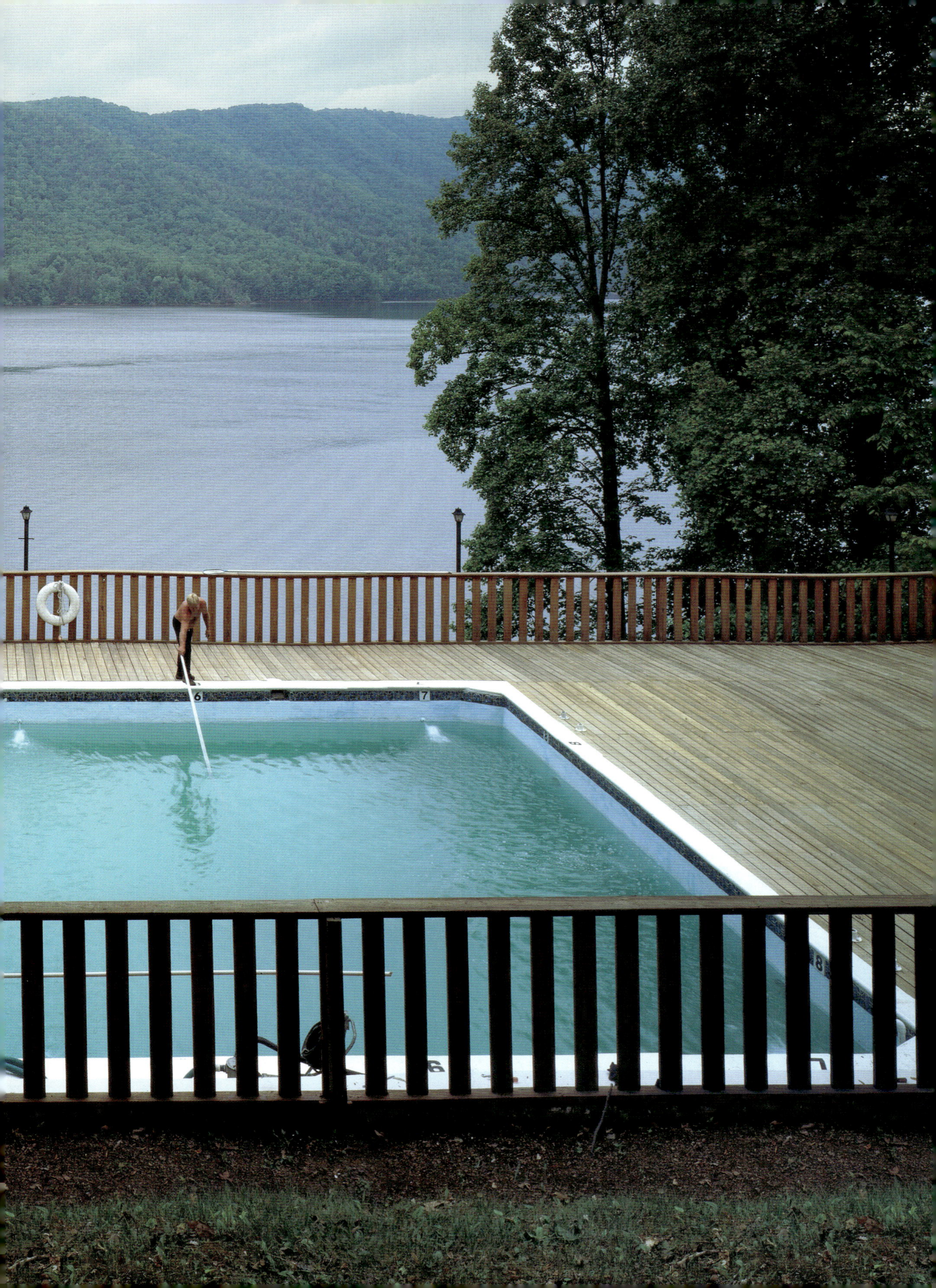

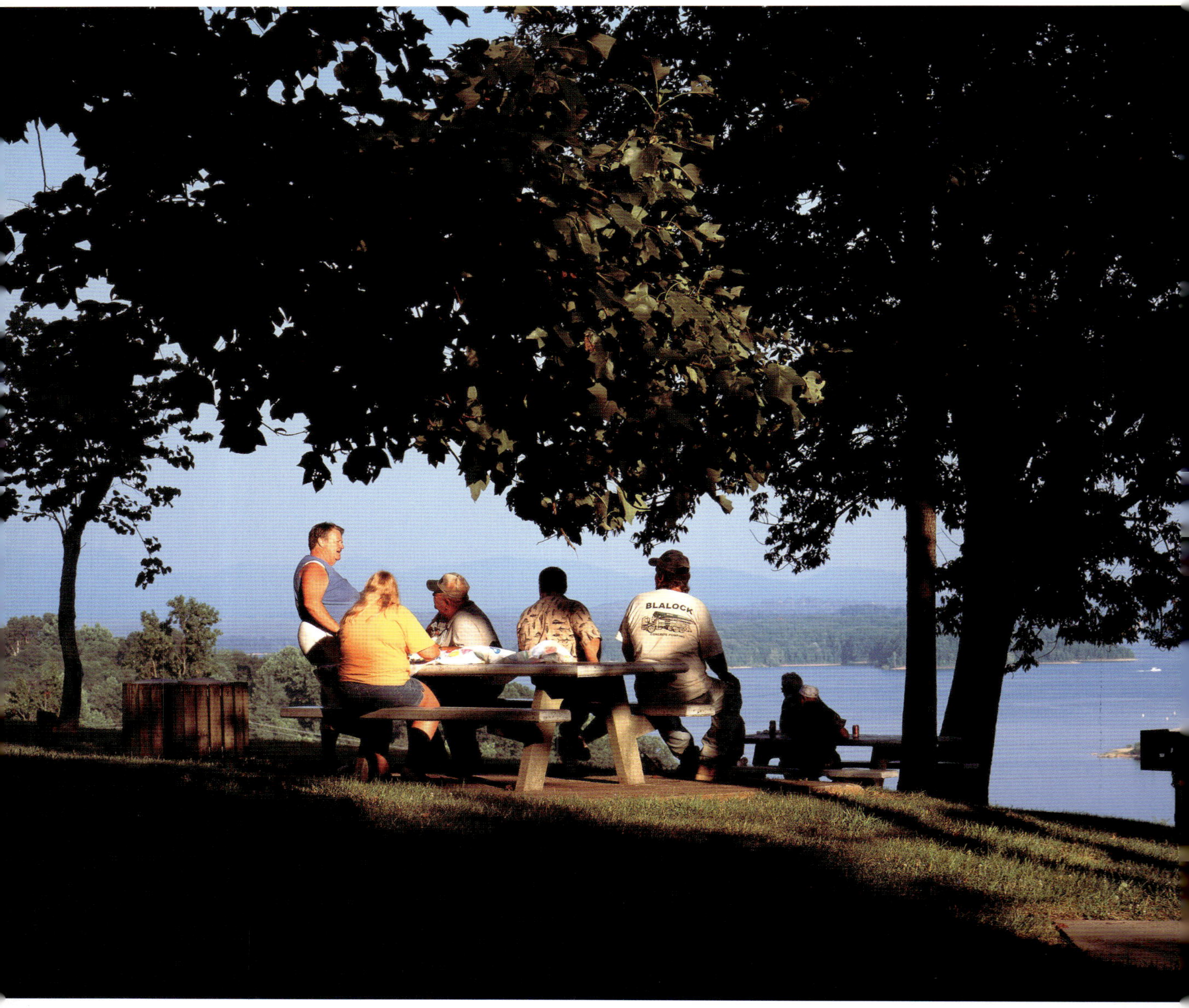
BLALOCK

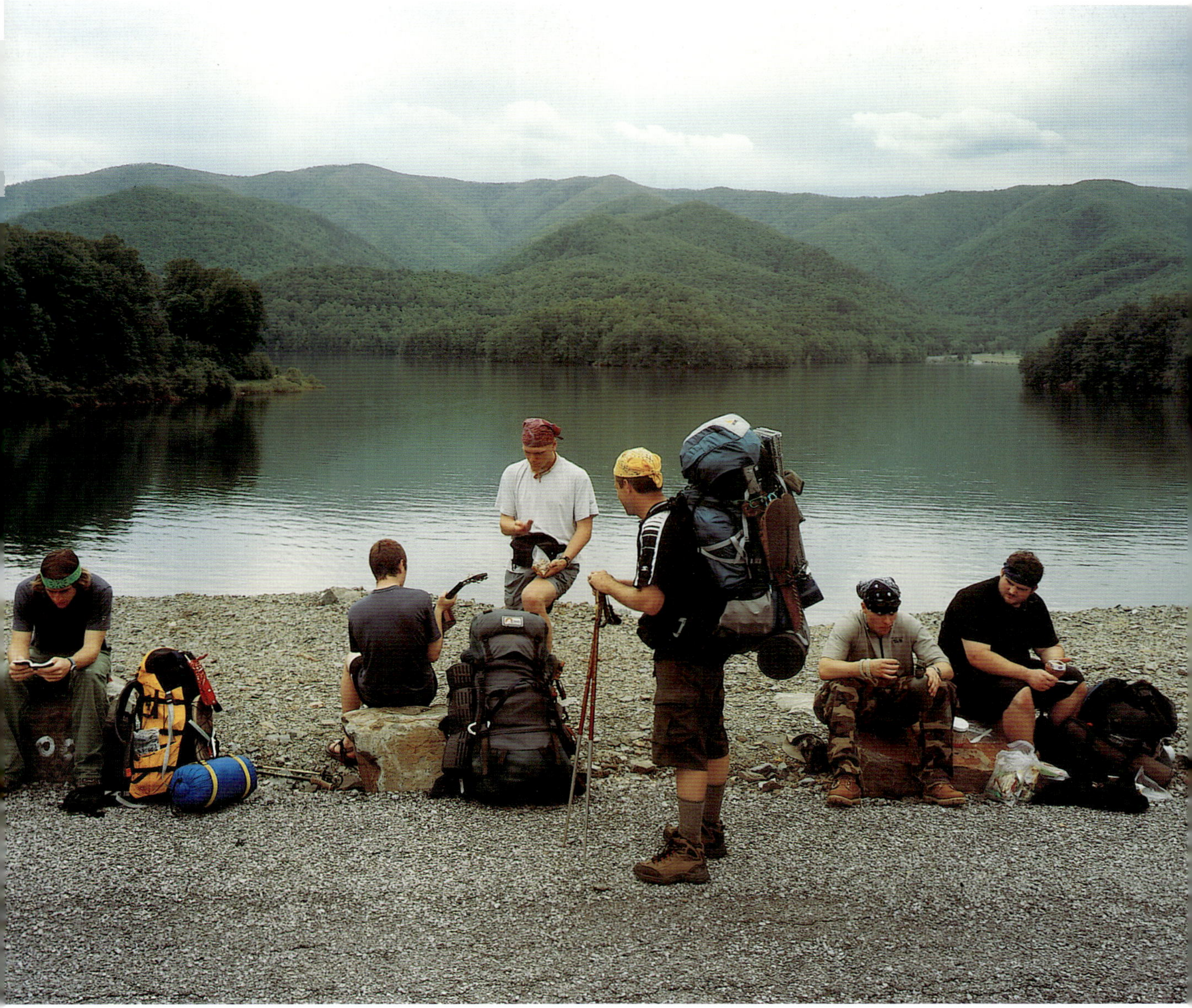

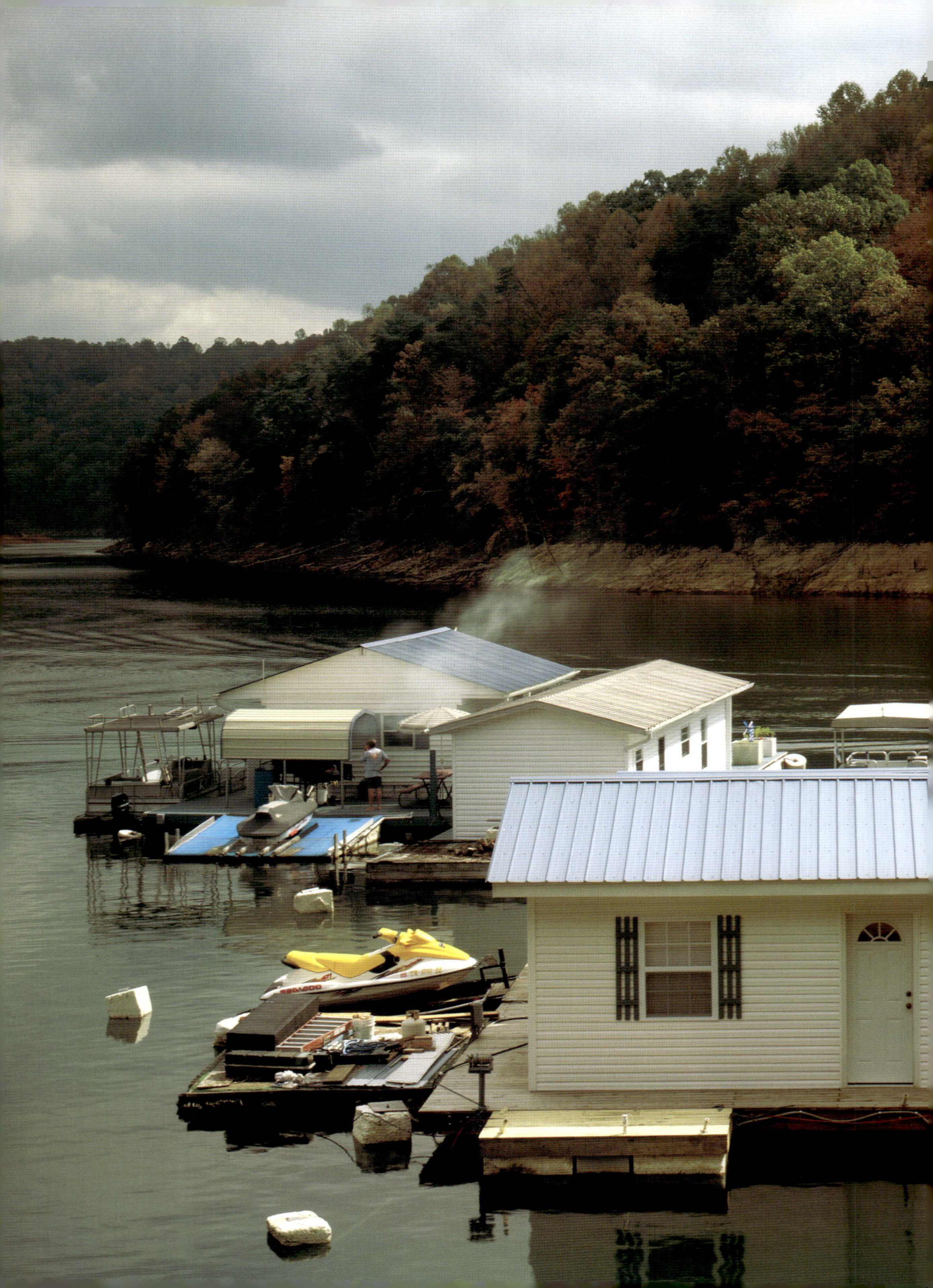

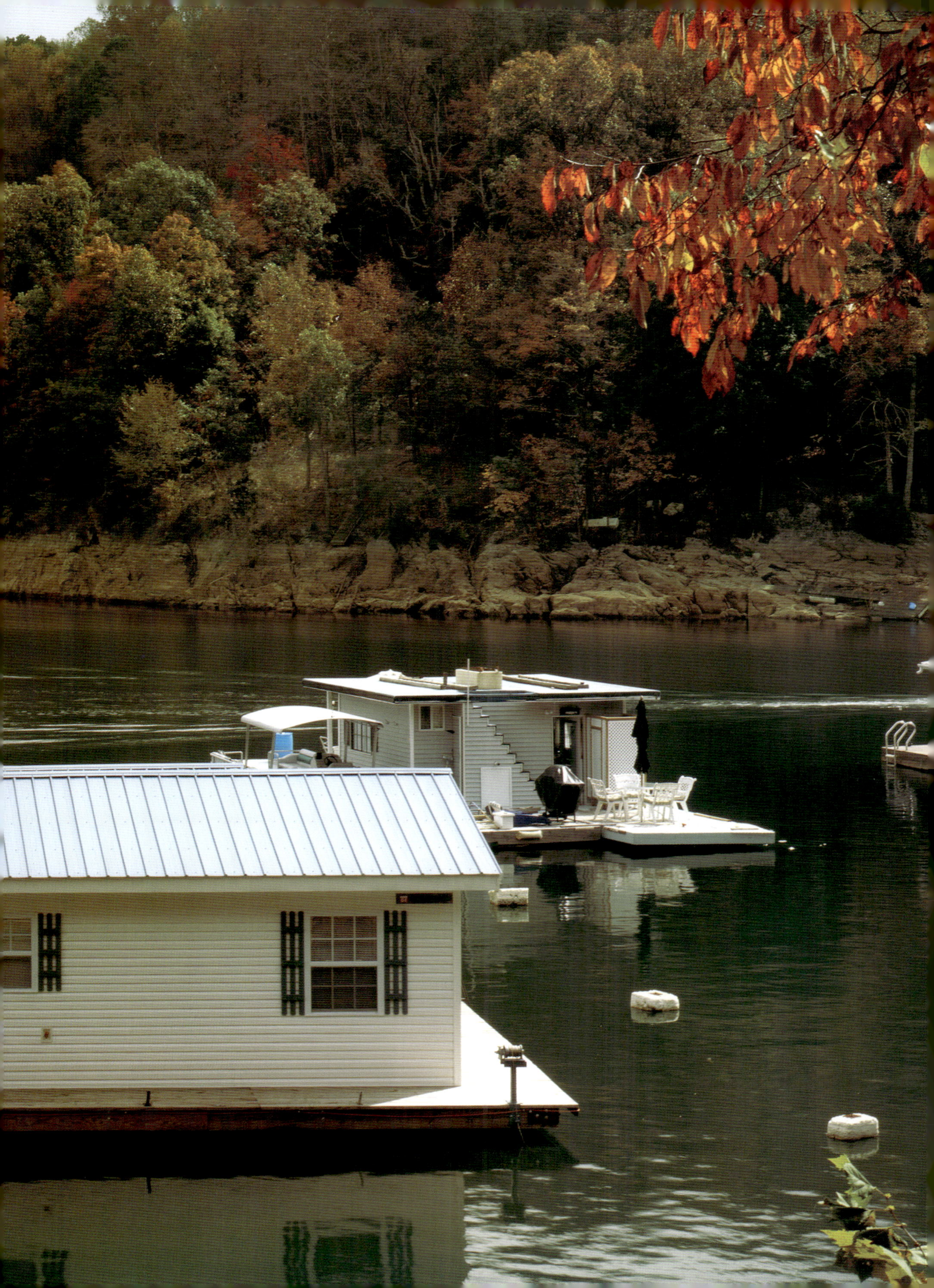

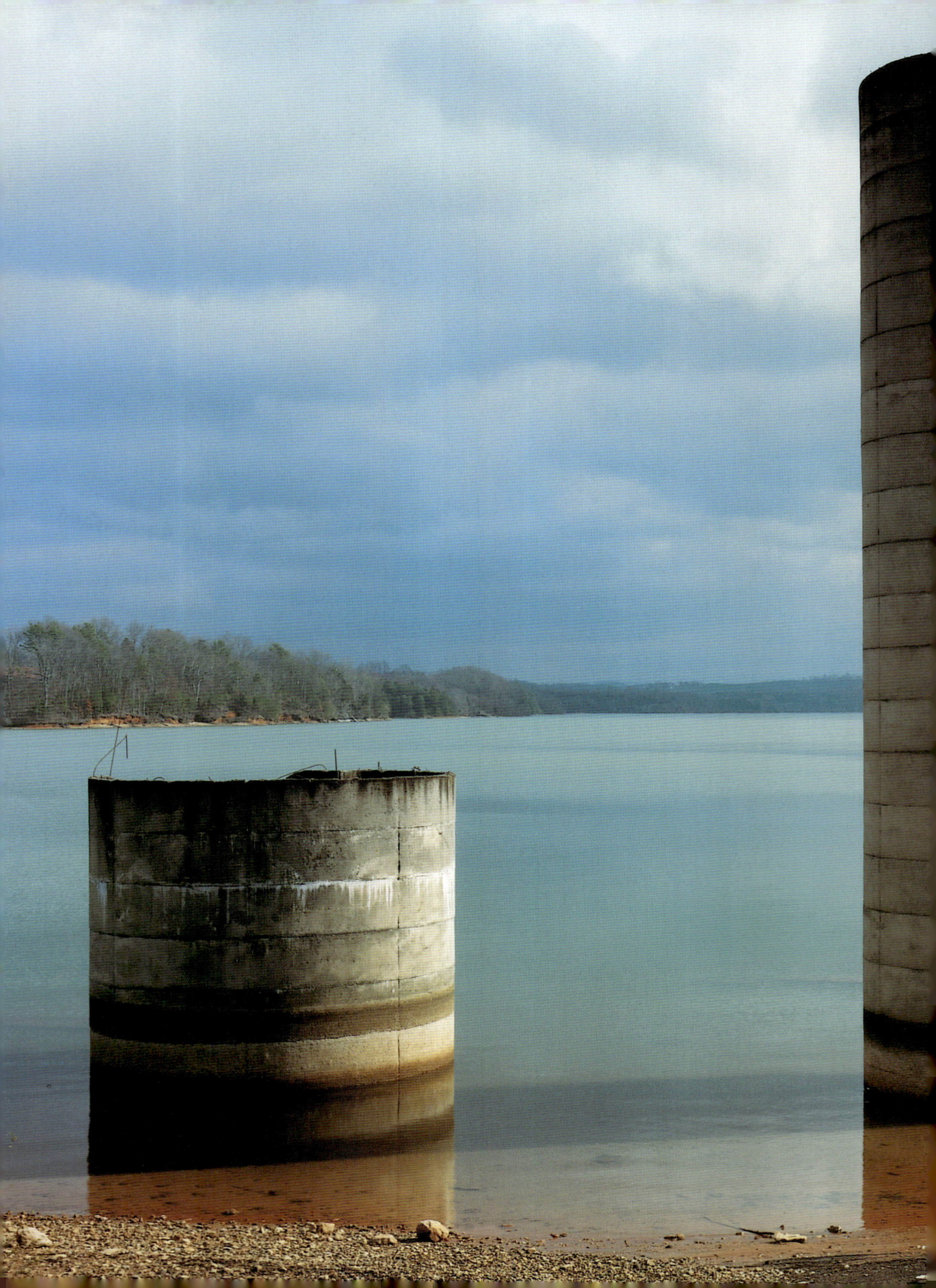

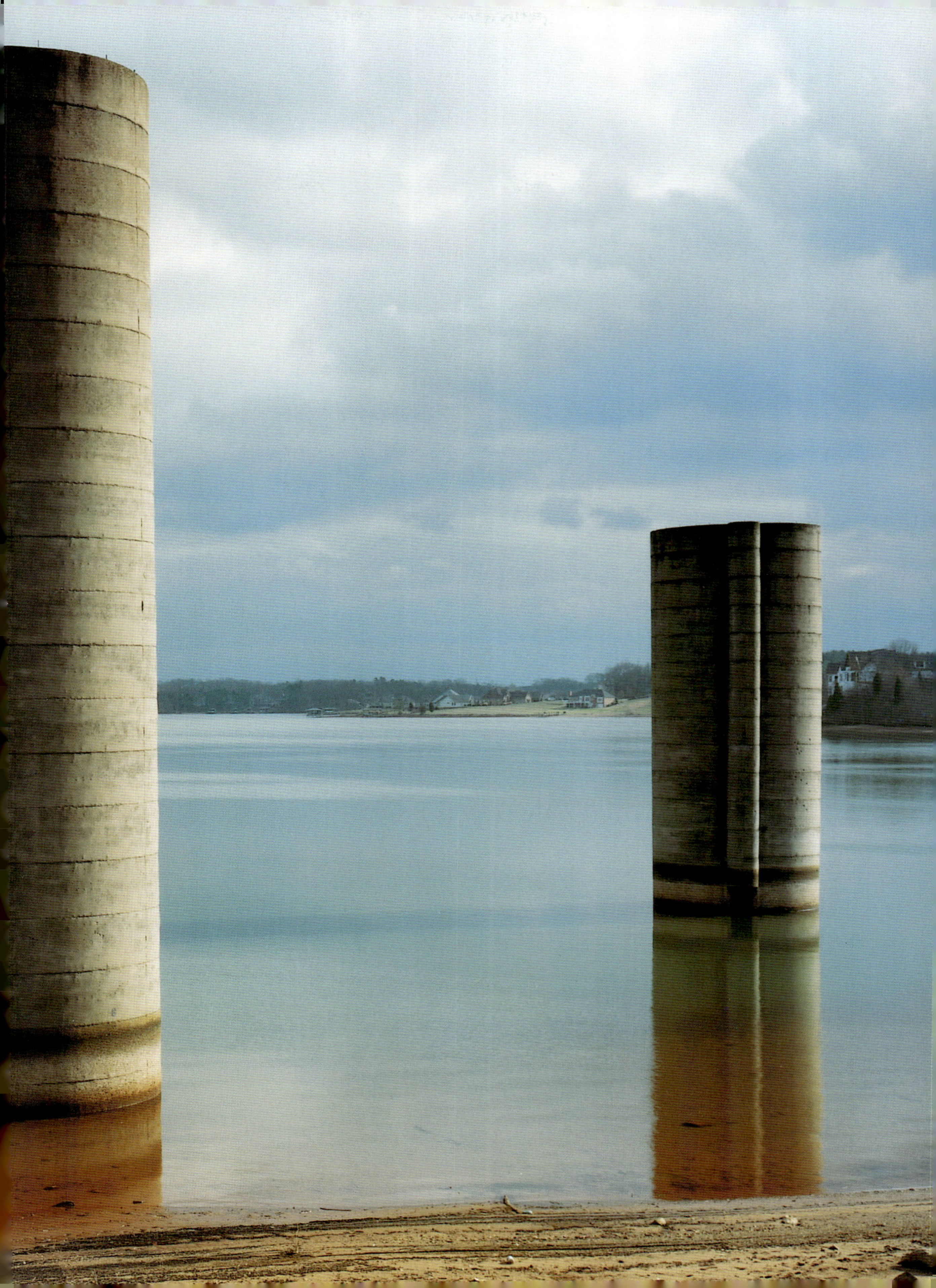

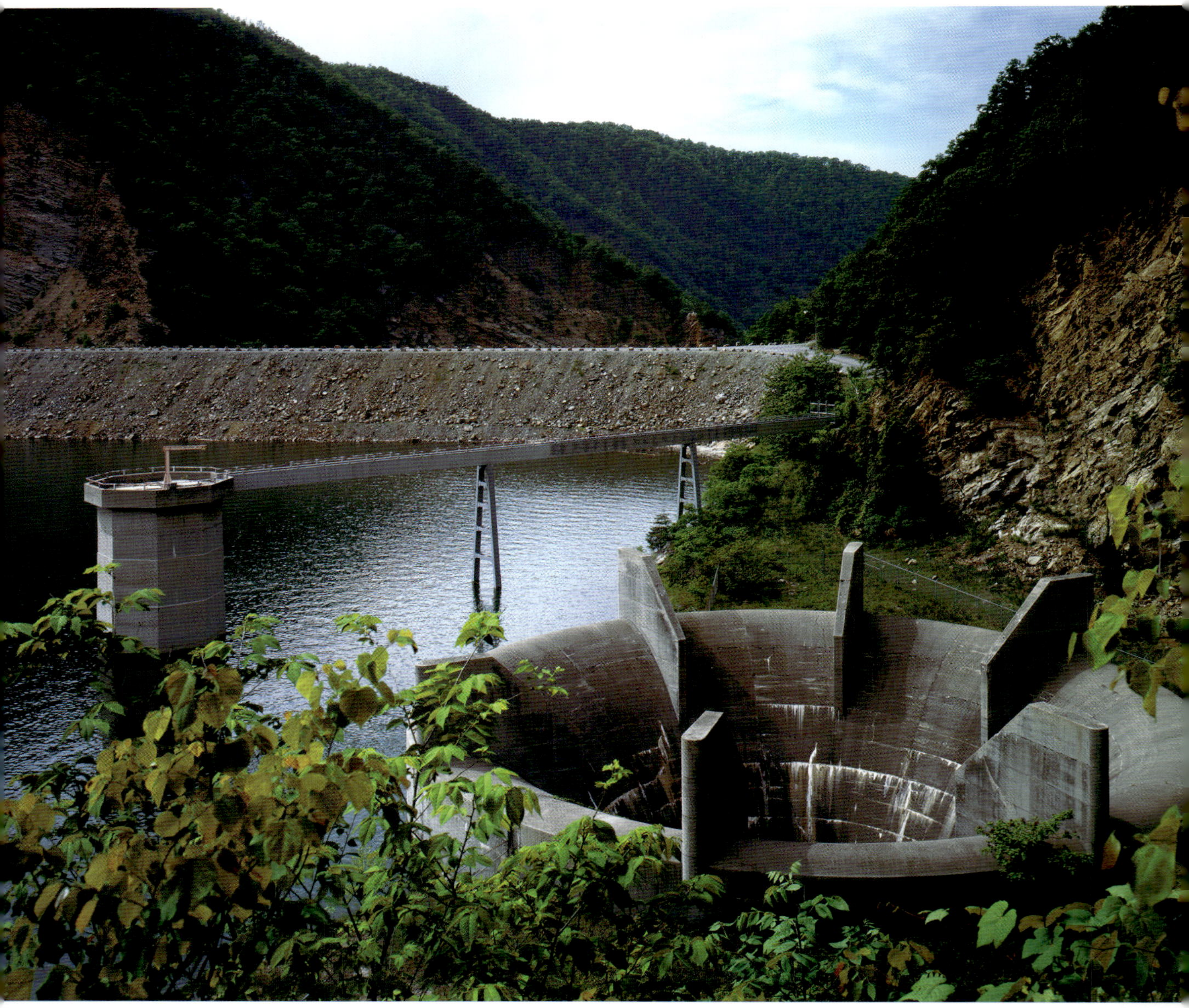

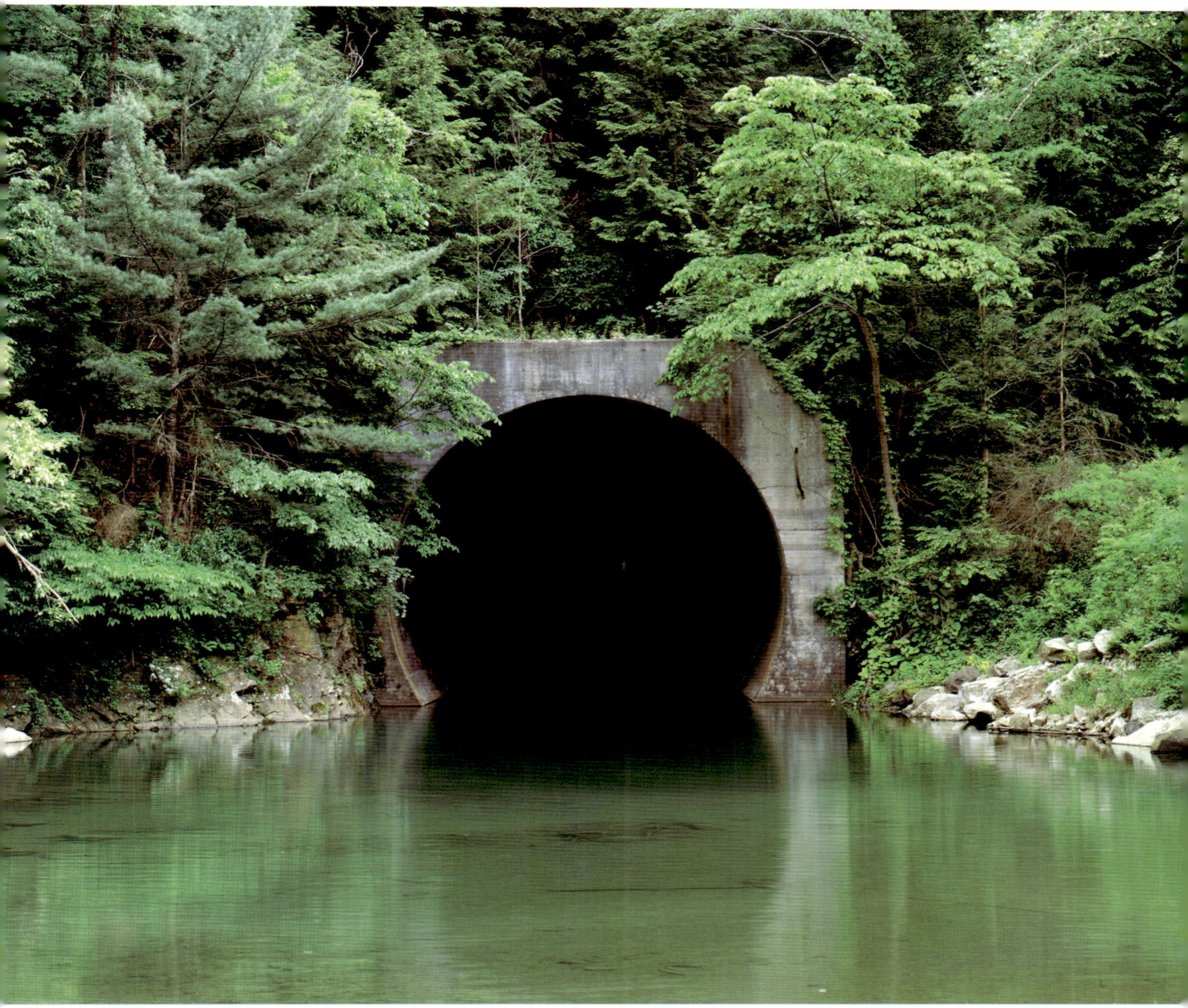

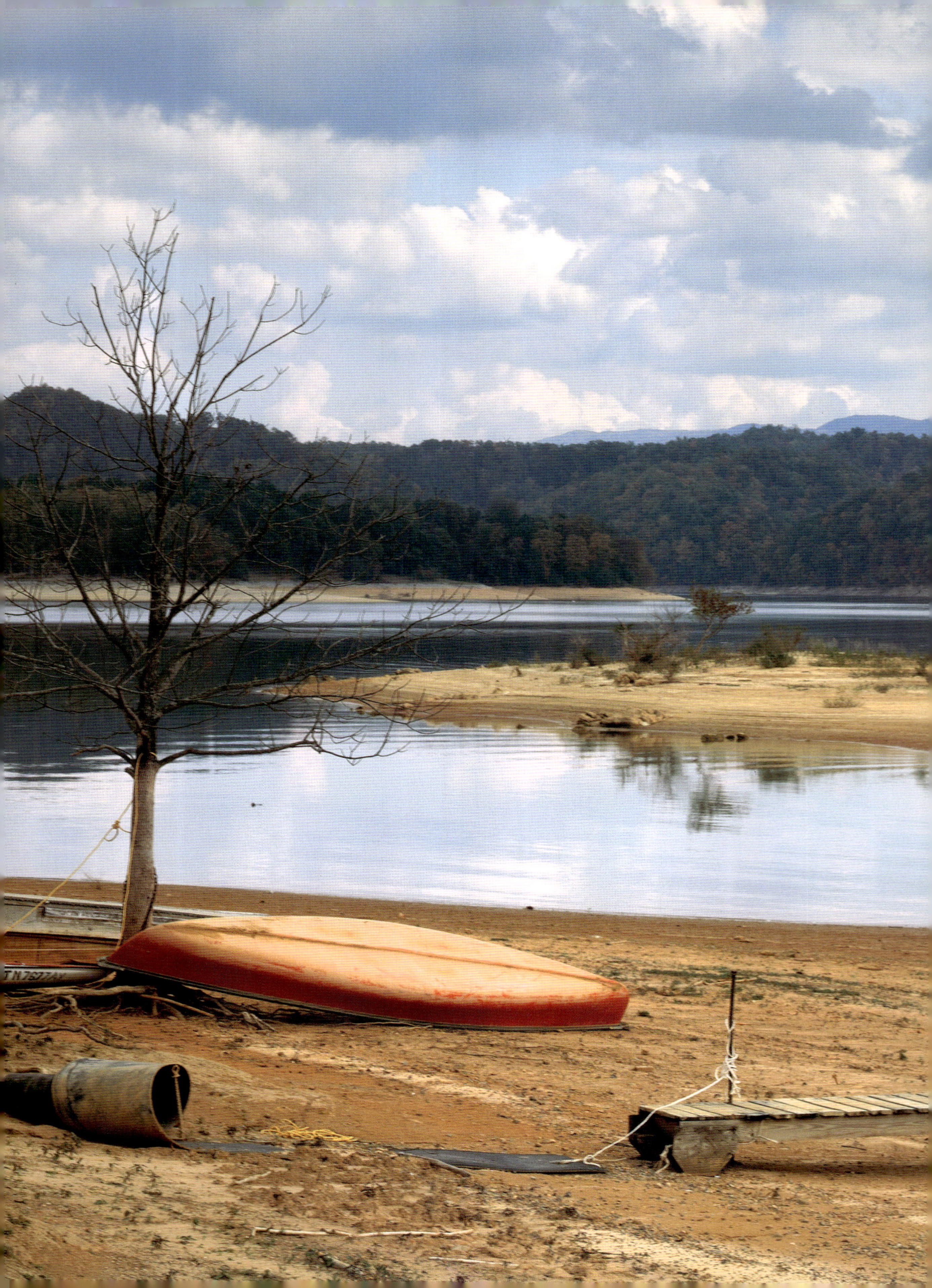

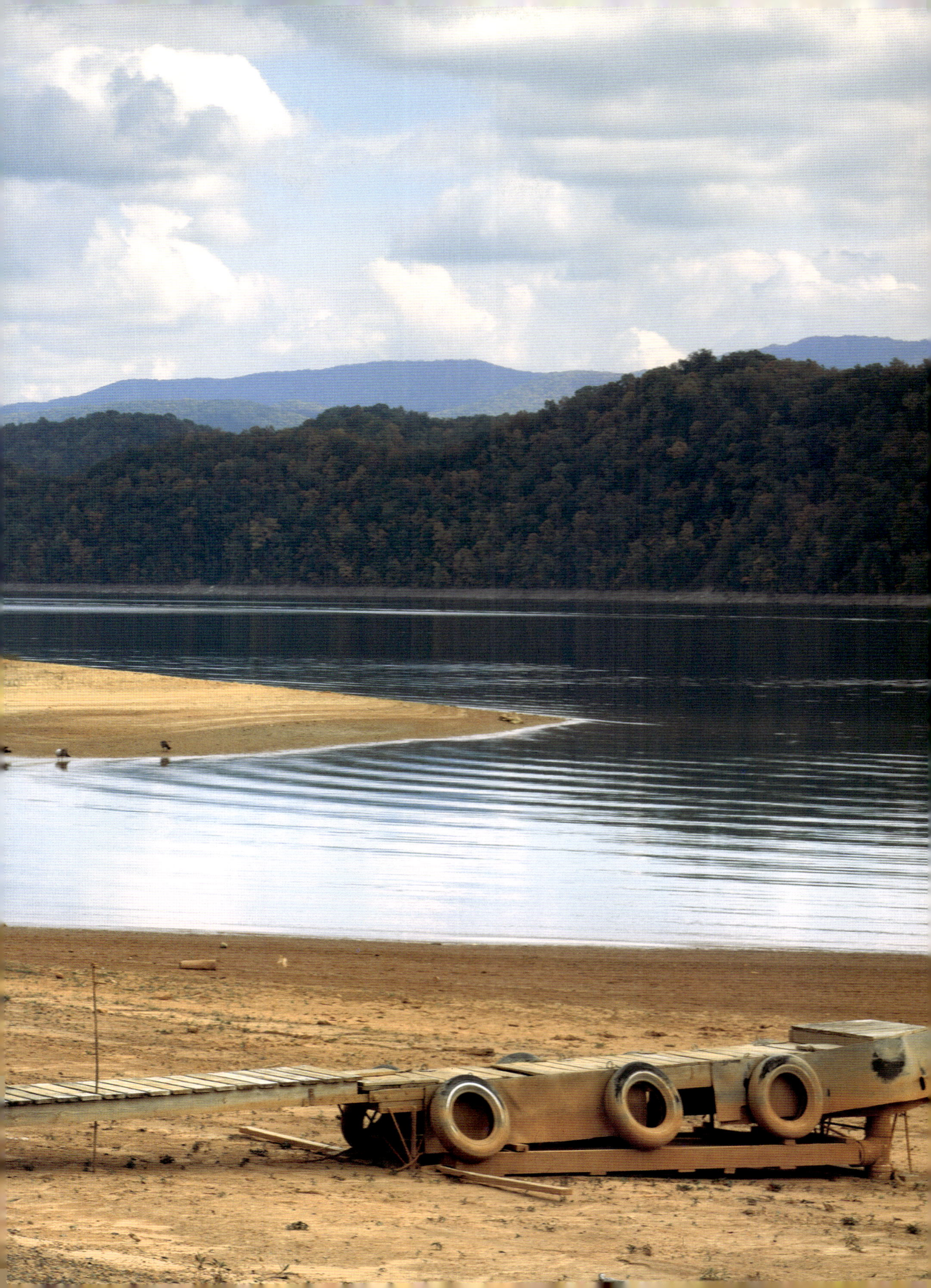

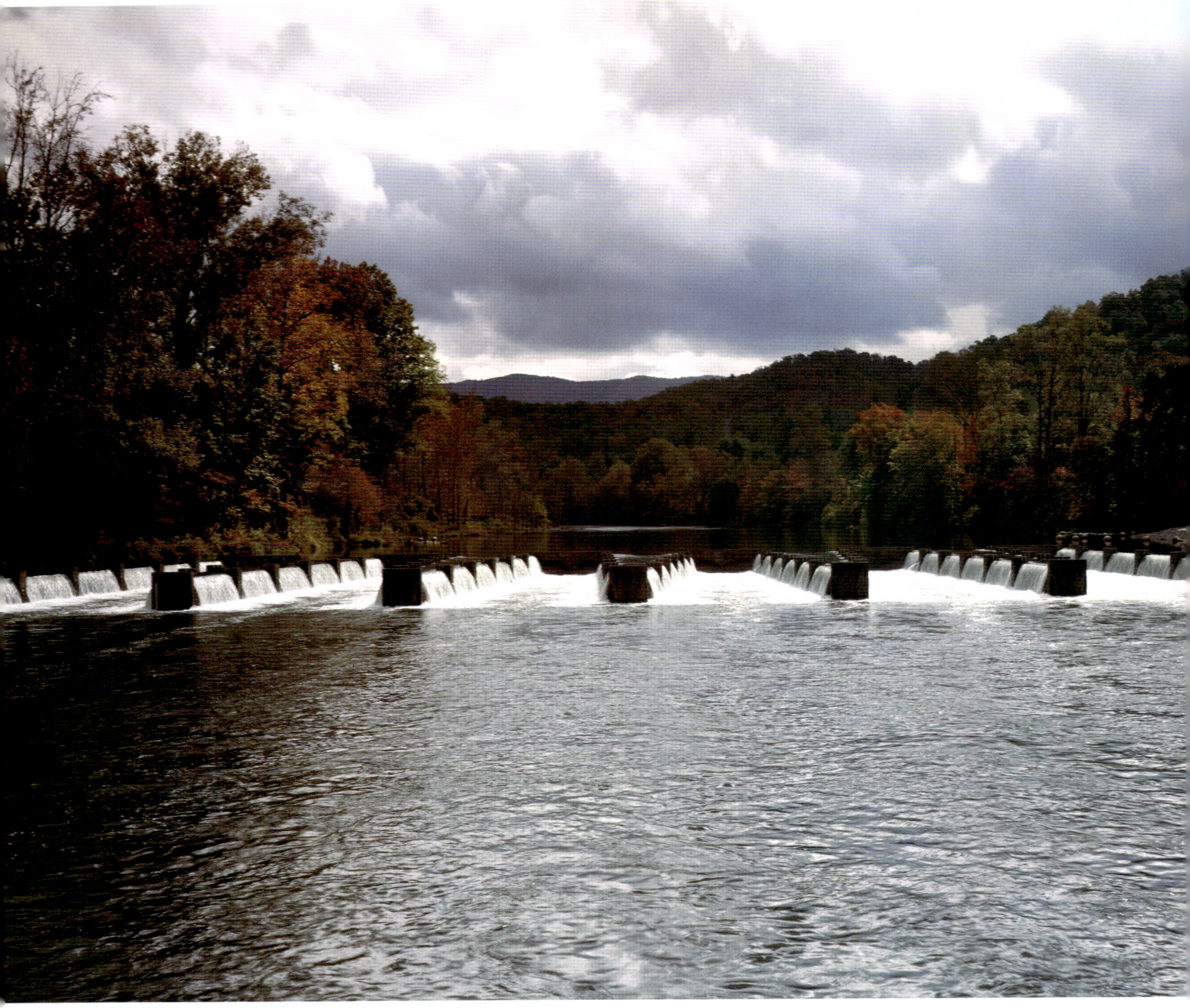

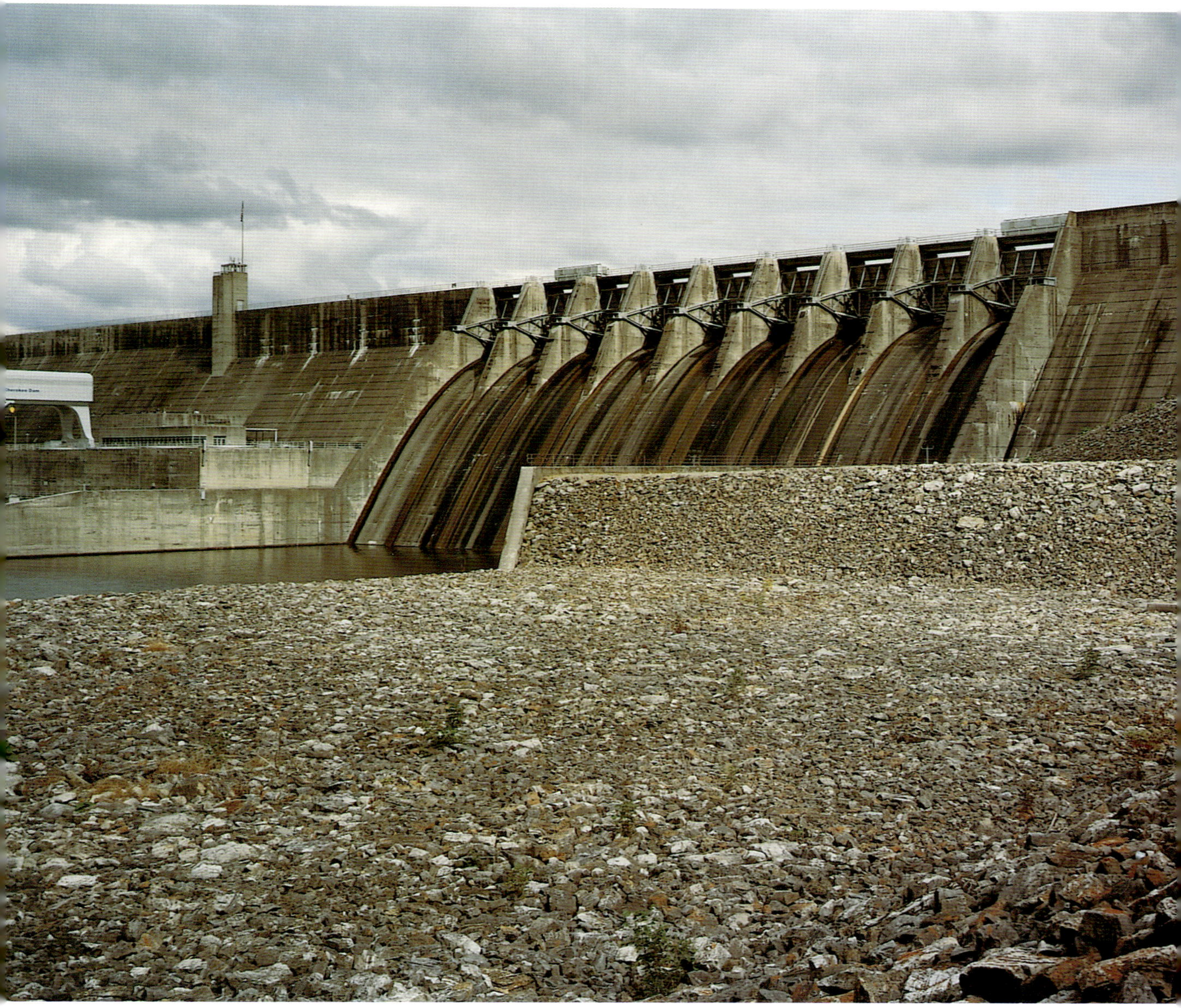

Ideology and Engineering in the Tennessee Valley

BARRY M. KATZ

On the floor of the Fontana Dam Power Station sits a wooden pallet piled with seventy-pound bags of powdered caulk—it is hard to imagine a more compelling metaphor for the Tennessee Valley Authority and its campaign to hold back the unruly forces of nature. One is reminded of the powerful conclusion to Goethe's *Faust*: "Those foolish dikes and dams," scoffs Mephisto at the pretensions of the modern, technological man. "All your labors are for naught: The Elements belong to us."[1] It is the nature of the physical universe to leak.

Faust's dream of rolling back the sea—"to open up to millions space to work in, build their dwellings"—was constrained not just by the forces of nature but by the recalcitrance of the moral and political universe. His schemes were financed by controversial economic reforms and advanced under the gathering clouds of war; a rural peasantry pursuing a traditional way of life would have to be displaced, and the devil himself lacked the wiles to persuade them that it was for their own good. The fortunes of Faust provide a striking parable for the vast undertakings of the TVA: Created by act of Congress in 1933, against the background of the New Deal and the growing threat of war, and over the resistance of much of the local population, the ambitions of the TVA were Faustian both in ideology and engineering. The bridge between them—then, as now—was design.

As the road to the Norris Dam straightens out and the colossal, 265-foot-high structure comes into view, visitors are struck not only by its scale but by the deliberate quality of the composition that unfolds before them—historian Walter Creese called it "an example of coordinated expression that was never again equaled."[2] Much of the integrated character of this panorama can be traced back to the program of Arthur E. Morgan, the iconoclastic visionary who served as the first director of the TVA, and to his interpretation of President Roosevelt's call for a planning

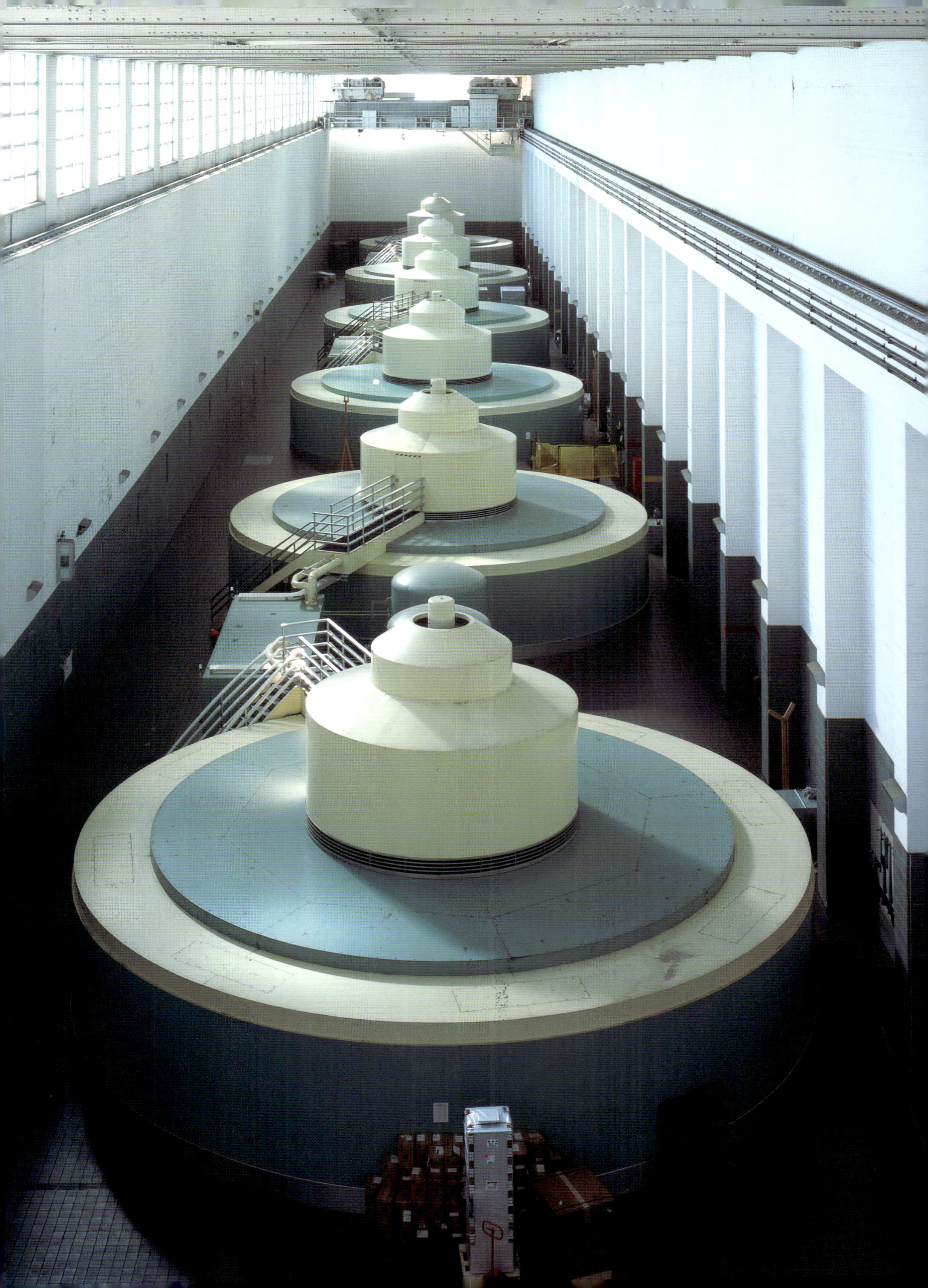

process that "touches and gives life to all forms of human concerns."[3] Morgan's almost religious commitment to a process that he variously called "dynamic design" and "multipurpose engineering" led to a system conceived across seven states but executed at a meticulously human scale.[4] Indeed, it was one of his core convictions—shared by his partner, rival, and then successor, David Lilienthal—that if the TVA were to rise above the sordid machinations of the political elite, it would have to fire the imagination of the public on whose support it depended: Large-scale planning was not the exclusive province of the Soviet New Economic Policy (NEP) but could take place in a democracy as well; monumentality could inspire rather than subdue the individual as it did in Fascist Italy. There was a middle way—an American way—between the gratuitous aestheticism of art nouveau and the austere functionalism of European modernism. "We wanted those dams to have the honest beauty of a fine tool," declaimed Lilienthal, "for the TVA was a tool to do a job for man in a democracy."[5] Design and engineering converged to become tools of social policy and instruments of New Deal ideology.

OVERLEAF Pickwick Dam powerhouse, 2004

This convergence came about not by accident, however, but very much "by design." The directors of the TVA understood that the Faustian projects they were undertaking needed broad popular support and that a singular but coordinated *experience* would be more effective in firing the public imagination than any mere publicity campaign. At the same time, the requirements of rigorous engineering design could in no way be compromised by costly and gratuitous aesthetic flourishes. To meet these twin objectives, they created an unusual parallel structure in which Roland Wank, chief architect of the Norris Dam project, and T. B. Parker, the TVA's chief engineer responsible for planning, design, and construction, would report independently and in parallel to the administrative officers.[6] Wank was, in any case, predisposed to work collaboratively with his engineering counterparts. A thoroughgoing Viennese modernist, he raged against "the perverted tendency of the Victorian era to regard utility as the antithesis of beauty" and advocated instead the "bare and bold masses and surfaces of contemporary work."[7] It is a measure of their success that the projects of the TVA remain so compelling not only to the public but also to historians of architecture and landscape.

But there is another dimension to the concrete dams, roadways, and buildings of the early TVA that has been typically—and literally—overshadowed by the vast structural and architectural projects associated with the Authority: a wide range of industrial objects was integral to its success, both at a technical and a political level. The program they embodied can best be understood against the twin background of a nascent American design culture and the politics of the New Deal.

The earliest of the TVA's hydraulic projects—Norris, Wheeler, Pickwick, Chickamauga—were designed and built in a decade bracketed by the Chicago Exposition of 1933, which looked backward with satisfaction upon A Century of Progress, and the New York World's Fair of 1939, which cast its gaze forward into The World of Tomorrow. Significantly, the decade that saw the birth of the TVA planning process also saw the birth of industrial design as a recognized profession that stood at the crowded intersection of architecture, the decorative arts, mechanical engineering, and advertising. By adding compelling gestures of style to otherwise functional products, energized by an uncanny, if largely intuitive, feeling for consumer behavior, the first generation of American designers popularized the idea that the artifacts of everyday life could be made to resonate with a larger system of symbols, codes, and values and deployed as a subtle but powerful means of persuasion.[8] The TVA was arguably the first undertaking to translate this program from the commercial to the public sphere, and it did so on a massive scale.

From the perspective of design history, the first decade of the TVA produced four types of industrial object that expressed in form and function the aspirations of the era. First, and perhaps most imposing in terms of its unprecedented scale and dazzling complexity, was the machinery designed to transform raw hydraulic energy into electrical power and deliver it to prospective users. Second, many smaller-scale fixtures and interfaces display "design elements" that went beyond the narrowly functional requirements of engineering and technology. Third, the grand engineering enterprise of the TVA would have been meaningless—for its intended customers, at least—were it not translated into a family of domestic products and electrical appliances. And fourth were experiments in regional craft through which the TVA hoped to show that, far from obliterating the past, cheap electricity could spawn whole new industries that might revitalize the traditional craft culture of Appalachia and link it to the future. Across this continuum we find that design—as the projection of an idea—and engineering—the solution of a technical problem—worked to complement one another.

I. Hydro-Aesthetics

> Instead of the stimulus of detail and gewgaws we want surroundings which know their place and don't infringe upon the energies urgently needed for thought and action.
> —Roland Wank

In 1934, one year after the TVA received its charter, curator Alfred Barr, Jr., introduced the selection of 600 industrial, scientific, and commercial objects on display at New York's Museum of Modern Art (MoMA) with some reflections on the aesthetics of industrialism. Some designs, he proposed, are the result of deliberate artistic intent. Others—his examples included a helical bearing spring and a Vernier micrometer—have an innate beauty that is the unintentional expression of clarity, integrity, and due proportion.[9] Significantly, when a selection of dignitaries was invited to select the most beautiful objects in MoMA's landmark Machine Art exhibit, they ignored the home furnishings and kitchen accessories in favor of the more purely technical artifacts: an industrial spring was the choice of aviatrix

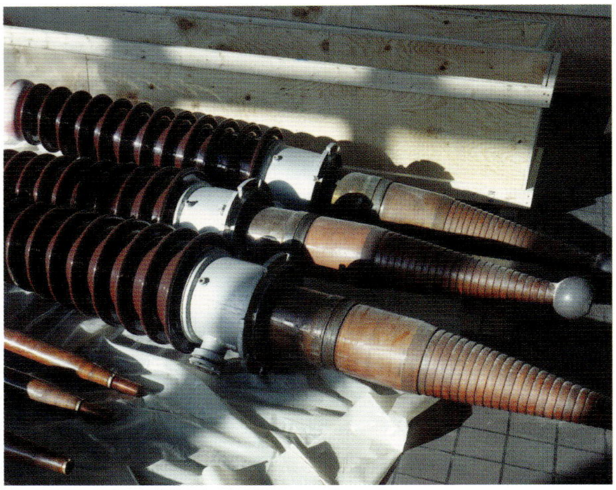

Electrical insulators at Norris Dam, 2003

Amelia Earhart; a steel ball-bearing assembly caught the eye of Charles Richards of the Museum of Science and Technology; philosopher John Dewey selected a serenely platonic ship's propeller manufactured by Alcoa—a hydroelectric turbine writ small.

Two decades after the Italian futurists sang their love of "the happy precision of gears and well-oiled thoughts," one decade after Commissar Anatoly Lunacharsky exhorted Soviet artists to "go into the factory where the real body of life is made," Machine Age America was beginning to appreciate the aesthetic implications of even the most highly technical artifacts. "Modular design, preassembly, and interchangeability of parts may [soon] achieve the status of major guiding principles," writes Wank of the expanding logic of mass production. Already, "smoothness of surface, accuracy of line, identical repetition of parts have become typical."[10] Attuned to the streamlined sensibility of the era, the planners of the TVA exploited every opportunity to domesticate their large-scale, engineering-driven systems and make their operation accessible to the public.

The electro-mechanical components that turn the erratic current of the Tennessee Valley waterways into a controlled current of electrical energy clearly belong at the technical as opposed to the artistic pole of Barr's continuum. Their formal geometries are compelling in and of themselves precisely because of their indifference to the humanist tradition according to which "man is the measure" of all things. The design of a bushing, one of the insulating posts mounted at the tops of large transformers and circuit breakers, for instance, is purely pragmatic: the taper of its ceramic coils serves only to minimize contact area, the luminous glow at the apex is of a nonconducting insulating oil intended to prevent the possibility of arcing. At the same time, the regimented armies of coils, insulators, sculptural bushings, and iconic masts, deployed like sentries in the switchyards

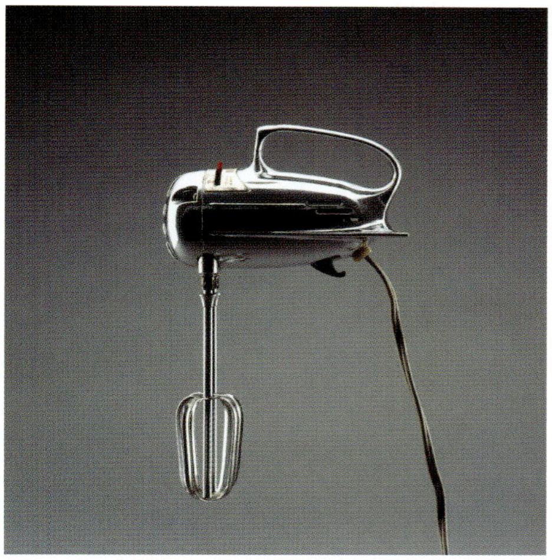

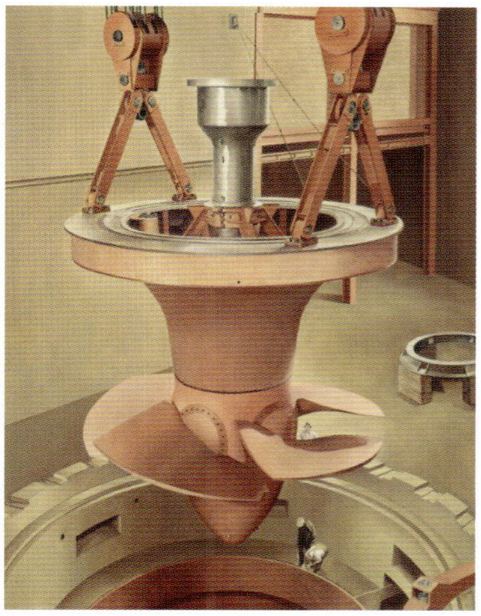

LEFT Designer unknown, *Mixall Jr.*, Portable Electric Mixer, 1945–55. Chromium plated steel, plastic, 17 × 25 × 7.5 cm. Produced by The Iona Manufacturing Company, East Hartford, Connecticut. The Liliane and David M. Stewart Program for Modern Design, Montreal, gift of Eric Brill. Photograph by Denis Farley.

RIGHT Charles Sheeler, *Suspended Power*, 1939. Oil on canvas, 33 × 26 × 2 in. Dallas Museum of Art, gift of Edmund J. Kahn.

and framed against the powerful massing of the dams, are striking expressions of the new technology and form part of the dramatic mise-en-scène of hydroelectric power generation. Years later, objects of this sort could still ignite the imagination of the Italian sculptor-designer Ettore Sottsass: "I want to make myself a filling pump where I can fill up forever on 4-star fuel, fill up my veins and set them alight."[11]

The same can surely be said of the most iconic of all of the machine parts, the hydraulic turbine generator, whose "suspended power" inspired Charles Sheeler's most dramatic painting and whose "pragmatic aesthetics" led Ezra Pound to conclude that "the beauty of machines (A.D. 1930) is now chiefly to be found in those parts of machines where the energy is most concentrated."[12] It was power, however, and not poetics that led the TVA to purchase for the Norris project two 68,000-horsepower Francis-type hydraulic turbines on October 22, 1934, from Newport News Shipbuilding & Dry Dock Company, Virginia, for $467,930. (That they should bear such an intimate family resemblance to ships' propellers is not surprising.) For Fontana Dam, the Authority bought two vertical Francis reaction turbines from the Allis-Chalmers Manufacturing Company.[13] There is not much room for applied artistry in the design of large-scale technical components—a variable-pitch turbine blade, whose specifications are determined by rigorous engineering calculations, does not need to be streamlined any more than it already is. The attempts by early industrial designers to transfer engineering design to product styling testify, however, to the profound symbolism of the new technology.[14]

As impressive as the artifacts may have been on their own terms, it was their deployment within the dramatically staged, theatrically lit, and finely scaled interiors of the TVA powerhouses that produced the most powerful aesthetic, and

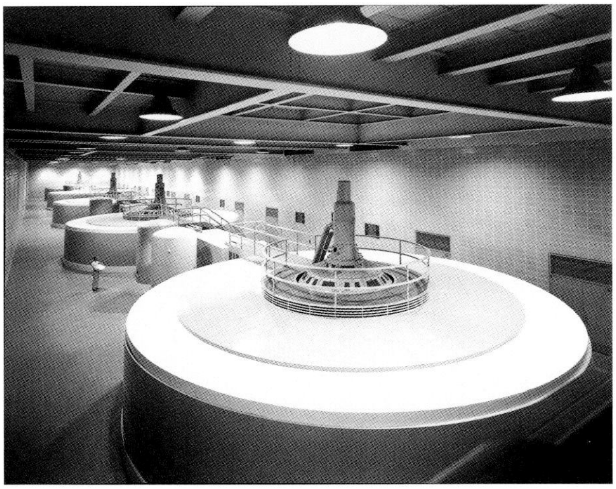

Watts Bar Dam powerhouse, 1939–42

even spiritual, effect. There is, at the very least, a suggestive visual affinity between the interior of the Watts Bar powerhouse—the powerful central nave paved in ceramic tiles; the catwalk ambulatory, accented by aluminum rails, connecting the iconic spires of its generators; the doors to its chapel-like control rooms framed by arches formed by the rhythmic chiaroscuro of the overhead arc lights—and a Romanesque basilica. It is impossible not to be reminded of "The Virgin and the Dynamo," Henry Adams's famous meditation on how technology has supplanted religion as the source of meaning in American life. "He began to feel the forty-foot dynamo as a moral force," the historian writes of his experience of gazing upon the giant Corliss steam engine on display at the Paris Exhibition in 1900. "Before the end one began to pray to it."[15]

This wave of emotion—the expression of what intellectual historian Perry Miller would call the "American technological sublime"[16]—was the deliberate and intended effect of installations that were, as the public was constantly reminded, Built for the People of the United States of America. Pilgrims were ushered into serenely appointed visitors' galleries and lofty observation decks—1,000 per day each at Wilson, Wheeler, and Norris within a year of their completion—where they could meditate upon the divine mysteries of hydroelectric power. "It was like history," effused one contemporary. "It was like epic poetry. It was like music."[17]

The aesthetics of TVA engineering express Wank's fervent belief in the "spiritual unity of modern design."[18] It is reflected both in the technically determined purity of its machine forms and in the evident premeditation involved in siting and displaying them to their best advantage. In addition, some of the installations carry deliberate elements of styling that situate them squarely within the persuasive language of industrial design. In a 1939 issue of the architectural

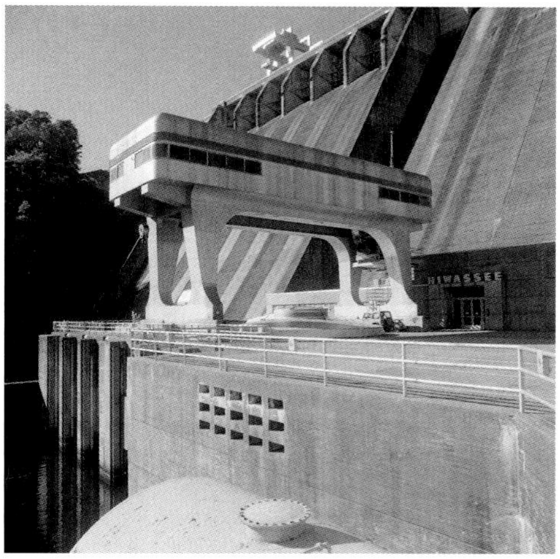

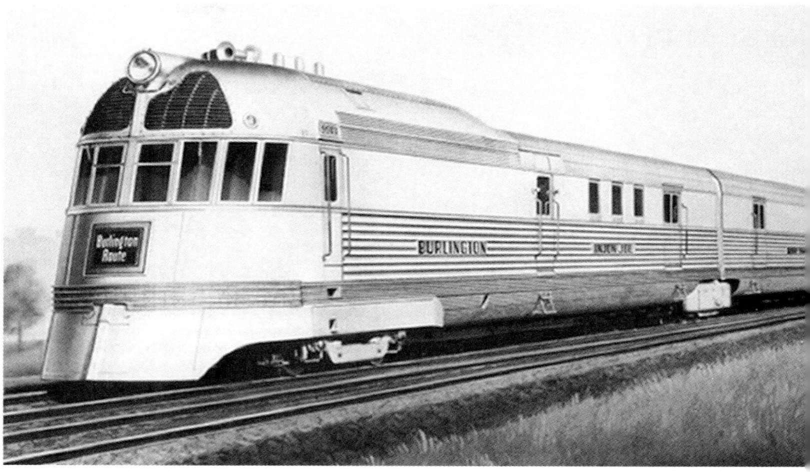

LEFT Hiwassee Dam, 1936–40

RIGHT Burlington Zephyr, produced by Budd Company, Troy, Michigan, 1934

journal *Pencil Points*, editor Kenneth Reid remarks perceptively on the huge traveling gantry crane at the early Wheeler Dam (1933–35), which he described as "a superb piece of engineering, dramatic in its forms, and full of that kind of complexity of pipes, conduits, pulleys, boxes, wheels, ladders, and riveted frames which is the conventional layman's idea of a great machine."[19] Wheeler had been built under plans developed by the Bureau of Reclamation, but by the time of later dams such as Pickwick Landing (1934–38), Chickamauga (1936–40), or Watts Bar (1939–42), the TVA's own engineers were in control and, as Reid notes, "the newer cranes and lifts...are totally different in feeling." The entire 112.5-ton structure had been radically simplified and sheathed in a sleek Streamline Moderne housing that has greater visual affinity with a 1936 Cord automobile or the back end of the Burlington Zephyr than with its own industrial ancestor.[20]

This sort of aesthetic intervention was becoming commonplace to a public that had, by this time, seen countless before-and-after images of refrigerators, cameras, office machines, and hotel lobbies that had been transformed by the seductive artistry of the industrial designer. What was new is the application of consumer-product styling to large-scale public works. As Reid concludes: "All the old false romanticism of the machine has disappeared."[21] It had been replaced by the new (but equally false) romanticism of design.

II. Human Factors

> In a dozen control buildings a handful of men will sit, and as they push buttons and turn switches the river will do as they wish.
> —Editors, *Architectural Forum*

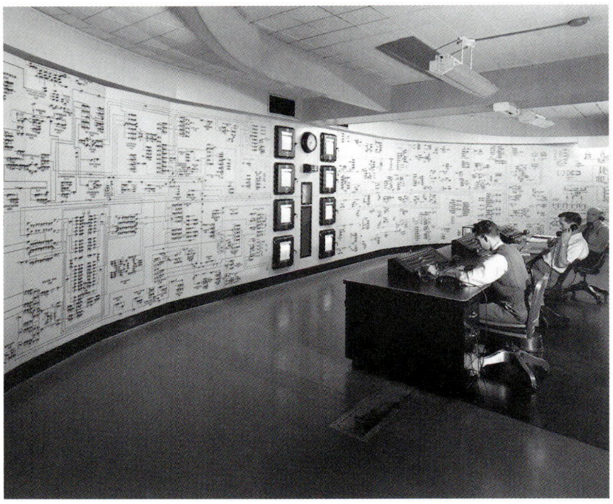

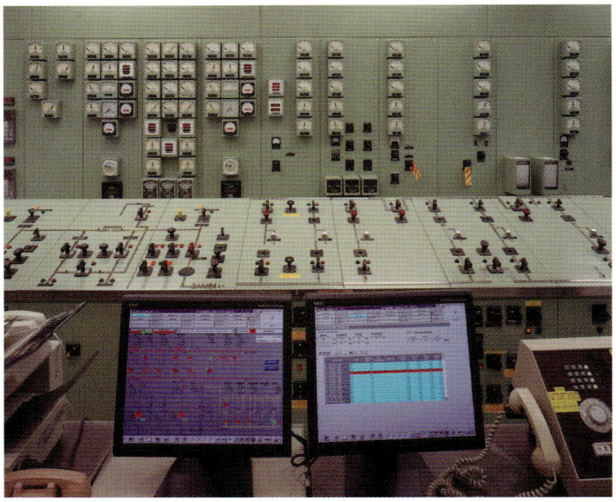

LEFT TVA central control board, Chattanooga, Tennessee, 1945

RIGHT Typical TVA dam control room, 2004

The overwhelmingly vast scale of the megatechnologies of the 1930s, not unlike the barely perceptible microtechnologies of today, made them seem remote, mysterious, and inaccessible. A laptop computer or a mobile gaming device implies discretionary consumer behavior, however, whereas the TVA was incorporated as a public utility and operated on the principle, as Wank put it, that "citizens at large are stockholders in the plant and are therefore entitled to all the courtesies and information due to plant owners."[22] This is an idealistic premise, of course, because the vast and unprecedented upheavals associated with the regional plan mobilized the anxiety, mistrust, and outright opposition of constituencies ranging from itinerant sharecroppers to private utilities to powerful real estate interests, not to mention individualists alarmed by the "socialistic" overtones of centralized planning. It was not simply a matter of "courtesies and information"; a skeptical and often hostile public had to be won over at a visceral level.

Harry Tour, a TVA engineer who frequently locked horns with Wank and his assistant, Mario Bianculli, captured the concerns of a public in search of a human scale in an interview with Creese:

> They hear the hum of the generators, and they are impressed by the size and the importance of it, but they don't understand it. It is completely foreign to their knowledge of things in the past, but the things that they do understand are handrailings on stairs, doorknobs, lighting fixtures, and floors.[23]

The directors, thus, made the bold decision to open the facilities to their citizen-owners and invite them to observe, in carefully staged settings, the operation of the technology that brought stability to their soil and electricity to their homes. This novel experiment in public relations resulted in the installation of visitor centers, educational panels, lookouts, and parks at all of the principal sites and in the design of galleries from which visitors could view, from behind double-glazed plate-glass windows, the technicians of the TVA as they artfully bent nature to their will. The domesticated electron was to the 1930s what the "friendly atom" was to the 1950s, and concerns about security, safety, or simply outright nuisance were overruled in favor of the propaganda value of engaging the public directly in the Promethean task of harnessing it. Wank's evangelical belief in the inherent beauty of honest technical forms predisposed him to share them with the public.

Despite some obviously theatrical gestures, the powerhouse control rooms were fundamentally designed around the requirements of the dam operators who monitored the entire facility from behind futuristic banks of controls. Whereas open, uncluttered spaces were an aesthetic preference in the design of modernist houses, visual access to all parts of the control room was a functional necessity. The indirect lighting that bathes the vaulted control room in an ethereal luminosity was intended to eliminate reflection and glare that could interfere with the reading of instruments. And although the visitor might experience "the hum of the powerhouse [as] truly the heartbeat of civilization," the technical operators were insulated from it by double windows set into thick rubber moldings and by the dampening effect of perforated acoustic ceiling tiles.

To be sure, the control room technician may have experienced something less than the ecstasy conjured by the futurist Filippo Tommaso Marinetti, who imagined this quintessentially modern type installed "in high-tension chambers where a hundred thousand volts flicker through great bays of glass."[24] Although it must remain a matter of speculation whether the employees of the TVA transferred to every button pushed and every switch thrown "the fullness and solidity of their own will," Marinetti's predictions were not entirely wide of the mark. In the decades before the system became computerized and automated, visitors could expect to see one or two operators seated at low, angled consoles, flanked by banks of cabinets containing monitoring and recording instruments. The filing cabinets from Steelcase and Speedomax recorders from Leeds & Northrup have long since yielded to digital readouts, blinking LEDs, and terabytes of storage. One can still see traces of the techno-aesthetics of the 1930s in today's TVA control room, in the vitreous-enameled rheostats and potentiometers supplied by the Ohmite Manufacturing Company of Chicago and the Westinghouse trip switches, circuit breakers, and synchroscopes, with their signature art deco styling, chrome accents, and Bakelite handles.

Most intriguing, perhaps, is the physical layout of the switchboards themselves, many elements of which survive despite the nearly constant stream of technical innovation that has marked the energy industry over the last sixty years. Just as interface designers today, recognizing their failure to wean us from the material world, are now striving to create the sensation of analog experience within a digital environment, so the instrument designers of the 1930s did not simply install banks of levers, panels of switches, and cascades of colored lights. The infant industrial-design movement was at this time groping toward the humanistic, "man-the-measure" concept soon to be canonized by industrial designer Henry Dreyfuss and his associates, according to which "the object being worked on is going to be ridden in, looked at, talked into, activated, operated, or in some other way used by people."[25] To soften the point of contact between operator and apparatus, the switchboards were laid out like subway maps to create a schematic, diagrammatic representation of the physical installation itself. At a glance the technician could follow the path of an electrical current, monitor the condition of the lines and equipment outside, and ultimately regulate the flow of water through the dam itself.

III. The Electrification of Everyday Life

> But what we are constantly keeping in mind in this electricity program is not dams, or generators or lines, but the everyday needs and desires of the men, women and children of the Tennessee Valley.
> —David Lilienthal

The ultimate aim of the TVA, as Senator Norris, its leading congressional advocate, always envisioned it, was to bring electricity to the homes and farms of the rural heartland. The vast structures, the state-of-the-art equipment, the armies of builders and operators, the garden villages of Norris and Fontana would have been for naught if the system had not connected what the fiber-optic industry today calls "the last mile." This program consisted of two initiatives: The first was to connect the surprising number of farms and rural communities of the seven states that still, by the early 1930s, had no electric service at all—to replace the kerosene lamp with the electric bulb. The second was to initiate the great majority of Tennessee Valley homes that had basic electric lighting into the further blessings of electric cooking, refrigeration, water heating, clothes washing, and the rest. It would be the equivalent, in today's information economy, of upgrading a home with a computer to a fully wired home.

For this program of social and electrical modernization to succeed, the TVA had to address the two interlocked obstacles that prevented the families of Appalachia from enjoying what its brochures tirelessly extolled as "the benefits of electricity": the cost of energy had to be driven down to a point where it became affordable by people of modest means. The only way to accomplish this, however, was to create the consumer demand—the "electric load," in the terminology of the industry—that would alone justify the massive TVA investment. "There is a vicious cycle which must be broken," declared the President, "and a wise public policy will break it."[26] The author of this wise policy was none other than the indomitable Lilienthal, who conceived a scheme that would induce private utility companies to lower their rates and manufacturers to produce high-quality but low-cost appliances. On December 19, 1933, Roosevelt signed an Executive Order creating the Electric Home and Farm Authority (EHFA).[27]

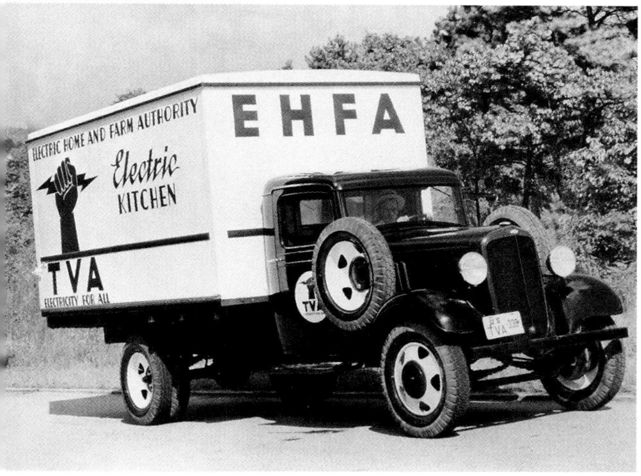

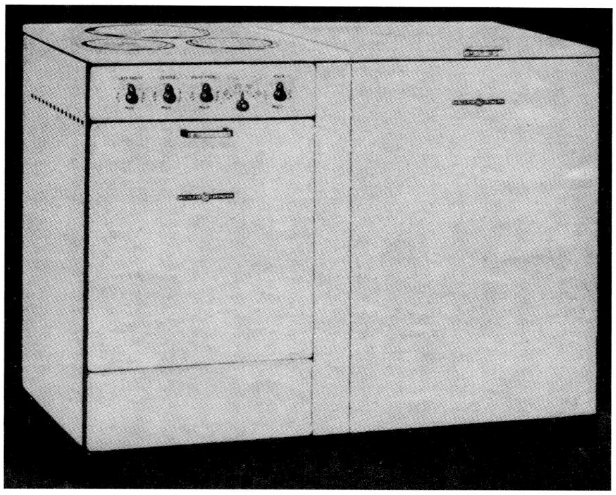

LEFT Truck sporting emblem of the Electric Home and Farm Authority, 1933
RIGHT Range and refrigerator, dubbed "Model T" by *Business Week*, produced by General Electric, Schenectady, New York, 1934. *Business Week*, June 16, 1934.

Under the terms of this quintessential New Deal program, the government would, in effect, jump-start the cycle at the demand end by providing ten million dollars in credits to help families purchase EHFA-approved electrical appliances on credit and at reduced prices. Lilienthal, director of the EHFA and its most tireless advocate, imagined a typical scenario in which a family would select a low-priced "standard model" refrigerator, water heater, or range: "She will order one of the special refrigerators, let us say, and her husband will sign the proper papers. If his credit is acceptable, a delivery will be made immediately and the dealer will be paid in cash by the Electric Home and Farm Authority."[28] Everybody wins, for as little as $5.33 per month.

At the heart of this complicated juggling act lay a disarmingly simple strategy of what a later age would call "counter-design." At a fraction of the cost of the sleek, full-featured models designed in the New York studios of Raymond Loewy, Lurelle Guild, and Walter Dorwin Teague, working families in the Tennessee Valley could buy stripped-down, dual-branded refrigerators, stoves, and water heaters bearing the trademark of a recognized manufacturer and the official seal of the EHFA—a blue fist grasping a lightning bolt above the TVA slogan proclaiming "Electricity for All."[29] Even as the industrial designers were easing their corporate clients out of a "top-down" and into a "middle-out" model of servantless, middle-class consumption, the EHFA was advocating a design program that was clearly "bottom-up."[30] Its aim was nothing less than to transform exhausted farmers and overworked housewives into dedicated energy consumers.

Yet, sales of the first generation of TVA-subsidized appliances proved disappointing: the manufacturers who responded to the TVA's great social experiment initially did little more than simplify hardware and remove accessories, and the trivial cost-savings that resulted did not meet the "base price" required to crack open the rural market and set in motion the whole cycle of rural electricity consumption. Under relentless pressure from Lilienthal, General Electric (GE) was the first to rise to the challenge with a fundamentally redesigned range-and-refrigerator set—a porcelain cooking range matched with a clean, white, top-opening icebox. *Business Week* heralded this ultraminimalist design as nothing less than "a Model T for the great mass market which will buy plain refrigeration just as it bought plain transportation."[31] The great mass market did not agree, however, and after only a year, poor customer response forced the EHFA to extend its financing program to a wider range of standard models. GE had produced a flawed and inconvenient design, but for the rural consumer, it was, in effect, the first piece of new design from the New Deal.

There was an obvious rationale to the EHFA's promotion of simple, high-quality, low-cost electrical goods: the more energy consumed, the cheaper it would become, and cheap hydroelectric energy meant prosperity and productivity. Electric pumps for individual wells would, for the first time, bring running water to remote farmsteads; plug-in radio sets would provide them with music, news, and "a knowledge of the interesting affairs of modern life."[32] In cities that were a part of the TVA power grid (including Knoxville, Tennessee; Chattanooga, Tennessee; and Florence, Alabama) people would learn to freeze their leftovers, iron their clothes, and entertain their children as never before. Our postmodern, postgendered, energy-exhausted age may find this image to be quaint, at best, but it needs to be appreciated within the broader social program of the New Deal. Energy was inexhaustible, women worked in the home, and cheap electricity did not serve simply to chill food and heat water. In the benevolent propaganda of the era, it represented the promise of happier and healthier families, of deeper understanding between farm and city, of a revived economy and a robust democracy.

As an unabashed agent of social modernization, the TVA waged an expressly ideological campaign whose twin targets were the appliance manufacturers and private utility companies that had refused to gamble on an economically underdeveloped segment of the market. *Electrical World*, the leading industry periodical of the day, recognized this when it editorialized that the EHFA could create the requisite consumer demand only by "extraordinary efforts to mold public opinion."[33] By this time the designers, self-appointed agents of persuasion, were already at work doing exactly that.

Symbolism Enough

With an expansiveness worthy of Goethe's autocratic Faust, Morgan reflected that "the Tennessee Valley is the first place in America where we can sit down and design a civilization."[34] The democratic ethos of the New Deal, however, required that the TVA win over the rural population—many of whom mistrusted the heavy hand of government or feared they would be physically displaced by the controlled flooding of the valley.[35] To do so, the TVA launched many schemes to promote local industry, mostly centered on the transformative power of electricity: as

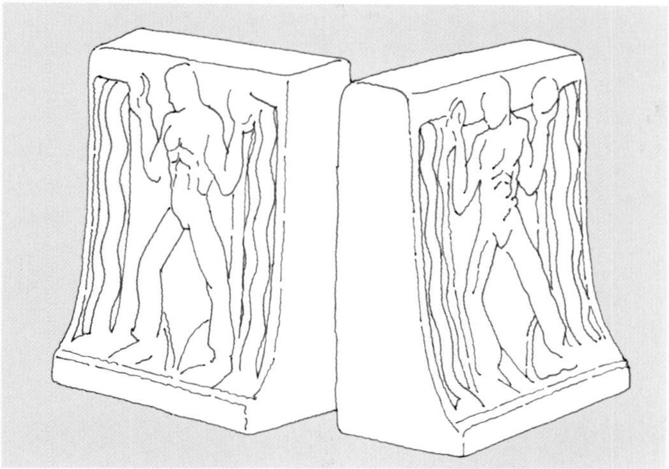

Bookends produced by the TVA Ceramics Laboratory, Norris, Tennessee, ca. 1936

hydroelectric power turned phosphates into fertilizer and bauxite into aluminum (used for everything from aluminum foil to long-range bombers), unskilled workers would find jobs that opened onto a dramatically different future. But the romantic-populist Morgan was committed to the survival of the Appalachian craft tradition, and under his guidance design was once again enlisted in the campaigns of the TVA.

In 1935, Morgan set up the Ceramics Research Laboratory in the model community of Norris in hopes of spawning an indigenous industry: its products would be crafted from the kaolin clay of the Appalachian hills, its electric kilns powered by TVA energy, and the traditional skills of the Tennessee Valley would be revived under the technical guidance of recently repatriated ceramics engineer Robert Gould. By 1938, however, Morgan's influence was rapidly waning, and shortly before his dismissal, TVA determined that "the primary objectives were approaching completion, and further operation [of the lab] was unwarranted."[36] By this time the lab had produced numerous prototypes: teapots emblazoned with power masts and bolts of electrical energy, souvenir ashtrays bearing the image of Norris Dam, and even some experiments with sanitary bathroom fixtures. Among the surviving artifacts, one particularly resonates with the ideals of the TVA and its use of design to win over a skeptical public: a pair of porcelain bookends designed to be lit from within by five-watt bulbs that illuminate a stylized bas-relief figure, Mosaic in his command, Promethean in his strength, Faustian in his spirit, holding back the raging waters of the Clinch River.[37] The heroic spectacle of civilization taming the destructive powers of nature was so appealing that a bill was debated in Congress that would have mandated the carving of such a figure into the face of the Norris Dam. The proposed bill was defeated: the designers of the TVA had done their work, and the dam was symbolism enough.

Notes

1. Johann Wolfgang von Goethe, *Faust*, 2:11544–6.

2. Walter L. Creese, *TVA's Public Planning: The Vision, The Reality* (Knoxville: University of Tennessee Press, 1990), 169.

3. Roosevelt, Franklin D., *The Year of Crisis, 1933*, vol. 2, *The Public Papers and Addresses of Franklin D. Roosevelt, 1928–1945* (New York: Random House, 1938), 22.

4. Arthur E. Morgan, *The Making of the TVA* (Buffalo, New York: Prometheus Books, 1974), 93–103.

5. David Lilienthal, quoted in R. L. Duffus and Charles Krutch, *The Valley and Its People* (New York: Alfred A. Knopf, 1946), 77.

6. As described by the editors of *Architectural Forum*:

> What really happened was this: Lilienthal and his administrative aid[e]s knew that the project must be made exciting and impressive to the people. They knew that it must also be designed by engineers. They feared that the engineers would destroy piece by piece many a fine architectural idea, not because of hostility but because of the engineer's inborn suspicion of things done for looks.

Building, U.S.A. (New York: McGraw Hill, 1957), 111.

7. Roland Wank, "Nowhere to Go but Forward," *Magazine of Art* 34, no. 1 (January 1941): 8.

8. These themes have been emphasized both by contemporaries and in recent scholarship. For a relevant selection, see the essays in Wendy Kaplan, ed., *Designing Modernity: The Arts of Reform and Persuasion, 1885–1945* (New York: Thames and Hudson, 1995).

9. Alfred H. Barr, Jr., foreword to *Machine Art* (1934; repr., New York: Museum of Modern Art, 1994); Sidney Lawrence, "Clean Machines at the Modern," *Art in America* 72, no. 2 (February 1984).

10. Wank, "Nowhere to Go but Forward," 8–10.

11. Ettore Sottsass, "Menhir, Ziggurat, Stupas, Hydrants & Gas Pumps," in *Ettore Sottsass: Ceramics*, ed. Bruno Bischofsberger, 86 (San Francisco: Chronicle Books, 1996).

12. Ezra Pound, "Machine Art" in *Machine Art and Other Writings: The Lost Thought of the Italian Years*, ed. Maria Luisa Ardizzone, 57 (Durham: Duke University Press, 1996). On the circumstances of Charles Sheeler's paintings, which were commissioned by *Fortune* magazine for a special Power issue, see Terry Smith, *Making the Modern: Industry, Art, and Design in America* (Chicago: University of Chicago Press, 1993), 432–40.

13. *The Fontana Project*, TVA Technical Report No. 12 (Washington, D.C.: U.S. Government Printing Office, 1949), 435; *The Norris Project*, TVA Technical Report No. 1 (Washington, DC: U.S. Government Printing Office, 1940). The author is grateful to Patricia Bernard Ezzell of the TVA Historical Archives for assistance in identifying these sources.

14. For contrasting perspectives on industrial design and the cult of streamlining, see Claude Lichtenstein and Franz Engler, eds., *Streamlined: The Aesthetics of Minimized Drag* (Zürich: Lars Müller, 1995); Christina Cogdell, *Eugenic Design: Streamlining America in the 1930s* (Philadelphia: University of Pennsylvania Press, 2004).

15. Henry Adams continues: "The planet itself seemed less impressive, in its old-fashioned, deliberate, daily or annual revolution, than this huge wheel, revolving within arm's length at some vertiginous speed." Henry Adams, *The Education of Henry Adams: An Autobiography* (Boston and New York, 1918), 380. Others have found this passage equally irresistible, including Richard Guy Wilson, Dickran Trasjian, Dianne H. Pilgrim, "The Machine in the Landscape," in *The Machine Age in America, 1918–1941* (New York: Abrams, 1986), 122.

16. Perry Miller, *The Life of the Mind in America from the Revolution to the Civil War* (New York: Harcourt Brace, 1965), 296–311. On the aesthetics of machinery, cf. Leo Marx, "The Machine," in *The Machine in the Garden: Technology and the Pastoral Ideal in America* (London: Oxford University Press, 1964); John F. Kasson, "The Aesthetics of Memory," in *Civilizing the Machine: Technology and Republican Values in America, 1776–1900* (Harmondsworth [London]: Penguin, 1977). The concept of the "technological sublime" has been reconstructed by David E. Nye, *American Technological Sublime* (Cambridge, MA: MIT Press, 1994).

17. Duffus and Krutch, *The Valley and Its People*, 78.

18. Wank, "Nowhere to Go but Forward," 7.

19. Kenneth Reid, "Design in TVA Structures," *Pencil Points* 10 (1939): 44.

20. Reyner Banham, "Valley of the Dams," in *A Critic Writes: Essays by Reyner Banham* (Berkeley and Los Angeles: UC Press, 1996), 203–7.

21. Reid, "Design in TVA Structures," 44.

22. Roland Wank, "Powerhouses," in *Forms and Functions of Twentieth-Century Architecture*, ed. Talbot Hamlin, 259–60 (New York: Columbia University Press, 1952).

23. Harold Tour, interview with Walter Creese, in Creese, *TVA's Public Planning*, 177–78.

24. Filippo Marinetti, *Le futurism* (Paris, 1912), quoted in Reyner Banham, *Theory and Design in the First Machine Age* (Cambridge, MA: MIT Press, 1980), 125.

25. Henry Dreyfuss, frontispiece to *Designing for People* (New York: Simon & Schuster, 1955). For a more recent perspective on technical affordances, cf. Donald Norman, *The Psychology of Everyday Things* (New York: Basic Books, 1988), 91–99.

26. President Roosevelt in an address of 1936, quoted in Ronald Tobey, *Technology as Freedom: The New Deal and the Electrical Modernization of the American Home* (Berkeley: University of California Press, 1996), 112.

27. Gregory B. Field, "'Electricity for All': The Electric Home and Farm Authority and the Politics of Mass Consumption, 1932–35," *Business History Review*, Spring 1990, 32–60; Thomas K. McCraw, *TVA and the Power Fight, 1933–1939* (Philadelphia: J. B. Lippincott, 1971), 123–24.

28. Lilienthal, "The Electrification of the American Home," 3.

29. The Madison Avenue firm of Young & Rubicam designed the emblem for the Electric Home and Farm Authority (EHFA), effectively a subsidiary of the TVA and governed by the same triumvirate of directors: David Lilienthal, Arthur H. Morgan, and Harcourt Morgan.

30. By "top-down" I mean to suggest the corporation's control of what the consumer will have; "bottom-up" characterizes the TVA/EFHA model of following the wishes of the people; "middle-out" is the transitional stage in which designers translated consumer needs into corporate strategies. Shelley Nickles, "'Preserving Women': Refrigerator Design as Social Progress in the 1930s," *Technology and Culture* 43, no. 4 (October 2002): 724–26. On streamlining, cleanlining, and the industrial design of the modern kitchen, cf. Jeffrey Meikle, *Twentieth Century Limited: Industrial Design in America, 1925–39* (Philadelphia: Temple University Press, 1979), 101–7; John Heskett, "Technological Innovation and Design for the Home," in *Industrial Design* (New York: Oxford University Press, 1980). Although it never lived up to Lilienthal's expectations, by 1938, when the EHFA was transferred to the Rural Electrification Authority, it had purchased over 100,000 installation contracts from over 2,500 dealers in 33 states. Tobey, *Technology as Freedom*, 113.

31. "Model T Appliances," *Business Week*, March 17, 1934, 10.

32. Electric Home and Farm Authority, "Toward an Electrified America," pamphlet, TVA Library, Knoxville.

33. Editors, *Electrical World*, 1933, quoted in Tobey, *Technology as Freedom*, 120.

34. Arthur E. Morgan, quoted in North Callahan, *TVA: Bridge Over Troubled Waters* (South Brunswick, NJ: A. S. Barnes, 1980), 95.

35. The numbers were not trivial. For its first major project, the TVA purchased 153,00 acres by eminent domain, displacing some 3,000 rural families from the Norris Basin. Michael J. McDonald and John Muldowny, *TVA and the Dispossessed: The Resettlement of Population in the Norris Dam Area* (Knoxville: University of Tennessee Press, 1982), 4.

36. Cited in "The Great Porcelain Experiment," Tennessee Valley Authority, http://www.tva.gov/heritage/porcelain/index.htm. On Morgan and the crafts of Norris, see also Christine Macy and Sarah Bonnemaison, *Architecture and Nature: Creating the American Landscape* (London: Routledge, 2003), 183–88; David Whisnant, *All that is Native and Fine: The Politics of Culture in an American Region* (Chapel Hill: University of North Carolina Press, 1983).

37. "Articles sent to the Norris Branch Library," a two-page, typed document, February 2, 1987, TVA Library, Knoxville.

TVA Graphics: A Language of Power

STEVEN HELLER

In the alphabet soup that was FDR's New Deal, the Tennessee Valley Authority was the most ambitious public works undertaking of them all. The Works Progress Administration (WPA) raised the nation's morale from the depths of Depression, the Rural Electrictification Administration (REA) illuminated the darkest segments of American society, the Civilian Conservation Corps (CCC) taught invaluable lessons about natural resources to the nation's youth, and the Federal Theater Project (FTP), Federal Writers' Project (FWP), and Federal Art Project (FAP) brought art and culture back into national prominence. But it was the regional TVA that proved that social-minded determinism could literally move mountains and divert rivers for the benefit of the "forgotten Americans." Much of this was realized through intelligent design.

The New Deal, President Roosevelt's historic plan inaugurated in 1933 to reinvigorate an economically traumatized nation, was controversial for how it flexed the federal government's muscle over states' sovereignty. Threatened by what they believed was the specter of socialism, reactionaries in Congress—of which there were many—tried but were unable to halt Roosevelt's engine of progress. Although individual states, especially in the South, had historically opposed Washington's intervention in their local and regional affairs, FDR found constitutional loopholes allowing his Democratic administration to institute and fund a slew of national programs designed to improve the fortunes of the downtrodden and create the solid bedrock on which vital social welfare systems were built. Government-sponsored optimism was at its peak, and although WPA financing was routinely curtailed and the entire enterprise was ultimately shut down by Congress in 1943, its short-term goals were met and long-term benefits continued for decades. Although the resolute dismantling by today's conservatives has virtually eliminated New Dealism (as though it were the devil's work) from American political life, the WPA's design scheme—its monumental architecture and graphic

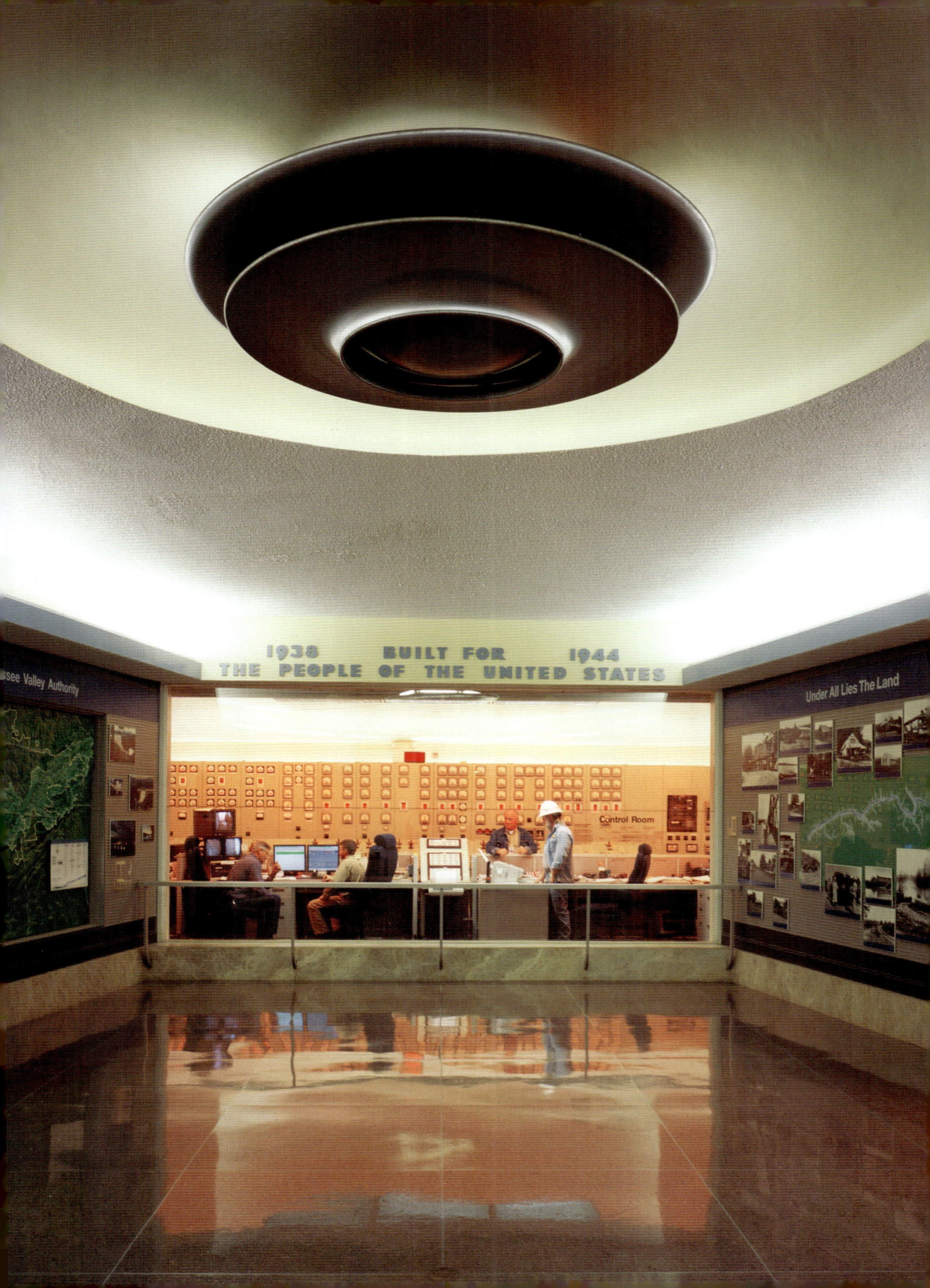
1938 BUILT FOR 1944
THE PEOPLE OF THE UNITED STATES
see Valley Authority
Under All Lies The Land
Control Room

artifacts—and coordinated design programs throughout the other public works agencies attest to its colossal impact on the nation.

Today, a curiously persistent longing for the 1930s continues, even among those who were not yet born. But nostalgia for this seemingly halcyon epoch (which, in fact, that chaotic time was anything but) when the federal government actively sought to improve the lot of its citizens is not the only reason for such interest in the New Deal in general and the WPA and TVA in particular. Pragmatically speaking, the WPA and TVA are still models during the current period of the United States' diminished worldwide prestige and eroding fortunes. The two agencies show how socially conscious collaborations between government and industry—not simply quests for excessive profits—can still spark national pride. The WPA and TVA were established during an enlightened moment in U.S. history when engineers, architects, and designers of all stripes joined together in a common cause to improve living conditions and thus ensure the greatness of the United States. It was an excellence symbolized as much by the outward trappings of the New Deal—its overall design style—as it was by the remarkable public works undertakings.

OVERLEAF Control room from visitor center lobby at Kentucky Dam 2005

The WPA director Harry Hopkins shrewdly invited artists from various disciplines into his ranks, not merely to fulfill the fundamental design requisites of his mammoth agency but to completely define its visual persona (or in today's argot, the total brand experience). As a consequence, the WPA brand, with its stark icons of progressivism, became as American as apple pie. Employing a bold visual language made up of expressive minimalist forms, designers replaced outmoded and dull graphic styles rooted in antiquated nineteenth-century traditions with demonstratively modern ones. The WPA's extensive fount of posters promoting everything from personal health and industrial safety to theatrical performances and art exhibits, as well as informational signs, charts, and displays with a variety of messages, used typography and emblematic illustrations adapted from modern sources including the Bauhaus, constructivism, and futurism, as well as French and Italian art moderne, or art deco, mannerisms.

American modernism grew and flourished within the WPA. And following its influential lead, the TVA introduced modernism to architecture—including dams, bridges, and power stations—to interiors—including offices, cafeterias, and educational public spaces—and to exhibitions and signage systems. During the 1930s, one of the most cataclysmic periods in twentieth-century American history, design was a principal tool of recovery. Nonetheless, modern design was initially suspected by some as having dubious political agendas, and this mode of communication was not embraced by all.

The Slow Embrace of Modernism

Following the unprecedented economic boom of World War I—which elevated the United States to a world power—national commerce started sagging under the weight of overproduction. The design of commercial products had stagnated. In

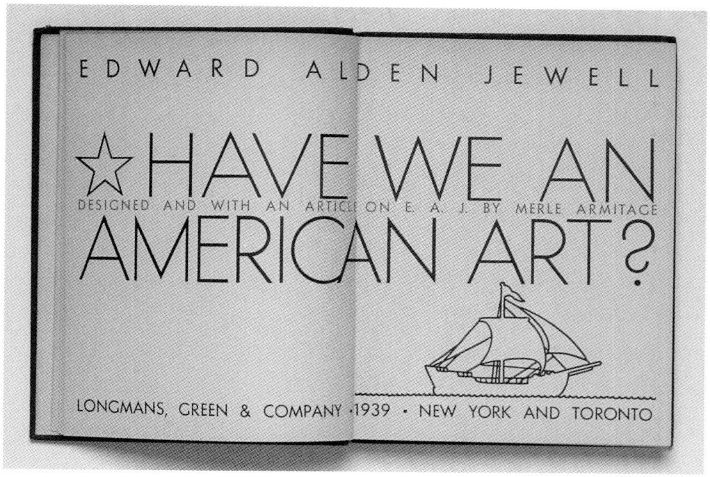

Title pages for Edward Alden Jewell, *Have We an American Art* (Longmans, Green & Company, 1939), designed by Merel Armitage. The designer was known for his startling moderne sans-serif typography that evoked the Streamline era.

fact, Henry Ford's 1910 exhortation when asked whether there would be stylistic variety in the automobile business, "You can have it in any color as long as it is black," symbolized the ongoing design malaise that contributed to the economic lethargy. In Europe during the mid-1920s, however, what can be termed commercial modernism—the widespread adoption and fusion of avant-gardisms into everyday production—was an alternative to both traditional and radical approaches.

The mannerisms born of this sensibility spread via France throughout the continent and the United Kingdom owing to the Exposition Internationale des Arts Décoratifs et Industriels Modernes (1925), the playground of modernity in Paris along the banks of the Seine. Laid out in boulevards lined with funhouses of consumerism decorated with geometric, planar ornament and neoclassical friezes incorporating functional and decorative designs, the exposition marked the rebirth of a pan-European (and ultimately an international) style. The world's leading clothing, furniture, and housewares manufacturers and many grand retail emporia were encouraged to exhibit their latest products and designs. But one player was noticeably absent. The United States, the largest industrial nation with the most expansive consumer culture, declined an invitation to participate at the urging of its industrial leaders. On September 21, 1925, U.S. Secretary of Commerce Herbert Hoover (the president on whose watch the Great Depression occurred in 1929) apologetically announced to the Fourth Annual Exposition of Women's Arts and Industries that although "we produce a vast volume of goods of much artistic value...[the United States could not] contribute sufficiently varied design of unique character or of special expression in American artistry to warrant such participation."[1]

Why was the United States so far behind? European radical modern avant-gardes—futurism, Dada, Bauhaus, De Stijl, constructivism—had already embraced

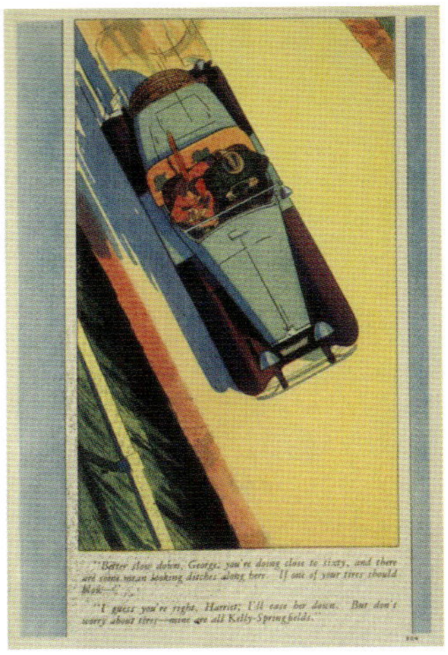

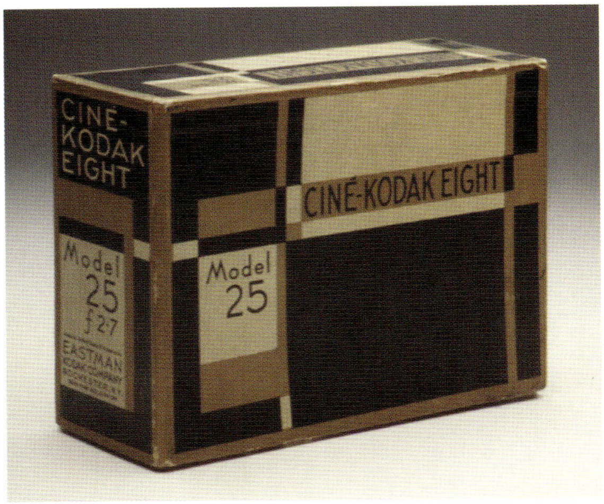

LEFT Advertisement for the Marmon automobile, c. 1928. The aerial view of the speeding roadster is rendered to evoke a sense of speed and motion in this static space.

RIGHT Package design for Cine-Kodak Eight movie camera, c. 1932. The quintessential art deco design for the most contemporary of film cameras.

the machine and proffered the integration of modern art and industry. Meanwhile, American industrialists, who could certainly afford to improve the look of their products, were either apathetic or suspicious of the socialist and communist implications of modernism. What they did not resist were marketing strategies that would ensure increased earnings. So, following a brief economic downturn in the early twenties and a subsequent boom, industry fervently sought new means of stimulating sales. The profit motive, not any transcendent utopian ethic or aesthetic ideal, paved the way for commercial modernism in the United States. It was ostensibly introduced by the advertising industry after 1925, specifically by Earnest Elmo Calkins, a design reformer and founder of Calkins and Holden Advertising Company. Like other American advertising and marketing executives, he visited the Exposition Internationale des Arts Décoratifs et Industriels Modernes and was wholly inspired by what he saw.

Describing the array of cubist and futurist graphics, Calkins writes in the 1933 article "The Dividends of Beauty": "Modernism offered the opportunity of expressing the inexpressible, of suggesting not so much a motor car as speed, not so much a gown as style, not so much a compact as beauty."[2] If this sounded like one of Italian futurist Filippo Tommaso Marinetti's earlier manifestos, it was because Calkins studied and borrowed from the European avant-garde. He was a tireless advocate of a formalist version of modernity in commercial art and industrial design, or what a leading advertising trade journal, *Printers' Ink*, in 1928 called "foreign art ideas." For most advertising art directors, modernism was a bag of tricks the artist could use to set an ordinary product apart, and advertising artists were indeed quick to appreciate the possibilities of modernism, since realistic art had reached what Calkins termed a "dead level of excellence."[3] It was

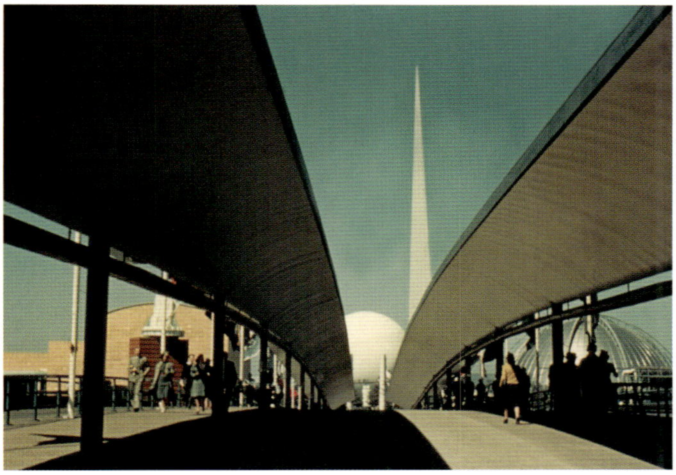

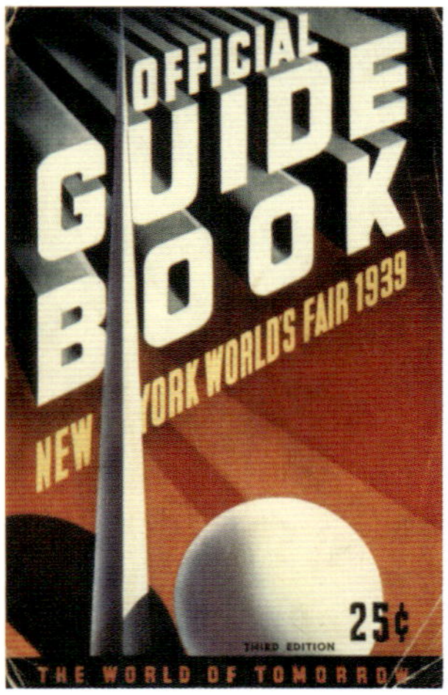

LEFT Kodachrome photograph of the Trylon and Perisphere, the centerpiece of the New York World's Fair ("The World of Tomorrow"), as seen from one of the futuristic walkways, 1939.
RIGHT Cover of the *Official Guide Book, New York World's Fair 1939*. The airbrush rendering of the Trylon and Perisphere is rendered in the Streamline style.

no longer possible to make an advertisement striking, conspicuous, and attractive using elegant still lifes.

Spearheaded by Calkins and Holden, and later adopted by such motivated agencies as N. W. Ayer (which opened its own galleries to display and promote modern advertising art) and Kenyon and Eckart, commonplace objects, including toasters, refrigerators, and coffee tins, were portrayed in advertisements against stark geometric patterns and dramatically skewed angles. These and other wares were shown in surrealistic and futuristic settings accented by contemporary typefaces with futuristic-sounding names like Cubist Bold, Vulcan, Broadway, Novel Gothic. Since the European New Typography (codified in 1925 by German typographer Jan Tschichold and practiced at the Bauhaus and elsewhere) proffered asymmetry as a sign of modernity, designers in the United States fostering the new aesthetics embraced such mannerisms. But this was ostensibly a packaging ploy, superficially eye-catching at best. The revolution was still to come in other design areas on a much larger scale.

Styling as a Prelude to Modernism

The dichotomy, for instance, between progressive advertising and dreary product design was a defining paradox. In Calkins's view, advertising was the Hy-test fuel running the engines of industry, and he saw in the next stage a new "styling" of manufactured goods. The term he used was "obsoletism." "We no longer wait for things to wear out," he added. "We displace them with others that are not more efficient but more attractive."[4] This cart-before-the-horse attitude, though intended to raise the standard of American wares through design, was greeted with considerable criticism.

Frederic Ehrlich, a columnist for design-trade journals, termed commercial modernism "a dark cloud," referring specifically to the decorative excesses in type, layout, ornament, and package designs created in the reflexive zeal to be modern. "'Modernism'...got off on the wrong foot in America," asserted advertising and industrial designer Walter Dorwin Teague in *Advertising Arts*. "It had been developing as a school of design for many years in Europe, outgrowing its absurdities and cutting its wisdom teeth. But it burst on America as a full-fledged surprise, and we've never quite recovered from the shock." He further argued that designers untutored in honest modernist principles merely exploited the trend for its novelty: "They figured that the queerer they made their stuff, the better....Such was the penalty we paid for barging into a full-grown movement, instead of growing up with it. We had measles late in life."[5]

Intense hostility to archaic traditions and promulgation of utopianism—the philosophical center of European avant-garde modernist movements—were not beliefs in the forefront of the domesticated modernity embraced by American business. Although certain visual conceits of radical modernism were influential, American designers were required to smooth out the edges or domesticate modernism by introducing certain ornamental conceits and accentuating a decorative rather than a purely functional sensibility, lest they rise too far above public tastes—or the ethos designer Raymond Loewy called "most advanced yet acceptable" (MAYA). Orthodox modernists disparagingly called this "modernistic," a vulgarization of true Modernism with a capital "M." From the perspective of the purist, this was valid description.

Yet modernism was never truly monolithic, nor loyal to one particular ideology. Indeed, the term is still quite slippery. Innovative technologies in the United States were considerably different from those in Europe, and design has always been a response to, if not collaboration with, technology. Modernity for the masses was epitomized in the United States by the setback, Aztec-styled silhouettes of distinctly American—particularly New York—skyscrapers, a product of engineering and design that surpassed European efforts and abilities. By the 1930s, industrial, product, and graphic designs—what many lumped under the rubric "industrial art"—were determined more by principles of science and engineering than style and aesthetics alone. Industrial art was as logical an expression of the 1930s as religious art was of the fifteenth century. "Business can and may be as stimulating a patron of the arts as the cardinals, prelates, and popes who represented the Church," writes Calkins.[6]

Maybe so, but despite such flowery punditry, American design took a while to find its distinctive footing. The impetus was there, but ultimately modern design required directed initiatives by designers to alter the status quo. From the late twenties and throughout the thirties—prior to and during the Great Depression—Designers for Industry, a self-proclaimed and often self-educated group of disparate graphic,

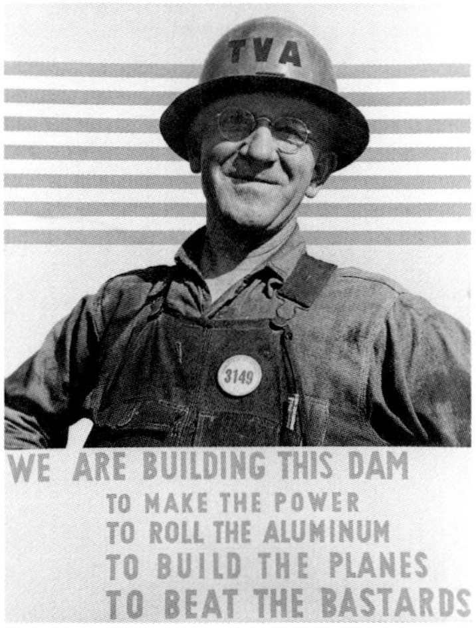

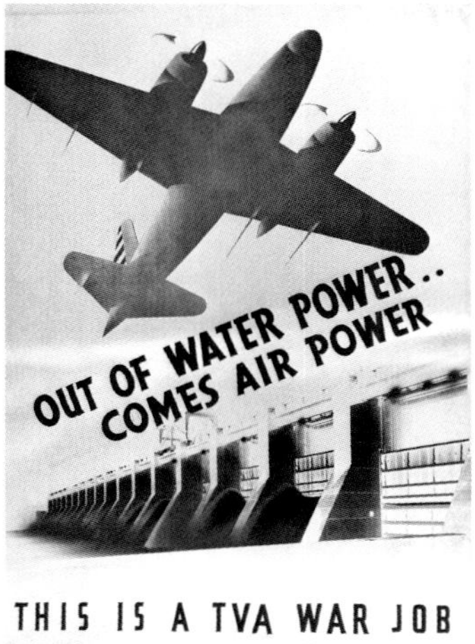

LEFT The worker was a common focal point for many WPA and TVA posters, 1942.
RIGHT TVA posters used the same photomontage techniques that were common in everything from American-government murals to Soviet propaganda tableaux, 1942.

product, industrial, and advertising designers, established themselves as the first wave in the transformation of dreary American design from staid post-Victorianism into Machine Age modernism. They propagandized and proselytized through manifestos, advertisements, and exhibitions aimed at the scions of business. Ultimately, they forged a new form and style to both symbolize and express the Machine Age in the United States: "Streamline."

Streamline, the American Style

These new designers for industry were not like nineteenth-century decorators, known for hiding machinery under layers of rococo, baroque, and art nouveau ornament, but were rather futuristic visionaries—inventors and form givers all. They believed fine and applied art should be of its time, and products must represent the era in which they are produced. The result was a distinct style rooted in functionality. Streamlining evolved from the pragmatic need to minimize wind and water resistance in the design of ships, trains, cars, and planes. The teardrop shape emerged because it allowed for faster movement. This practical, if somewhat shocking, form-language was gradually embraced by the mass population and came to symbolize the mechanized tempo of daily life. The semantics of streamlining implies a modicum of artifice—the application of aerodynamic and other progressive engineering principles to products and machinery does not result in significantly increased efficiency for all applications. Yet Streamline design signaled the good and bad of Machine Age retooling. Although not as pure in its rejection of ornament as members of the Bauhaus would have liked, the American Streamline ethos was nonetheless progressive within the strictures of popular art. Modernistic graphics, characterized by sleek, airbrushed veneers (the airbrush was

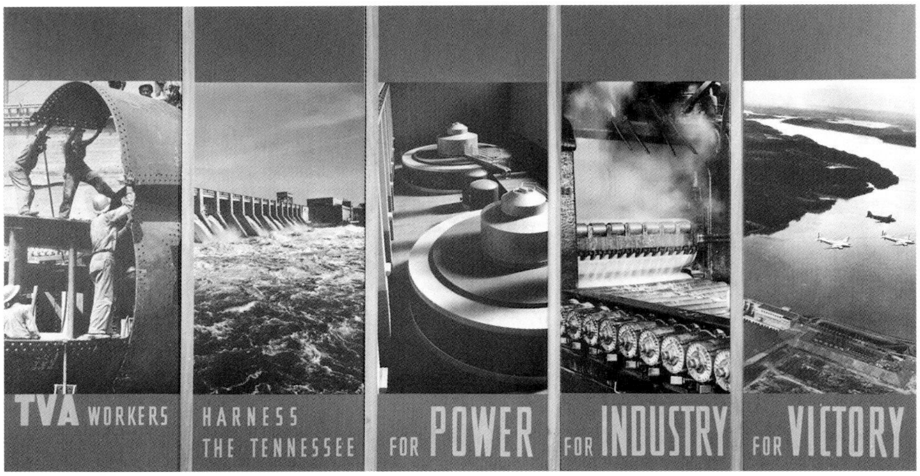

"Power for Industry and Victory" poster takes a page out of *Life* magazine in using extreme close-up photography to heroicize the architecture and machines of the TVA, 1942.

the key tool in altering the fundamental look of type and image) triggered a sense of optimism, if for no other reason than because it suggested forward movement—change.

By 1938, streamlining was such a widespread (indeed vernacular) practice that the leading design chroniclers of the day, Sheldon and Martha Chandler Cheney, write in their popular analysis of American industrial design, *Art and the Machine*, that "everywhere, there is...merchandise distinguished by the beauty that is peculiarly a product of artist and machine working together."[7] Their survey includes everything from automobiles to pencil sharpeners to posters and books. But the real fulcrum of their survey was not merely the household appliance with Streamline veneer but the grand machines, the great turbines and transformers built by the TVA and other public works, which both defined and produced American power. These facilities and their designs identified the United States as the most powerful industrial nation.

The greatest testament—indeed, coda—to design for the public good, with Streamline design as its foremost agent, was the 1939–40 New York World's Fair. Its majestic Trylon and Perisphere, designed by Wallace K. Harrison and J. Andre Fouilhoux—with the idealistic, theme-centered diorama *Democracity*, suitably housed in the enormous Perisphere, a white futuristic temple—served as the fair's indelible architectural trademark. The Perisphere was the largest "floating" globe ever built by man—180 feet in diameter and eighteen stories high, twice the size of that other art moderne gem, Radio City Music Hall. The theme center emerged after more than one thousand sketches and models and, despite its unique form, was not without design precedents, including references to the Bauhaus and constructivism. Not just a mere trade show, the fair was endowed with mythic qualities; it was called "The World of Tomorrow," and "The Dawn of

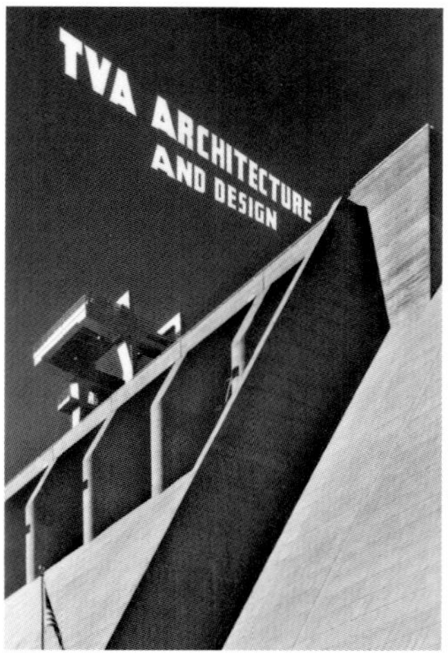

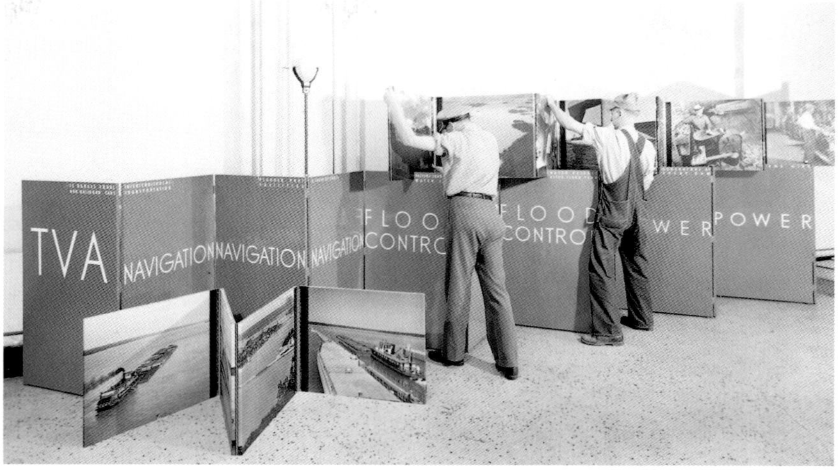

LEFT A synthesis of graphic and architectural form in TVA posters, 1941

RIGHT This photographic display was a tried-and-true means of telling the narrative about the TVA, 1940.

a New Day," a "masterpiece of showmanship," the "epitome of stagecraft"—a Land of Oz indelibly etched in the memories of those who attended and in the imaginations of those who did not. It celebrated city planning and public works, by implication touting the accomplishments of the WPA and TVA, which had taken the lead in such endeavors. Through a critical mass of graphic displays, the fair proffered the notion that public works were at the core of highest American values, and design was key to its success. Although the Second World War would soon put a halt to such works, it was clear design would continue to play a role in the United States' progress.

Propagating the TVA

The TVA was the most far-reaching design experiment of all the New Deal initiatives, encompassing not only architecture but interior, exhibition, environmental, and graphic design. Graphic designers held staff positions in several divisions of the TVA, notably in the Information Division and the Public Relations Department, which were responsible for exhibitions and displays documenting the TVA's achievements. Charles Krutch was the TVA's chief photographer and head of graphic arts for the information division until 1954. Chronicling the TVA was a key aspect of its aggressive public-relations campaigns.

The more iconic posters and printed ephemera preserved in contemporary graphic-design histories were produced for New Deal projects other than the TVA (Lester Beall's exquisite 1937 series for the REA, for example, are well documented and celebrated today because, through their colorful simplicity, they characterize a modern style that is unique to the United States). Yet, the TVA arguably initiated the most uniform design scheme of all New Deal activities. Each administrative office, power station, and turbine housing was adorned with simple, stark Gothic

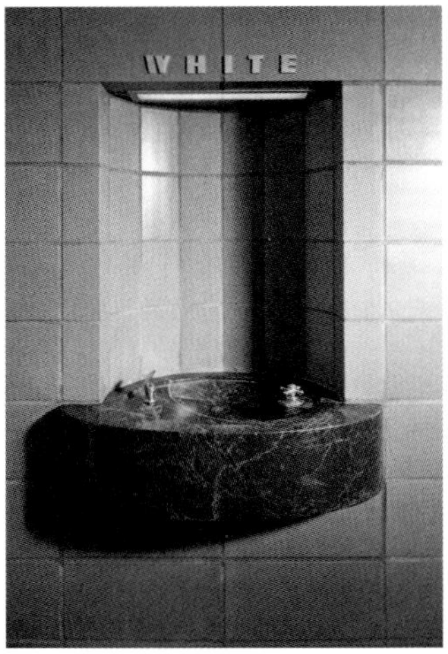

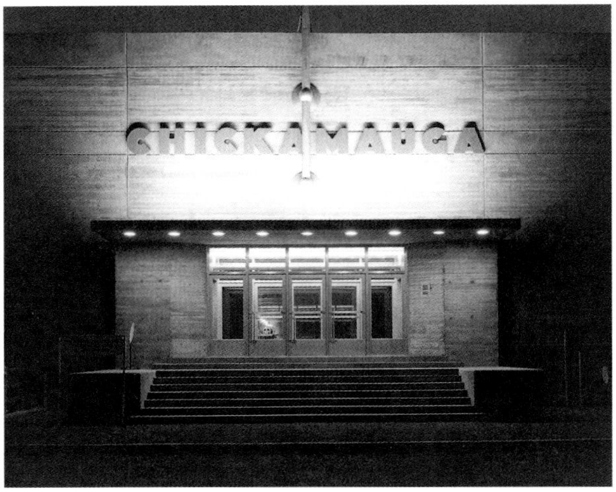

LEFT Water fountain at Guntersville Dam, 1940. The distinctions of the then-segregated South were, like every element of TVA design, rendered in spare, elegant typography.
RIGHT The lettering on the entry of the Chickamauga Dam powerhouse is consistent with the modern sans-serif type styles used on all the TVA architecture, 1940.

(modernist) signs in a monumental style that evoked both potency and optimism. While graphic design seemed to play a comparatively less memorable role in the overall TVA campaign, typographic details were not insignificant. Even routine metal signs for the local post offices, information centers, and restaurants, all designed in the dominant Streamline aesthetic, were indications that an overarching yet benevolent authority was pulling the real and metaphorical switches.

Power was key in more ways than merely reclaiming and harnessing natural resources of the region. Through design the populace was not only overtly, but also subliminally, persuaded that the federal government had the power to control their destinies (for the good, of course). Branding the various TVA facilities with uniform typefaces and harmonized icons helped instill both popular confidence and pride in the overall endeavor.[8]

Propagating the TVA's image required maintaining a visual language that was consistent with the architectural style born of the Machine Age and the technological requisites of the day. Graphically, nothing was left to chance or nuance; each structure and artifact had a deliberate rationale. Building the future—fueling the engine of progress—could not be done without employing a monumental aesthetic. The TVA's assets were larger than life because, by controlling nature, it would raise the disadvantaged. The graphics that served this cause had to be not merely tasteful but dynamic, monumental, and imposing.

Notes

1. Herbert Hoover Papers: Articles, Addresses and Public Statement, 511, Women's Arts and Industries, address telephoned from Washington, D.C., to Fourth Annual Exposition, New York City, Herbert Hoover Presidential Library, West Branch, Iowa.

2. Earnest Elmo Calkins, "The Dividends of Beauty," *Advertising Arts*, September 1933, 13–18.

3. Ibid.

4. Ibid.

5. Walter Dorwin Teague, "Will it Last," *Advertising Arts*, March 1931, 13–19.

6. Calkins, "The Dividends of Beauty," 13–18. See also Calkins, "Whither Industrial Design," *Advertising Arts*, May 1934, 9–12.

7. Sheldon Cheney and Martha Chandler Cheney, *Art and the Machine* (New York: Whittlesey House, 1936), 6.

8. In retrospect this visual propaganda has some curious, if unsettling, parallels. Similar design languages were used at the same time to promote totalitarian regimes in Germany, Italy, and the Soviet Union. While the commercial modern and Streamline aesthetics in the United States were decidedly unauthoritarian—or more commercial and capitalist—than in dictatorships, similar visual principles were in play. The Nazis, Fascists, and Soviets also emphasized public-works projects, with very similar architectural and graphic styles. The graphic iconography, whether modernistic in the Italian mode or neoclassical in the Nazi manner, employs techniques and tropes that can be found in the WPA, like the use of the airbrush to give futuristic luster. Even the TVA logo—a powerful clenched fist holding a lightning bolt—the red, white, and blue patriotic palette not withstanding—is evocative of numerous totalitarian national, military, paramilitary, and political symbols. And the murals, a hallmark of the WPA's public art initiatives, were often rendered in either an overt or stylized heroic realism, not unlike the more turgid versions of Nazi and Socialist realism in Germany and the Soviet Union, respectively.

Almost Fully Modern: The TVA's Visual Art Campaign

TODD SMITH

To consider the achievements of the Tennessee Valley Authority from only the perspective of engineering and architectural virtuosity would overlook its forays into the visual realm. The Authority complemented its massive building and topographical redesign with a visual program that tempered the bold assertions of the built structures with a more traditional approach to storytelling: murals. The murals, created to enlighten the public, were purposefully traditional and modern at the same time and demonstrated the Authority's understanding that its avowedly modern design needed to be balanced with a more traditional aesthetic strategy. By choosing nineteenth-century symbols of Manifest Destiny peppered with images of American heroes, along with well-proven spectatorship strategies, the murals of the TVA told a different story from that expressed by the massive architecture—yet one equally necessary.

At the height of the TVA's unprecedented construction campaign, the Museum of Modern Art (MOMA) in New York City presented an exhibition devoted entirely to the TVA project. Opening in April 1941, the show took place in the shadow of the United States' growing movement toward war. President Roosevelt had just signed into law the Lend-Lease Act on March 11, 1941, which provided war material to the United Kingdom and the Soviet Union. As the exhibition closed, Germany invaded the Soviet Union, and in a mere six months the war would hit the U.S. forces at Pearl Harbor.

Reading the architectural criticism of the exhibition, it is not surprising to find a strong political message within the published commentary. Critic Geoffrey Baker in the *New York Times* states that the exhibition "should serve as an effective bracer for those who doubt the creative power of democracy."[1] In comparing the TVA dams to the Egyptian pyramids, historian Lewis Mumford in the *New Yorker* reasoned that "both pyramid and dam represent an architecture of power. But the difference is notable, too, and should make one prouder of being an

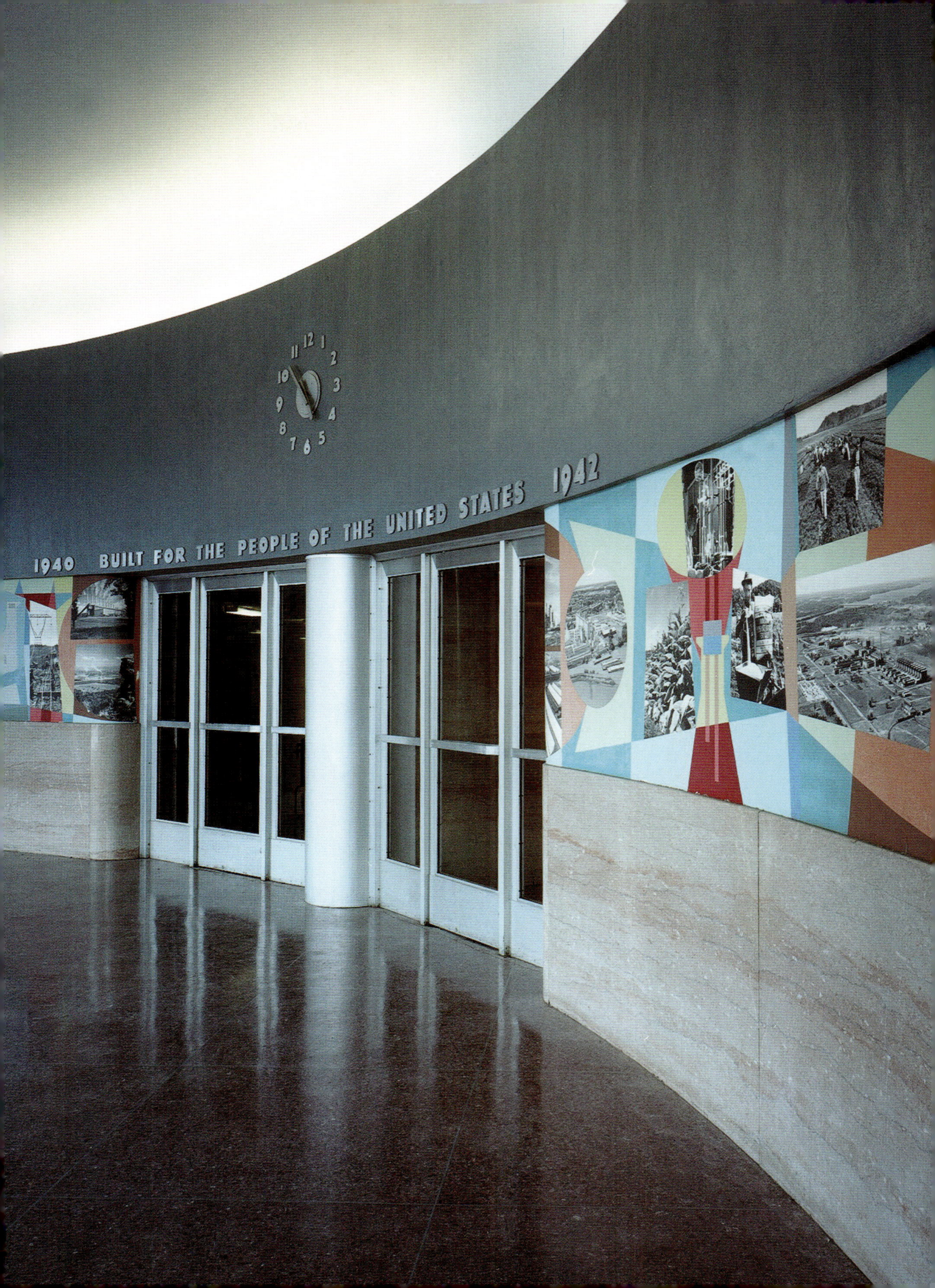
1940 BUILT FOR THE PEOPLE OF THE UNITED STATES 1942

American. The first grew out of slavery and celebrated death. Ours was produced by free labor to create energy and life for the people of the United States."[2]

Beyond the overriding political rhetoric that punctuated these cultural elites' take on the TVA project and accomplishments, these commentaries also offered insight into the artistic vocabulary needed to appreciate the scope and magnitude of the project. The audience for these reviews was predominantly East Coast urbanites who had never visited the Tennessee Valley and who sat at the opposite end of the socioeconomic spectrum from the millions of residents of the valley who suffered poverty rates double those of the rest of the country. Additionally, the illiteracy rates of those ten years of age and older were four times higher in the valley than in other regions of the country. In other words, the criticism of the architecture and the exhibition that spoke so highly of the lofty democratic principles was as alien to most of the affected residents as a foreign language.

There was an American boosterism at work surrounding the feats of the TVA's campaign. And this boosterism drew heavily upon existing (and often unquestioned) devotion to long-held American values. The TVA and its supporters knew that modernism could only go so far and that it must be complemented by references to traditional, and in this case visual, clues.

OVERLEAF Photographic mural at Cherokee Dam, 1941

Picking up on this tack, Mumford writes that "in these dams and power stations the largely unconscious precedents of our grain elevators and storage warehouses and coal bins reach the final mark of a conscious expression."[3] By relating the undertakings of the TVA engineers and architects to that of unknown earlier agricultural and industrial builders, Mumford drew parallels between the photography of the dams (the main feature of the show) and the Precisionist landscape images of artists Charles Sheeler and Charles Demuth. By the early 1940s, these artists had established enough credibility within the art world that Mumford's subtle reference would have been significant.

This desire for the codification and celebration of indigenous American forms might seem at first completely antithetical to the plans of the TVA—plans that included developing a new aesthetic style for architecture and design. Yet it was in the 1920s and 1930s that a full-scale desire to conserve, restore, and exhibit objects of the American past had reached a fevered height. Industrialist Henry Francis du Pont amassed 85,000 objects of American decorative arts for display at his family's house, Winterthur, in Delaware. Henry Ford established Greenfield Village in Dearborn, Michigan, to commemorate and preserve traditional (i.e., premodern) Midwestern village life. From these efforts to the restoration of the colonial capital in Williamsburg, Virginia, by the Rockefeller family and their well-known collecting of American folk art in the late 1920s, the period was intent on marrying capitalist might with the preservation of a distinctively American "usable past." This conservation mentality was counterbalanced by the 1933–34 Century of Progress World's Fair in Chicago, which celebrated one hundred years of American industrial progress. The period, to be sure, was schizophrenic—clinging to a past, which

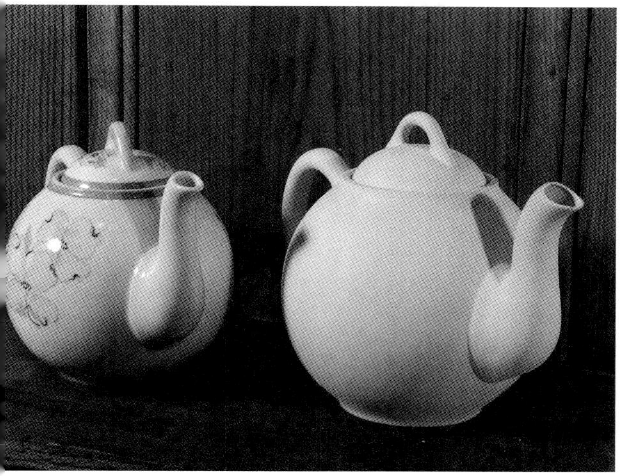

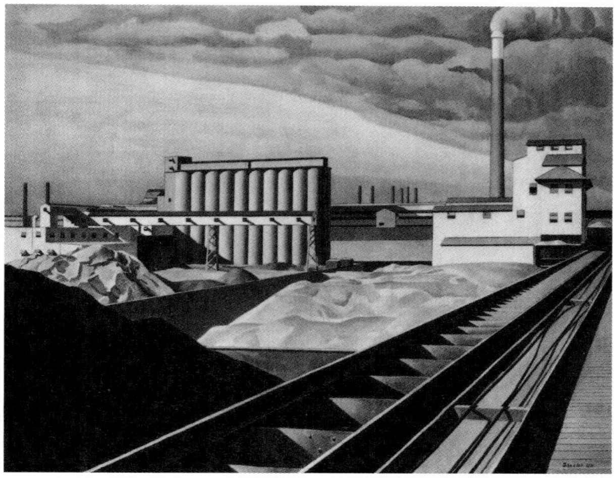

LEFT Porcelain tea pots, Norris Ceramic Lab, 1936

RIGHT Charles Sheeler, Classic Landscape, 1931. Oil on canvas, 25 × 32 ¼ in. Collection of Barney A. Ebsworth. Image © 2006 Board of Trustees, National Gallery of Art, Washington, D.C.

provided stability, while yearning for a future of hope. The TVA occupied a similarly uneasy position, hovering between the cultural and historical richness of the traditions of the Tennessee Valley and the need for improvements to agriculture and the standard of living of its citizens in the twentieth century.

From the beginning the TVA was committed to the visual arts as part of a larger public-relations and education campaign. The Authority embraced the indigenous culture of the valley and did much to promote its uniqueness both locally and nationally. Adult education courses offered to its employees and residents included woodworking and weaving. A woodworking shop was established at Norris in 1934, where employees produced furniture inspired by local antiques. The TVA also joined forces with the Southern Highland Handicraft Guild and in 1935, with the efforts of the TVA's first chair, Arthur Morgan, was instrumental in getting sales outlets for the guild's inventory at Norris (for the thousands of visitors) and at the Plaza at Rockefeller Center in New York City. Also, recognizing the potential for fine-quality porcelain to be produced from the local kaolin clay of the valley, the TVA created a ceramics laboratory at Norris to remove the impurities from the clay and produce porcelain for use in ceramic design.

The Visitor Experience

The TVA sought to regulate and direct all aspects of the visitor's experience. The dams were celebrated as much for their status as wonders of the world as they were for the benefits they brought the residents through improvements in agricultural productivity, employment, and increased access to inexpensive electrical power. From the outset, the leaders of the TVA understood that what they were creating would also be a great curiosity. Visitor centers and overlooks and recreational areas surrounding the dam sites were primary concerns. The TVA wanted

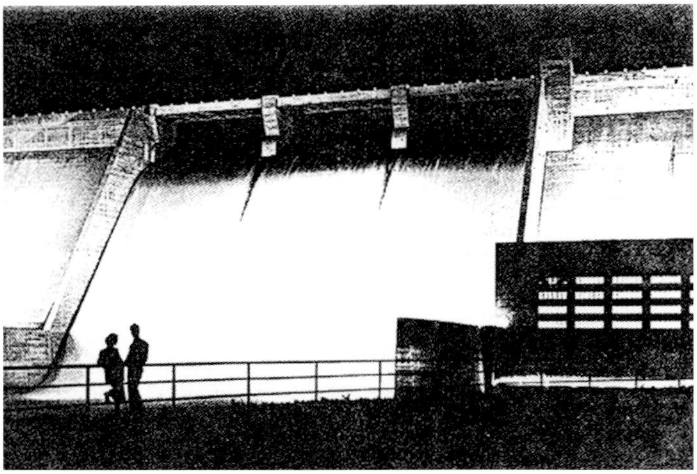

Image of couple at Norris Dam, ca. 1940

and needed visitors, and it correctly assumed that the visitor wanted access to the spectacle of the unfamiliar and the novel. The TVA was happy to oblige.

As a writer remembered on the death of the TVA's primary architect, Roland Wank, in 1970:

> Wank saw to it that [the dams] were approached as one would the Acropolis, seen suddenly as one came from around the wooded flank of the mountainside, and presented with a heightened appreciation of scale. He led one up to the best view. There he provided a "lookout" where a subtle combination of technical information and TVA philosophy was offered.[4]

The entire landscaping and topographical reshaping around the dams was orchestrated in such a way as to provide perfect "views." The public-relations function of the TVA recognized the power of this strategy. In a characteristic image taken at Norris Dam, a happy couple is perfectly framed in silhouette, complete with her leg flirtishly resting on the railing, set before the beauty and awe-inspiring power of the dam.

Could this as easily have been an image from a honeymoon scene at Niagara Falls? Of course. The visual strategies are strikingly familiar. For a couple at Niagara, their union has been ordained by the forces of nature and God; for our friends at Norris, however, their union is blessed by nature, science, and the government—a forceful trinity in mid-twentieth-century America. Nineteenth-century audiences regarded Niagara Falls as a covenant from God—that theirs was the chosen land and that the rushing force of the falls was a clear sign that such natural features of the New World foretold a rich and promising future. Norris Dam and its accompanying visual clues, however, were significant prompts to the

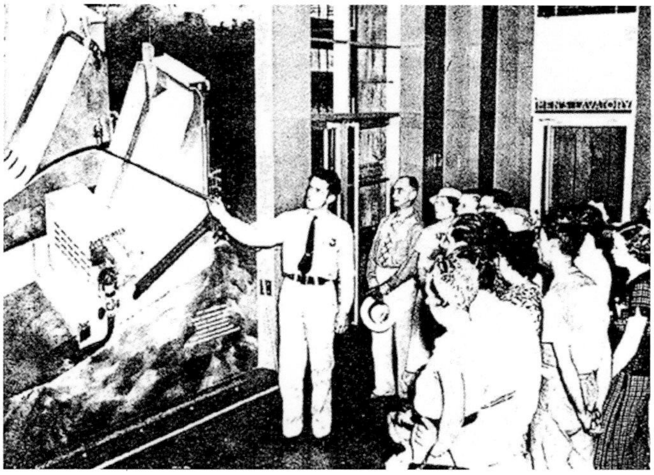

Guide instructing visitors at Norris Dam, ca. 1940

visiting public that only with the strong hand of science and government could the true beauty (i.e., God's beauty) of the Tennessee Valley be made evident. Nature alone was no longer enough.

Within the visitor centers themselves, considerable time and effort were placed on visual storytelling. Much as medieval cathedrals had used decorated capitals to inform and educate the mostly illiterate congregants, the visitor centers at the dams relied on visual programs to instruct the tourists about the power and purpose of the TVA. The earliest pictorial undertaking was at Norris. The powerhouse was used as the original visitor center and placed squarely in the public's view in a 1936 mural. The large painting provides a cross-sectional, laboratory view of the dam and serves as an instructional tool for the guide stationed next to it. The aesthetics of the painting are at the service of the pedagogical needs of the Authority.

By the time of the MoMA exhibition in 1941, the TVA had honed its picture-making skills further, and by the early 1950s, the mural program was in full operation. In a review of the 1941 exhibition, critic Douglas Haskell of the *Nation* reported that the "director of the Museum of Modern Art in New York City, in the course of opening the current show, said bluntly that the architecture of the TVA was the 'greatest that America had yet produced.'"[5] But would the art that the TVA commissioned to adorn and punctuate the visitor centers be comparably regarded? If not, why not?

The Daniel Boone Mural

A single mural typifies the TVA's approach to picture making in the modern era, joining a modernistic aesthetic with nineteenth-century tactics for storytelling. Located near the cities of Kingsport, Johnson City, and Bristol in northeastern

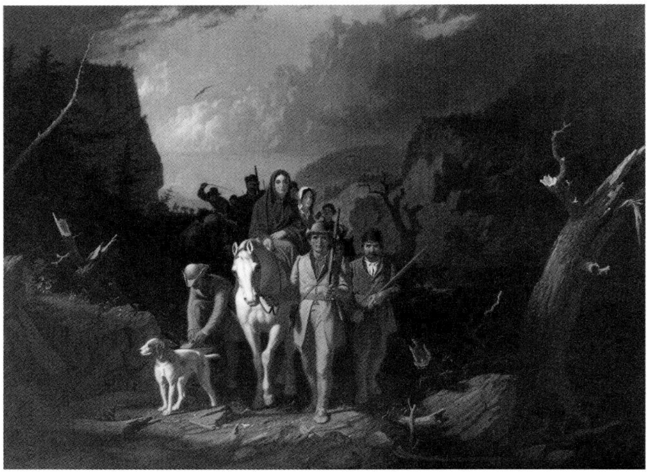

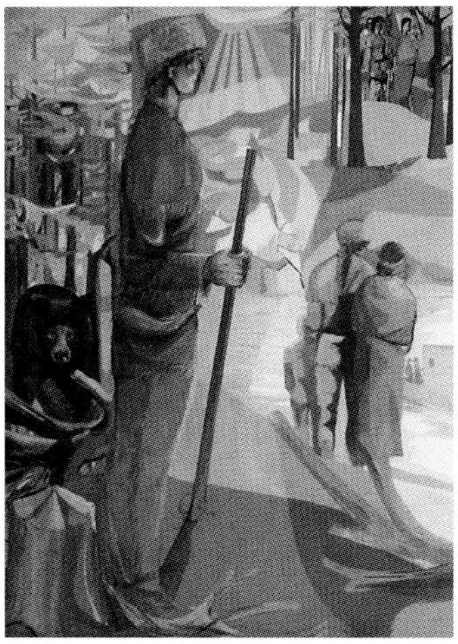

LEFT George Caleb Bingham, *Daniel Boone Escorting Settlers through the Cumberland Gap*, 1851–52. Oil on canvas, 36½ × 50¼ in. Mildred Lane Kemper Art Museum, Washington University in St. Louis.
RIGHT Robert "Bob" Birdwell, detail of Daniel Boone mural at Boone Dam, 1955

Tennessee, the Daniel Boone Dam and the accompanying Boone Lake were created in 1952 and named for the early American pioneer. The pictorial landscape of the mural is straightforward. As the viewer begins on the left side of the composition, the narrative of the region and the TVA's presence and positive influence unfold, or, more correctly, are revealed to the viewer. Three significant male figures are present: the namesake of the dam on the far left, pictured in his coonskin hat; the TVA engineer, the central figure; and the fisherman on the far right. These men provide moments of entry for the viewer, but it is only Boone whose face is visible. As one moves through the composition, the gun in Boone's hand is replaced by technical drawings in the hands of the engineer and ultimately a fishing pole. The progress from pioneer to professional to leisure enthusiast is carefully orchestrated. Other figures present are a Native American family, a pioneer family, a farmer, boatmen, workers on the TVA site, and a second fisherman. The composition weaves over two hundred years of regional history into a diorama punctuated by abstracted panels of color and perspective.

Boone had become the visual stand-in for the American pioneer by the turn of the twentieth century. Made famous in the 1850s by George Caleb Bingham's opus, *Daniel Boone Escorting Settlers through the Cumberland Gap*, Boone by this time had taken on religious trappings. Contemporary writers and ministers in the nineteenth century regarded him as a Moses figure leading his people through the wilderness to safety and prosperity. As seen in a popular engraving based on Bingham's painting, Boone is depicted as the leader of a group that winds its way through the middle ground and extends into the distance. He is bathed in light and cuts a striking figure, as he and his similarly lit horse burst through and make their way past the gnarled tree on the left. His wife, appropriately shrouded for the toils of cross-country travel, is the Mary who will bring new life to wherever they

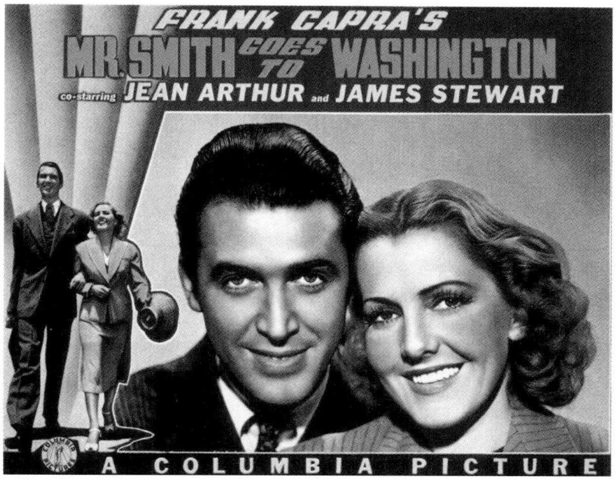

Movie poster for *Mr. Smith Goes to Washington*, 1939. Courtesy of MPTV.net.

settle. To be sure, it is a mixing of Old Testament and New Testament elements, but for nineteenth-century viewers, the connections were strong and meaningful.

Historian Henry Nash Smith asks in *Virgin Land: The American West as Symbol and Myth*: "Which was the real Boone—the standard-bearer of civilization and refinement, or the child of nature who fled into the wilderness before the advance of settlement?"[6] Long regarded as an uncomplicated hero in popular parlance, Boone was, by the time the TVA mural was completed, the subject of increasing academic inquiry. Smith reveals the conflicting nature of Boone's legacy: was Boone a figure who blazed the trail into and through the wilderness, or was he a failure in the land-speculation business that grew up in the early years of the nineteenth century?

Boone was not simply an issue for academic historians, however. As a symbol, he was still alive and well in the twentieth century. In 1939, the actor James Stewart rose to prominence with his Academy Award–nominated performance as Jefferson Smith, the Boy Ranger turned U.S. Senator in Frank Capra's paean to grassroots political chutzpah and American "stick-to-it-ness," *Mr. Smith Goes to Washington*. Framed from the start as the outsider and the naive dope who unwittingly ends up as a senator, Smith accepts the mantle of the traditional country bumpkin coming to the big city. When Smith disembarks in Washington, D.C., and wanders off from his handlers to join a tour-bus journey around the nation's capital, his anxious and rather cynical new secretary, Clarissa Saunders, played by Jean Arthur, wonders out loud if this Daniel Boone is lost, or if he will be able to find his way. The references to Boone continue with a mention of a coonskin hat and subsequent snide remarks made by Saunders before her boss arrives at his new office.

Boone represents a type—a country rube full of wide-eyed naiveté, who is the laughing stock of the cosmopolitan environment. Smith, aka Boone, only

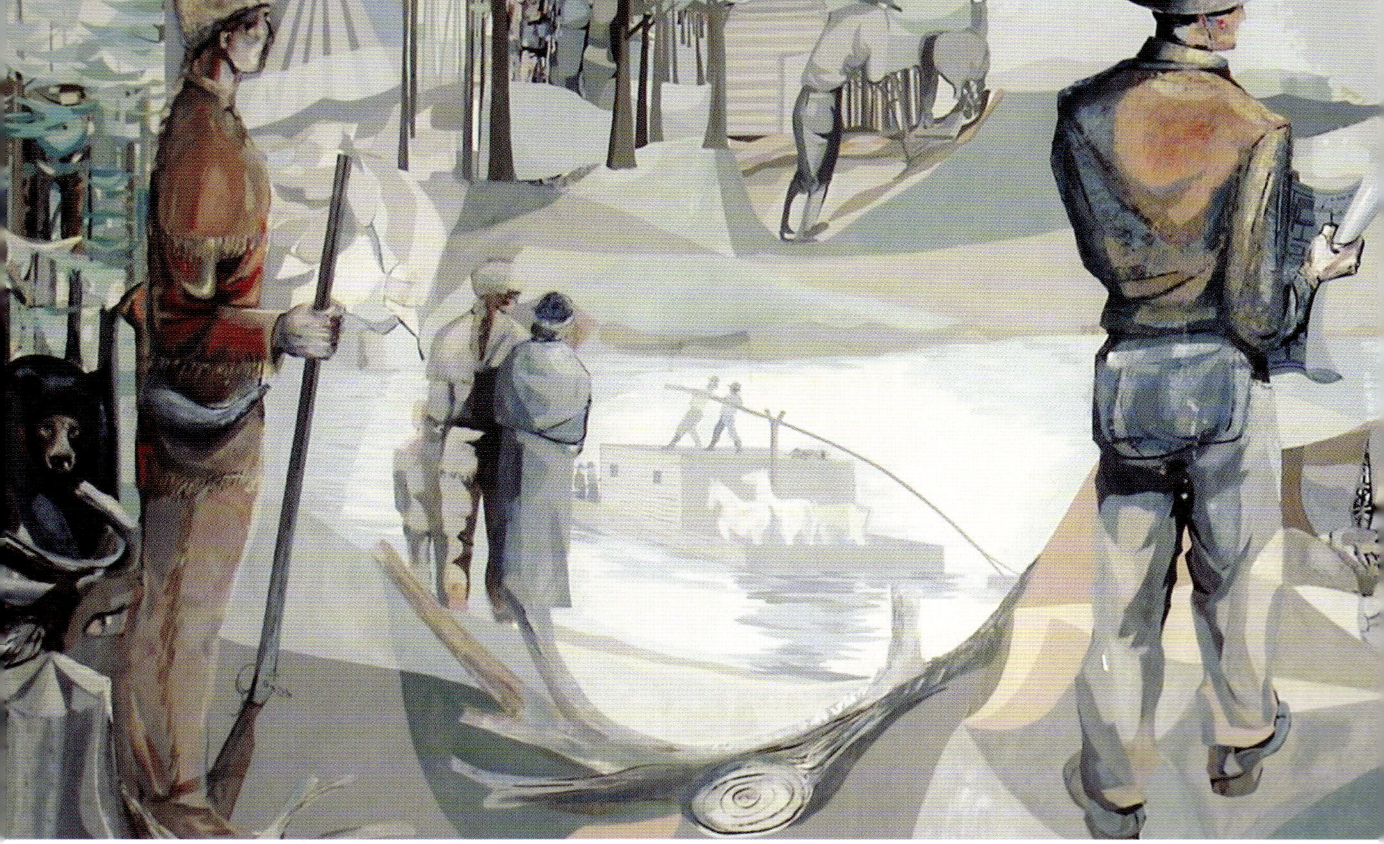

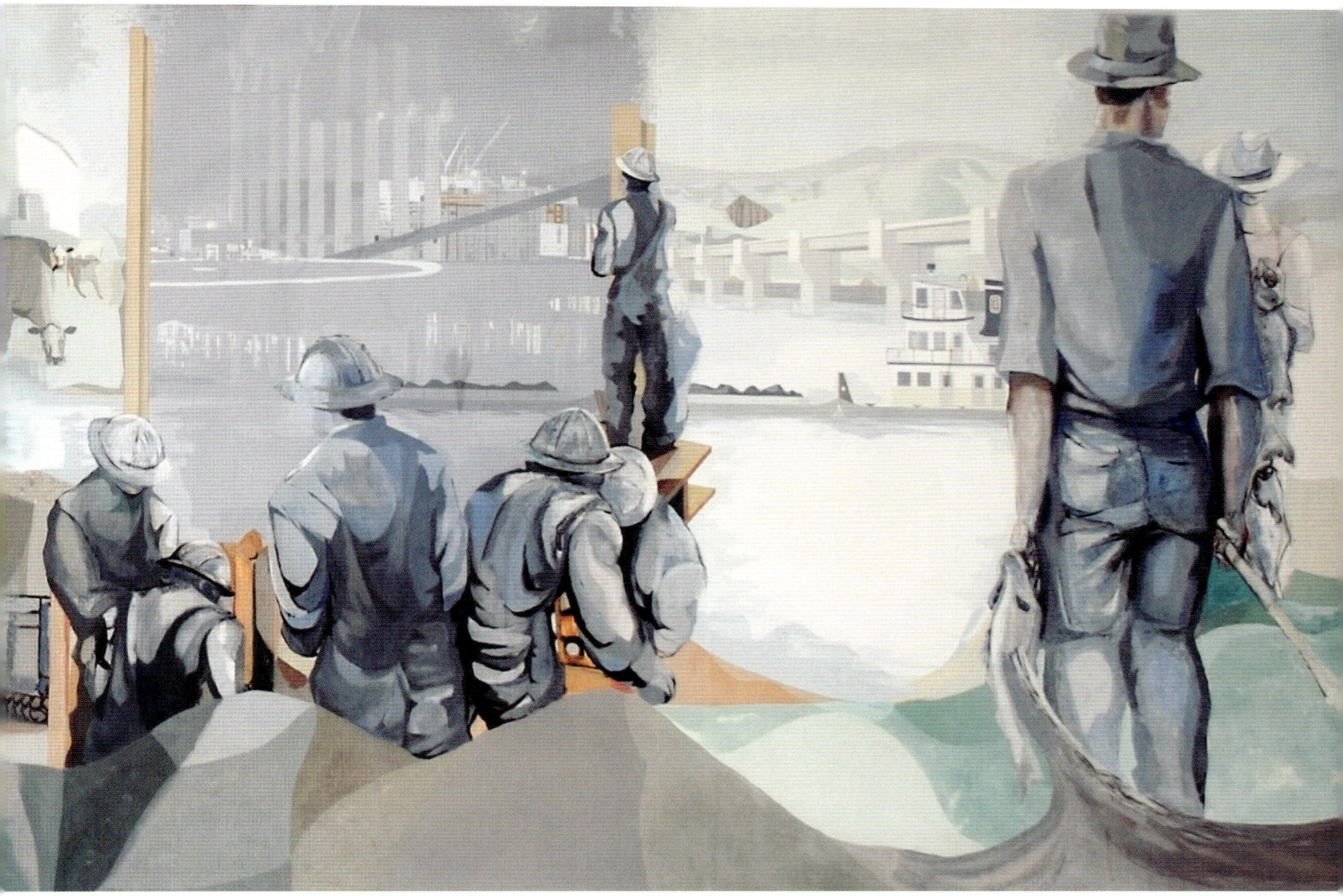

Birdwell, Daniel Boone mural at Boone Dam

gains credibility when he perseveres, holds steadfast in his beliefs in the goodness of men and institutions, and is able to uncover a major instance of corruption. The project under scrutiny was none other than the building of a dam. Of all of the potential pork-barrel graft projects around on which to base an entire screenplay, a plot driven by a dam project undoubtedly raised eyebrows and drew connections to the massive TVA project well underway.

For the powerbrokers in the film, the proposed dam on Willett Creek would reap windfalls for those, including the senior senator and the governor, who have direct interest and investment in the land that surrounds the creek. For Smith and his dream of a national Boys Camp, the creek offers the perfect location for the teaching of the American values of patriotism and civic duty. Is it too much of a stretch to suggest that a decade later, when the TVA commissioned the Boone mural, the artist(s) had Capra's film in mind?

While Boone is certainly caught up in the rhetoric of nineteenth-century Manifest Destiny, his treatment in the TVA mural differs from the previous century's pictorial treatment. Unlike his nineteenth-century predecessors, this Boone is not an active agent in directing the course of an empire. His role is to introduce the story and frame the conversation. Turning further away from earlier prototypes, this hero does not direct his followers westward, toward a promised land; instead, he is firmly planted on the left bank of the composition. The established iconography of nineteenth-century American visual boosterism places the leader at the right side of the composition and through a variety of devices moves the action from the right of the composition to the left, recalling the physical movement of the country from the east (the right) to the west (the left). In a reversal of placement, the TVA mural places Boone facing toward the right (i.e., east).

Why such a shift? By the middle of the twentieth century, the connection between a quasi-political, quasi–big business enterprise such as the TVA and a visual campaign to sell the advantages of massive topographical, economic, and psychological upheaval could be more transparent than nineteenth-century business-cum-progress Manifest Destiny imagery. The mural purposefully reconfirms the connections for the real-life experience of the visitor in ways that nineteenth-century canvases could not. The Boone mural is placed in a typical TVA visitor center. With its modern design, flat roof, use of local stone, and disavowal of ornament and expensive decorative features, the visitor center at Norris Dam signals to its audience that this place and this experience are about today. While the center itself is relatively small, the mural is featured prominently in the limited space, and its impact is impressive—both outside and inside. Standing in the center, the visitor is overwhelmed by two complementary visual experiences: the mural itself, which commands the primary wall, and, opposite it, several large picture windows that offer an expansive view of nature. The correlation of views (an odd mixture of manmade and natural) is the key to the mural's ability to narrate the TVA story. Starting at the left side of the mural and slowly turning clockwise, the viewer experiences both the history of the project (as told through the iconography of the mural) and the modernity of the project (as conveyed through the choice of an abstracted style). As the painted experience ends, the real-life experience picks up, and the visitor gazes out to the landscape, the authentic scene "to be looked at." No detail goes unnoticed in guiding the visual experience. And none other than Boone, as Boy Ranger, as U.S. Senator, as champion of the common man, is there to introduce and lead the view.

Almost Modern

At the moment that Jackson Pollock and others were becoming the critical darlings of the New York art scene, works such as the Boone mural were created quite a distance away. The mural speaks to a pattern within the history of our visual heritage, that the "shock of the new" represents only the smallest fraction of the leading edge in any society. Traditional aesthetic sensibilities and expectations linger, and their use remains necessary for the telling of the story. TVA is rightfully considered in the forefront of progress for its early adoption and promotion of starkly modern principles of design, land management, and the reconceptualization of disparate areas as a single, specific region. But for all of its progressive beliefs and values, it relied heavily on established and well-regarded methods for visual instruction. The TVA brought much-needed modernization to the country's least modern residents, but in the arena of public information and visual iconography, it knew when there was such a thing as too much modern.

Notes

1. Geoffrey Baker, "Exhibition at the Museum of Modern Art Reveals Democracy In a Mood of Creation on a Project of Gigantic Size," *New York Times*, May 4, 1941.

2. Lewis Mumford, "The Sky Line: The Architecture of Power," *New Yorker*, June 7, 1941, 60.

3. Ibid.

4. Frederick Gutheim, "Roland Wank, 1898–1970," *Architectural Forum* 133, no. 2 (September 1970): 59.

5. David Haskell, "Architecture of the TVA," *Nation*, May 17, 1941, 592.

6. Henry Nash Smith, *Virgin Land: The American West as Symbol and Myth* (Cambridge, MA: Harvard University Press, 1950), 51.

Watauga

JENNIFER BLOOMER

The wake of the cabin cruiser widens, slows, and swells, rhythmically lifting and dropping everything that floats and diminishing in calculable progression until it laps the shore. School is done for the year. Haynes and Vesper are celebrating the long summer ahead. Vesper has risen early this morning to fry a chicken, make potato salad, and bake a big can of Bush's beans with mustard and ketchup mixed in, three strips of ruffled bacon across the top. She has packed it in Tupperware and Alcoa aluminum foil in a picnic basket with paper plates and plastic forks. On top she's laid a batch of iced fudge brownies, made from Mama's recipe, and a generous stack of paper napkins. The whole of it is wrapped with a blue checked cloth tucked all around. It waits for noon in the shade of the gunwale.

Haynes cuts the motor and the boat drifts in bobbing tranquility. Vesper is startled, then calmed by the retreat of sound. Slowly she registers the lapping of the water, and the susurration of a host of pine needles in the distance. She thinks: "This is a perfect day. I'm going to remember it forever."

It is the summer of 1968. Sly and the Family Stone's slow boogie oozes from Haynes's transistor radio. The sun encourages the heat radiating from the oiled bodies of the two teens: Haynes shirtless in Lacoste whites, still crisp after a morning of tennis; Vesper in the pink gingham two-piece she'd sewn on Grandma Kannie's foot-treadle Singer. Something sultry and forbidden lurks beneath the surface of this moment of two fresh human animals alone in the middle of a lake—Hot Fun in the Summer Time. The whole of Watauga surrounds them, bits of fickle sky dancing on its teal mystery.

Heat builds. Haynes has that look on his face and begins to murmur in his sleepy drawl words that both flatter Vesper and make her skin crawl. Vesper knows the look and knows that she does not want to end up like Ginger and Peggy, mothers at seventeen. She wants to go to college; she longs to become somebody, to

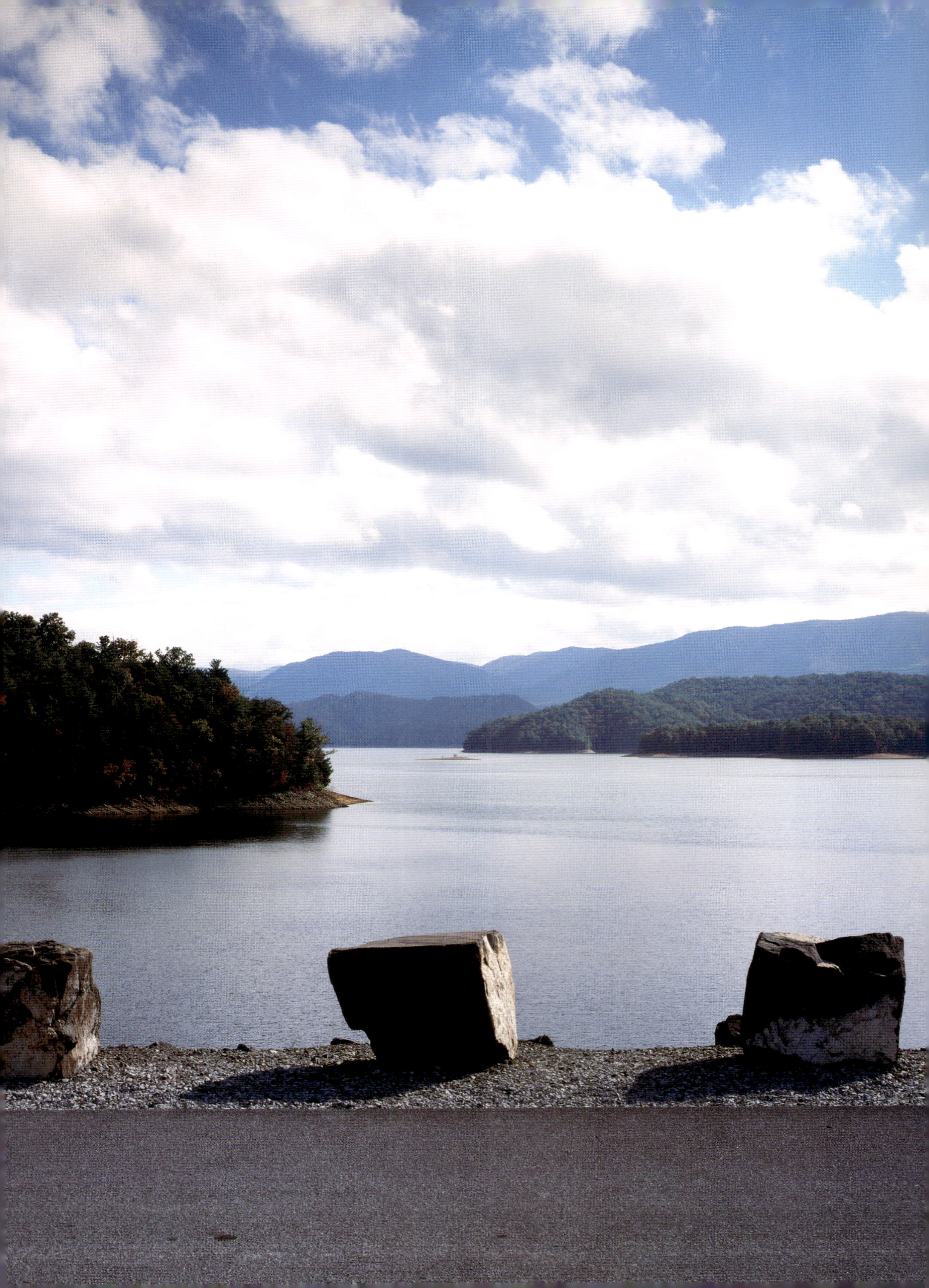

make Mama proud. She stands, turns abruptly, and steps up nimbly onto the gunwale. Just escaping Haynes's grasp, she leaps into air. An icy, dark shock sends her body heat packing. Sinking, will-less, and praying her feet will touch nothing but water, she kicks and gratefully ascends into the silky top layer, warmed by the sun. Tall witnesses on the shore stand stark and still against a cerulean backdrop. Between their canopy and her nose only water, delicious and daunting. Blue smoky mountains roll beyond. The lake and the day brim.

Vesper is glad he does not follow. For a time she floats face down, suspended thirty stories above a thousand ancient stumps, the rubble of rock foundations and disinterred graves. The slimy, scavenged landscape is a full-scale map of the lives of people long gone, put to rest and covered by a moon-breathing blanket of cold mountain water. Fish swim where birds flew. This thought frightens her.

Behind her eyes seeps a memory of snorkeling in the Crystal River: the breathlessness of cold water, the silence and mystery of the aquifer's baroque formations of limestone and orifice, the terror that rived her body as the bottom fell away beneath. All the old, animal parts of her brain had screamed Falling! Falling!—yet she had remained suspended, dream-flying over the holey landscape, cradled by the invisible weight of water.

Were the blue-green miasma of sediment and life strained from Watauga's waters, Vesper would be able to see the cavernous bottom as she floats leisurely, angel-like, over its drowned history. It is a suspended history, for centuries untethered to the forces of progress and causality, a history rather in circles—rolling vectors of generations, each one living pretty much the moments of the others.

Down below these waters, the Cherokee had lived for centuries with the rhythms of land, air, and water; then, her people, greedy pupils of those they so uncharitably displaced. Daniel Boone had walked beneath these waters toward the Cumberland Gap, seeking a way through the mounds of Appalachia, toward Manifest Destiny.

Up until 1944, all below was mountain land laced by paths of trickling and flowing water, and over time the village of Butler had grown up at its heart. But in that year, eleven years after President Roosevelt and the U.S. Congress brought into being the Tennessee Valley Authority, work began on an enormous construction of earth, rock, and concrete that would block the open end of the valley at Carden's Bluff and cause the water in all the mountains' streams and creeks to back up until, foot by foot, a great reservoir rose into being: Watauga Lake.

Watauga is a wonder of human imagination and artifice. It is the first link in the chain of lakes that were created by the TVA and draped across Tennessee. A contrivance masquerading as nature, the long mountain lake was shaped by 10 million hours of men arguing, persuading, negotiating, sawing, hauling, disassembling, demolishing, designing, and building. Like most things tending toward the sublime, Watauga is usually described in quantities. Watauga Dam: 318 feet

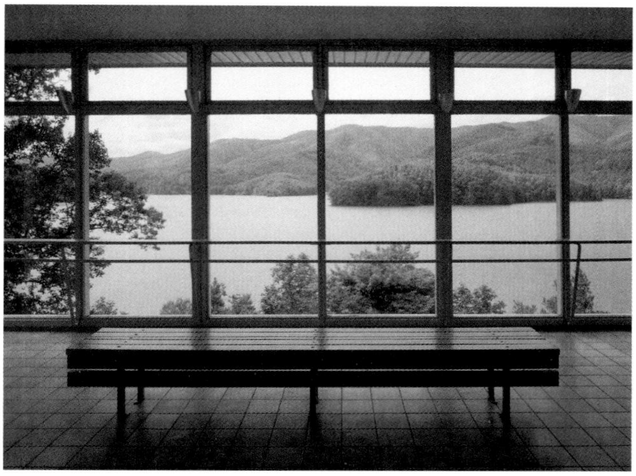

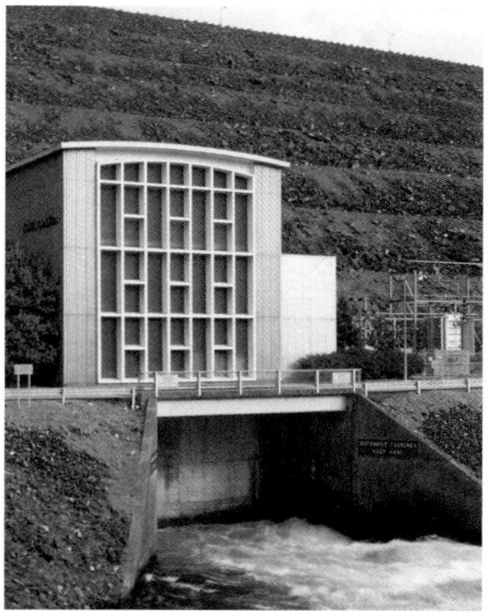

LEFT The pristine beauty of Watauga Lake, from the Watauga Dam visitor center, 2005. Largely surrounded by national forest, most of the lakeshore remains safe from development and its injury to the nation's natural resources.
RIGHT Watauga Dam Powerhouse, 2005

high, 900 feet long, 80,400 cubic yards of concrete, 65,400 cubic yards of grouting; 48 injuries, 1 death; 761 families; 1,282 decomposing bodies moved; 1,663 acres of trees cut down. Construction began in 1942, was interrupted by World War II, and was completed in 1948. Watauga is one of the largest earth- and rock-filled dams in the United States.

The crooked, finger-shaped lake edged by the dam also is mapped by numbers: 1,915 feet above sea level, 6,430 acre feet of water, 330 feet deep, 106 miles of shoreline, 85 percent protected by national forest, the third cleanest lake in America. A succession of dramatic and devastating floods—1867, 1886, 1901, 1902, 1916, 1924, and 1940—finally brought to an end.

One town—Butler, Tennessee—under water: before the final, planned inundation, the people of Butler relocated to nearby higher ground. Buildings had been carefully disassembled and carried away piece by piece for reuse. Their foundations and unusable material remained to lie with the stumps of trees and scrub that would become the bottom of an immense bowl of water. The concrete jail and the City Shoe Shop were left standing. Seeds, scions, tubers, and corms had been gathered, cut, and unearthed, then packed carefully to await replanting in new garden sites. Graves had been excavated and the remains carefully carried to drier resting places.

Fourteen years from the day that Vesper wafts far above Butler, Watauga will be drained and the people of the town will stand on the shore and behold for the first time in forty years the remains of their town: 125 homes and 50 businesses. Like a shipwreck revealed by the parting of the sea, the setting of their memories will sit drenched and dripping before their eyes. There will be the Fish Springs Bridge, intact and spanning nothing, its engineered supports stuck deep in mud. As the water recedes and the earth dries, people will walk down into Old Butler, tell stories, and pick over the remains. Men will pry a church cornerstone from the muck. Then the dam's sluices will close, and the entire town of old Butler will disappear once more, never to be seen again by people who lived there.

Beyond Watauga's statistics are other numbers—57,600 kilowatt hours generated per day, thousands of appliances electrified, men put to work, families fed, children clothed and educated, farms fertilized, crops increased, acres of erosion stopped.

There are sadder numbers—the number of human tears shed as people were forced to abandon the land their families had occupied for generations; the number of families who stood on safe ground to watch the hollows fill, their tears flavoring the waters that poured over the remains of their homes and gardens; the number of hours of impotent rage and indignation; the 2,170 graves not moved, 2,170 earthly remains left to lie beneath two billion gallons of water; the number of dollars' difference between their land's value and what farmers and homesteaders were paid. These numbers are absent in the literature of the lake.

Vesper lifts her head for breath, frog-moves her body forward, and returns to her quiet floating, at one with surface, rising and falling gently, rhythmically, still pondering the map that she cannot see, far below.

Nobody really knew what the word "Watauga" meant. People said it was Cherokee for any number of watery things—clear waters, beautiful waters, village of many springs, river of islands, broken waters. The Cherokee claimed the word was not even remotely Cherokee. Vesper figured it had just been made up to make the area sound more Indian-y and mysterious.

History was a peculiar thing, allowing people to make up things that got written down and were later learned as facts. These stories about people lived on after they were gone. People, things, and stories—that was about it for history. Who here today was in the memory of the drowned land? Vesper knew: people like her people, the grandparents of her grandparents, and even some of their grandparents. She recollected that her people had been living in the surrounding hills since long before the American Revolution. The war for independence had been fought and won, creating scarcely a ripple in the rhythms of her kin.

Haynes called his people ancestors. They were here, too. They had been hundred-acre farmers whose grandsons became merchants and surgeons who owned boats and second homes. Their descendants belonged to the country club, an alien presence nestled in a hollow, with its nine amoebas of unnatural green and spotty puddles of sand on swerving mountain fairways. Men drank and guffawed in the "nineteenth hole," daughters of the Daughters of the American Revolution lay by the club pool in John Meyer of Norwich, slathered in baby oil and iodine and combing lemon juice through their hair. Their brothers were tennis-tanned and sleek as seals. Their madras shorts, with sinister white pocket innards

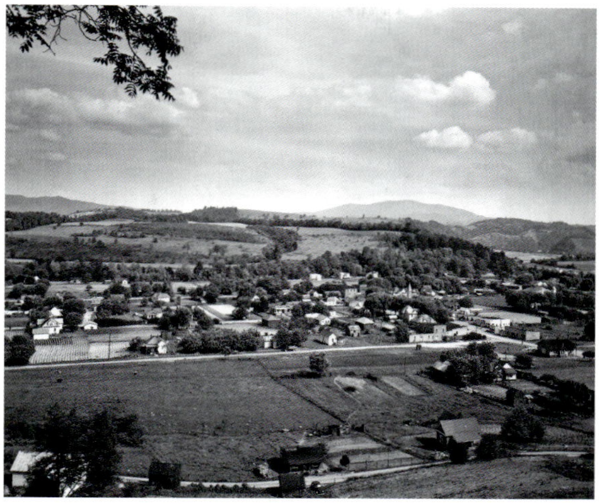

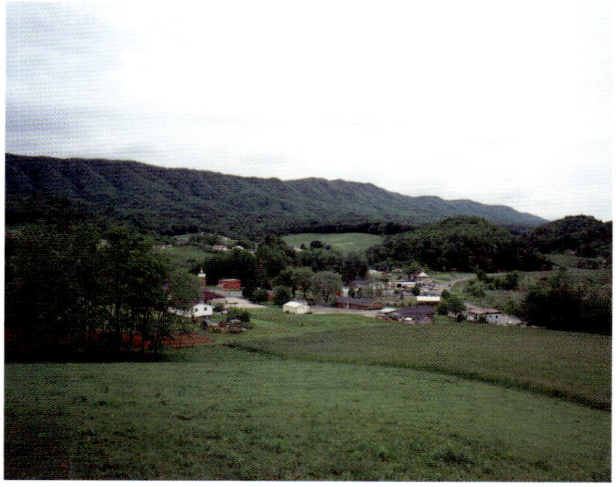

LEFT Butler, Tennessee, before its relocation, ca. 1940

RIGHT Butler, Tennessee, 2005

exposed, were carelessly tossed onto the plastic-tubed, green-and-white chaises longues that flanked the pool.

Their mothers went to luncheons and garden club. They pored over civic and church records seeking proof of their American aristocracy. They dressed up in suits with brooches pinned just so, and hats and white gloves, and gathered to swan around, giving each other ribbons and awards. This represented to Vesper both a seductive cachet and a repulsive silliness. Although her family had come to America long before the qualification date, she would never be invited to join this group. She knew that real colonial dames were mostly the shipped-in wives of exiled ne'er-do-wells. They had been adventuresses, disgraced girls and old maids desperate for husbands, willing to spend perilous weeks on damp, stinking wood boats on miles of sea to have chances at hooking up with colonial jailbirds with bad teeth. Where was the pride in that? Nonetheless, the ancestors were worshipped in shrines of oil portraits and hard leather albums of daguerreotypes, in tired gold lockets and bracelets of braided hair, on monogrammed silver spoons and porcelain portrait plates, in wills and deeds, and with the odd, military-looking medals pinned on the fine wool bosoms that made Vesper think of pigeons.

Her people were different. The evidence of their existence, beyond the flesh-and-blood that lived on and a group of illegible grave markers, was sparse: Bibles, quilts, spinning wheels, plows, knives, shotguns, and handed-down cast-iron pans constituted the historical documents of a people not given to portraits and Sevres. Heritage resided in the stories that were told, scraps that by turns were funny, tragic, outrageous, and inspiring.

Born a decade before anybody had heard of the TVA, Vesper's mama had grown up in a two-room house in a mountain hollow. Seven people dwelled there, eight until J. P. died from water on the brain. They ate what Granddaddy could shoot and the produce of green, slope-hugging furrows. The children wore no shoes but for a pair of scuffed oxfords that were used by each child until his feet grew too large, then passed to the next in line. They walked two miles down to their one-room school, the girls' hair combed and braided fresh every morning. Mamaw had taught them all to read from the Bible before they started school. In the summers they ran over stony meadow clearings through chigger weed and goldenrod, gorged on blackberries warm in the bramble, got ringworm, and worried about the dreaded lockjaw when bare feet met rusty nails. An old hound with mange and an impossibly long tail lazed in the yard. Nero. Mamaw's pink and white cosmos bloomed by the door. Red-bellied spiders spun and webbed in the evil-smelling dark of the outhouse hole.

Washing and ironing were all-day chores, with water carried from the creek and boiled on the fire. Clothes were scrubbed on a washboard with soap made from wood ashes and pork fat—washed on Mondays and ironed on Tuesdays with heavy flat irons sizzling from the fire. On Sundays they gathered at a white wood Baptist church to worship and then had dinner on the grounds with people who had walked for miles to be there. Fried chicken, baked beans, potato salad, stack cake, and fruit cobblers.

The children were no strangers to life's extremities. Most everyone they knew had lost a brother or sister still in didies, as surely as they had sat just outside the door and heard a mama's anguish as the next child worked his way into the world. Everyone had watched aunts, cousins, or grandparents suffer, struggle for breath, and succumb to the Lord's will, propped up in an iron bed as the work of the household went on around them. The only doctor anyone saw was a traveling man with a mysterious black bag who came around twice a year. Grannies delivered babies and helped with ailments. The woods were their medicine chest. There they harvested coltsfoot, ginseng, goldenseal, false unicorn, the cohoshes, and all the healing gifts the mountains offered.

In the house sun streamed through neat, homemade curtains, yellow with curlicues all over, and shed its light over an ancient upright piano that was out of tune and had six notes that wouldn't play. Every one of the kids could play hymns, Bach and Mozart, thanks to Mamaw's insistent efforts. In winter the wind whistled its own tunes through the house. The fire banked for the night, the kids slept five to a bed, head to toe to head, under the quilts that Mamaw had stitched. The girls made a game of recognizing scraps of dresses and overalls in the patchwork and of telling their stories until Papa shushed them. Decades later Uncle Mack would entertain the nieces and nephews at every family gathering with a song called "A-Sleepin' at the Foot of the Bed." Vesper's favorite part was a line about cold toenails scratching your face and a footboard rubbing your head.

Pinto beans were often on the menu, cooked all day with a hunk of fatback and cornbread baked in the cast iron pan greased with lard. In summer, fresh tomatoes, corn, and greens complemented the tender, soupy beans. Toward summer's end, collards. Varmints like groundhog and squirrel made for good eating, and, on special occasions, one of Mamaw's yard chickens.

Vesper could not remember ever visiting Mamaw's house on the mountain, as they had all moved to town when the TVA came in the 1930s. She did have vivid memories of the house of Grandma Kannie, her Daddy's mother. Sunday chickens running in slowing spirals round and round the dusty yard, heads abandoned on the stump next to Papaw's bloody ax. After it ran itself out, the chicken was plucked, cleaned, and hacked up into pieces. Once the chicken's parts had been dipped in flour, salt, and pepper, dropped into the sizzling lard of Grandma Kannie's heavy black frying pan, and spent an hour simmering under the lid, they were presented, redolent on the pink-flowered Sunday platter. The kids would call dibs on the "crispies" left in the pan and hope for a drumstick. As long as she didn't think about those parts running around without their head, Vesper thought there was nothing better on this earth than the juicy meat in its salty crust. "Bless this meal, O Lord, and God bless Senator Gore and Mizriz Pauline."

Vesper loved Grandma Kannie's yellow Double Wedding Ring coverlet that her grandma had made before the war between the states. Tiny pieces, tiny stitches never slept under, handed down from mother to daughter. Kannie had been waiting for Aunt Lorene to straighten out before she gave it to her. Vesper had hoped that it would come to her instead, to pass on someday to her own oldest girl. But before Grandma Kannie was cold, Aunt Lorene had snatched the earbobs out of the ballerina jewelry box and the precious quilt out of the chiffarobe. The Double Wedding Ring laid on Aunt Lorene's bed until it gave out from too many wet trips through the wringer, the result of Aunt Lorene letting BoBo sleep on it. Vesper asked for Grandma Kannie's black frying pan and thought that one of her own granddaughters would treasure it someday, if there were still chickens to be fried and Crisco to fry them in.

Plasters of spit and tobacco soothed the inevitable wasp stings from drinking Coca-Colas without watching what got between your mouth and the bottle lip. Vesper never thought of Grandma Kannie without picturing her pillowy bosom and the little tin of Red Man she kept handy—recalling the sweet punch of the snuff on her breath and Kannie pausing in midsentence to send lazy dollops of nasty brown juice into the dark blue Granger Tobacco can at her feet.

Grandma Kannie had married at fourteen and had had no formal education, but she was wise. "Don't you never be ashamed of being poor," Kannie said. (She pronounced it "pore.") "Be ashamed of lying and cheating, be ashamed of ignorant, be ashamed of mean, but don't never be ashamed of poor."

Education was to be everything for Vesper. It would take her far out of the Tennessee hills, to private dinners in the bowels of the Guggenheim and the Getty, and onto the podia of foreign capitals. Haynes's life was to follow the road of local privilege—the SAE house at Hampden-Sydney, tennis pro at the club, alcohol problems, whispers about a meek and long-suffering wife with suspicious bruises. There's a big difference between ignorant and stupid, Mama said. Ignorant you can fix; stupid is forever.

Four of Mamaw's sons and daughters, including Mama, had graduated from Berea College in Kentucky, where African-American and Appalachian Mountain children could receive college educations with the help of a work program and financial aid. Both Mamaw's sons who lived to adulthood worked for the TVA, one as a mechanical engineer and one at Headquarters.

Vesper had conflicting feelings about the TVA. Most everybody did. Before the dams, floods had come with unpredictable regularity. Grandma Kannie told stories about the floods. With little warning the waters swept through the hollows and valleys, leaving in their wake uprooted, drowned crops, the bloated bodies of livestock, and the houses that were left standing thickly iced inside and out with stinking muck. Privies were washed away, and wells were tainted. Grandma Kannie's three-year-old brother, Rueben, had been lost in the flood of 1886, carried off by water sluicing through their land. His body had been found days later, after the filthy water had subsided, caught six feet off the ground in a nest of broken branches and debris, his little dress torn, muddy, and wrenched up under his armpits. Flooding was a dramatic interruption of the daily cruelty of life. It was a sign of God's wrath, not to be questioned. It was just, and it was to be endured. Kannie as a little girl had been taught to read the Bible, the only book in the house, and she knew about floods.

Grandma Kannie and her family had moved to town in the 1920s. The timing was bad. When the Depression came along, town folk, with their dependence on each other for food and trade, had it much worse than country folk, who went on pretty much the same as before: poor, growing and storing food on the land, sleeping and rising with the sun. In Knoxville food was scarce and jobs scarcer. But Papaw was a carpenter and could build anything out of wood. When the TVA came along in 1933, he applied for a job. The job took him miles away, helping to build the housing for construction workers that was to become the town of Norris and also the formwork for Norris Dam, the first of the TVA projects. Papaw came home once a month and brought a paycheck so Kannie could pay the rent and buy a sack of flour, and the occasional pair of shoes handed down from one child to the next. Uncle Jake, the youngest of the six who lived past infancy, joked that by the time the shoes got to him, they were nothing but patches of cardboard and hide held together by twine and hardly worth the trouble of putting on. As an old man, Jake joked and laughed about his "air-conditioned" shoes.

Papaw was a Melungeon, one of the mysterious people of unknown heritage who holed up and kept to themselves up in the counties of upper East Tennessee. Melungeons were different. Most of them had dark hair, dark eyes, reddish brown skin, shovel-shaped teeth, and prominent ridges on the backs of their heads. They were skilled craftsmen. Some people thought that they were of

Mediterranean origin, came to the North American continent in the sixteenth century and intermarried with Cherokee, Powhatan, and other tribes. Some think they were originally Portuguese, and many believe that they were descended from the Lost Colony on Roanoke Island. No one could ever determine whether they were black, white, or Indian. In the 1830 United States Census, Melungeons were labeled "free persons of color." Their name remains to this day tinged with shadow. When Vesper was growing up, Melungeons were much maligned, equated with boogeymen and trolls. "You better watch out or the Melungeons'll get you." It wasn't until she reached adulthood that she knew what a Melungeon actually was, and that her taciturn, distant grandfather was one. She never knew how he met Kannie, but one thing she knew for sure: Kannie had been enough of a draw to lure him out of the tight-knit and interbred Melungeon territory up in Grainger County and leave it behind for good.

Vesper never knew Papaw to say much at all and certainly never to talk about himself in any way. But she knew that he had built the desk at which David Lilienthal had sat and monitored the workings of the TVA system. Lilienthal had moved his family from Chicago to a modest house in the TVA company town of Norris. Papaw's carpentry skills had come to his attention while he was observing the building of the town. Family legend had it that Papaw had chosen the tall, straight pine, sawed, cured, and milled it, and meticulously cut and joined a sturdy piece of furniture for the TVA board member and future director.

Years later Vesper was to find an old *Knoxville News Sentinel* photo of Lilienthal sitting at the desk. The caption described the desk as rustic and homemade. The photograph belied this: the desk was simple but silky smooth, substantial, and sparse of knots. She figured that "rustic" ran better in the press, the dapper young man in his suit and tie, who would become the director of the TVA and of the Atomic Energy Commission, graciously condescending to sit at a crude artifact crafted by an ignorant hillbilly. It was true that Papaw had had no formal education at all and had never traveled outside Grainger County until he moved his family to the four-room shotgun house in west Knoxville. He never traveled across more than half a dozen counties in his life. Papaw might have been ignorant of much of the world, but he was a deeply thoughtful man who knew more about mitering corners and making dovetail joints than most anyone around. In old age he would become a self-educated expert on grafting and growing roses. In summer his tiny backyard plot burgeoned with the colors and fragrances of velvety bourbons and hybrid teas growing in neat mounds next to the rabbit hutches that provided a grand source of nutrients for the roses and, more often than not, housed dinner for Papaw and Kannie. That is the way Vesper remembered her grandfather: shiny scalp dappled with spots of café au lait, its topography dominated by a high ridge between his ears—his spine bent with age and pain, eyes closed in a private ecstasy, his Melungeon nose buried in the petals of a full-blown Boule de Neige.

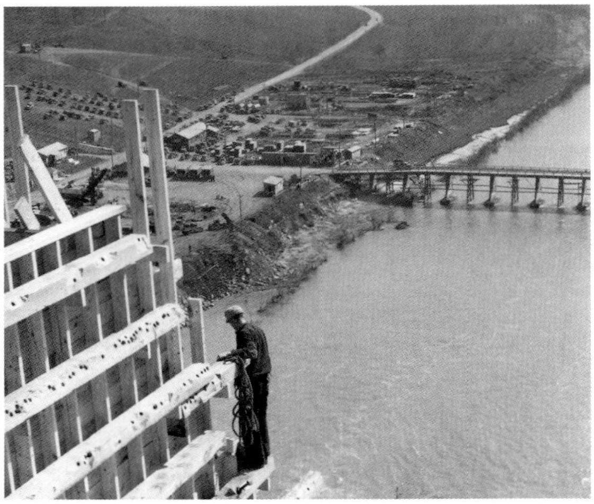

A lone construction worker labors on formwork for Norris Dam, 1936.

Papaw had never heard of the famous little Frenchman who came to see his work at Norris Dam: Jean-Paul Sartre, whose name and ideas would grace the writings of his granddaughter. The philosopher came to East Tennessee in 1945 and visited the TVA headquarters in Knoxville, as well as Norris Dam and two others. Sartre in the French newspaper *Le Figaro* would remark on the lightness of the temporary housing. He described the little wood houses clustered about the great gashes in the land as if they were floating, weightless, in water or air. Like the American city itself, he said, the village at Fontana Dam seemed to leave no mark of human presence upon the earth.

By the late 1940s, the TVA dams had put an end to flooding in most parts of East Tennessee. The TVA had brought paid employment, electricity, and—perhaps most significant—fertilizer. By the 1920s the hollows and valleys, vessels of potential and hope once prized for shelter and fertility, had been farmed out. Virgin forest had been razed, the rich top layer of the soil had been washed away, and the land carved with narrow gullies of erosion. The soil no longer offered nourishment to corn and beans. The TVA fertilizer program, an offshoot of the water-generated wartime production of nitrates for munitions at Muscle Shoals, Alabama, had brought new life to the depleted soil in East Tennessee. As if by magic, the land produced robust cabbages and fat ears of corn in abundance.

But progress always bears a cloudy lining beneath its silver sheen. The shining promise of the TVA masked an underbelly of resentment. Folks in East Tennessee had been forced to sell their land to the TVA. It had not been a question of choice, but a question of how long they could hold out before giving up the land of their fathers and their fathers' fathers before them. They had not asked for the

TVA and did not welcome the government's intrusion on the heritage that lay in their bones. Floods, erosion, barren land, sleeping and rising with the sun's rhythms, working and making do with what was available were woven into their lives. Grandma Kannie had said that people didn't wish for what they didn't know about, that they had never felt poor until people from outside came and told them about their lack. Life had been hard but so was everyone's around them, and it was punctuated by the small pleasures of living close to nature. Folks were suspicious of other folks coming in from outside telling them what to do and resentful of the loss of say-so about their ways of life.

There was no question that the lives of East Tennessee folk had been made easier by the TVA. Yet in the end they were right to be suspicious of the charitable motives of President Roosevelt and the triumvirate TVA board of Arthur Morgan, Harcourt Morgan, and David Lilienthal. The TVA was meant to serve the nation, not simply the poor folk of the Tennessee Valley. It had been nurtured in a web built of fear and the threat of war. The spring of 1933, when Congress authorized the TVA, was the same spring that Adolf Hitler rose to power in Germany. Not two years later, Arthur Morgan, testifying before Congress, emphasized the dependence of national defense upon a vast and unified source of electricity.

The TVA headquarters in Knoxville was only one point of a triangle of operations critical to the wartime effort. Sartre was given a tour, in addition to the headquarters building and the three dams, of two towns south of Knoxville that were vitally fed by the electrical power generated by the TVA dams: Alcoa and Oak Ridge. Tiny Alcoa, to the southeast, was the site of the largest aluminum plant in the world, run by its namesake corporation, the Aluminum Company of America. Here, men processed bauxite ore into aluminum, the light, bright metal that formed the skins of the 50,000 fighter planes that the president would demand in preparation for war. Oak Ridge, to the southwest, was the secret, planned town developed for the refining of plutonium. Oak Ridge was an important building block of the Manhattan Project, the development of the atomic bomb. Descendants of the isolated mountain families who had remained relatively removed from the nation and its wars became instrumental in the making of two of the most sophisticated and world-changing war machines ever known. They would send far more than their fair share of sons and daughters to fight and die in France and the Pacific, in Vietnam, and in Iraq.

For Haynes's family and others, the TVA had meant farmland and homes taken at unsatisfactory prices. It then signified progress and opportunity for undreamt-of fortune in the newly fertilized and electrified East Tennessee and a recreational landscape for Chris-Crafts and weekend cabins. Between the war and the close of the century, East Tennessee would become as interstate-highway-crossed and connected-by-cable as any other part of the country. Progress and money would be made, and their fruits—subdivisions, fast-food joints, big-box

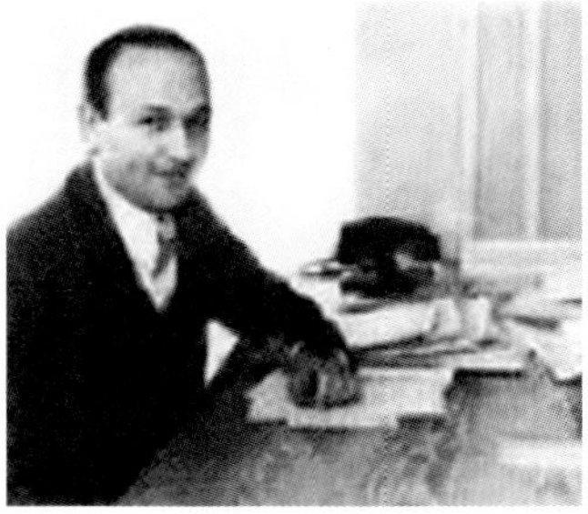

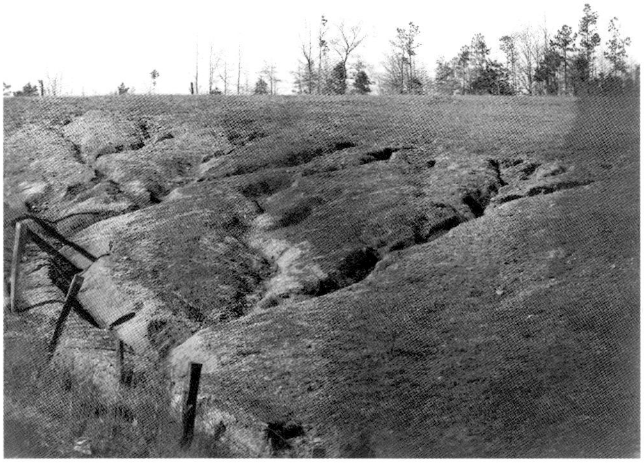

LEFT TVA Director David Lilienthal at the desk crafted by the author's grandfather, TVA headquarters, Knoxville, 1933 from *The Knoxville News-Sentinel*

RIGHT A sharecropper on worn-out land, 1936

chains, and Williamsburg-wannabe office parks—would be shoved into a landscape butchered to accommodate them. Cheek-by-jowl 6,000-square-foot manses of Styrofoam, steadily dripping the lake toward eutrophication, would replace the old lakeside cabins.

Watauga, nuzzled by national forest at its shoreline and fed by mountain streams, would be protected from most of these changes. Long, thin, and deep, Watauga would remain as if suspended in time and place for decades, change simply a matter of the cycles of the seasons and the quiet rising and falling of the water.

Vesper turns over and rests on the surface with her arms floating lazily over her head, her legs apart and curved down to catch the perfect still moment, floating, floating, her body one with the lake. Cool dark flips to dazzling, bright warmth. She closes her eyes and thinks of the continuum of water—how it is the first home, how it flows through bodies, released as sweat, urine, blood, tears, streams, cascades, steady drips from mountain rocks, over the smooth river stones, rising and falling with the moon, evaporating into the air and falling as rain, over and over and over again. She thinks of how the flow of water is a map of progress—from buckets dipped in creeks and carried, to buckets raised from wells, through the spigots of backyard pumps, right on into the houses themselves, and held captive and controlled behind the great dams that generate power for a nation. She thinks of Nimrod's Dam, built across the Tigris in Mesopotamia 4,000 years earlier. She is in this moment innocent of what is only a bit down the line: water flowing through the five and six bathrooms of single houses in which two people live, flowing through whirlpool baths, personal steam rooms, and six-headed showers through which fifteen gallons of hot water flow each minute from the behemoth water heaters needed to supply them.

For Vesper, Watauga means this suspension of innocence. But it is the fictional innocence of nature and of youth, without awareness that every moment arrives just for that moment. It might be remembered, and might not, and then it is gone. Vesper does not yet know this. She will never swim twice in the same Watauga, the lake that covers Old Butler and looks up at New Butler and its old, moved houses and new window-boxed double wides nestled in the hills. The lake made by many grandfathers, that fed and clothed their families, that fostered stories that will go on and on, like the soft, rolling mountains of Appalachia. The lake that 4,000 years from this moment may be polluted and decayed, all organic matter gone to slime, teeming with the anaerobic life that flourishes in an atmosphere without oxygen. When there may be no great-great-grandchildren, no chicken for the pan. Life as Vesper knows it will cease. Nevertheless life will go on, perhaps remembered, then submerged beneath the next new thing.

> The striking thing is the lightness, the fragility of these buildings. The village has no weight, it seems barely to rest upon the soil; it has not managed to leave a human imprint on the reddish earth and the dark forest; it is a temporary thing.
> —Jean-Paul Sartre

I dedicate "Watauga" to my grandparents: Ida Dora Archer Bloomer, Sarah Gustava Bowman Irwin, Mack Latham Bloomer, and William Haskew Irwin, whose bones lie in the hills of East Tennessee, but who live on in memory, and in "Watauga."

I still cook in "Idy" Bloomer's cast iron frying pan, well seasoned with her bountiful love.

Afterword

FORMER SENATOR HOWARD H. BAKER, JR.

The Tennessee Valley Authority has been an important part of my life since I was a young boy (a condition from which I have long since recovered). My father took me to Norris, Tennessee, to watch the construction of the TVA dam there. I remember being fascinated by a system of overhead cables and buckets being used to transport and pour the concrete for the dam. I remember my father saying the dam's engineers had calculated that it would take at least thirty years for that volume of concrete to completely cool, and I was sure that neither I nor anybody else could possibly live long enough to see that day come.

I remember watching the first water come over the spillway at the Norris Dam—and thinking it must be as grand as the Niagara Falls. I remember the manmade lake above the dam flooding Baker's Forge, where my great-grandfather had lived, and the family cemetery located there. The TVA disinterred the bodies of my relatives and moved them to a new location, which my cousin J. T. Baker and I could not find (nor could anyone else). At length, the TVA bought and erected a tombstone in my great-grandfather's honor, though his actual final resting place, somewhere under Norris Lake, has been lost.

The TVA, though the brainchild of President Franklin D. Roosevelt and his Depression-era New Deal, was nevertheless very popular with the Republicans of East Tennessee from the very beginning and has remained so ever since. Even an occasional scandal has not been able to dampen the enthusiasm of our people for this wondrous work of human skill and imagination. When President Roosevelt fired the first chairman of TVA for contumacy, a reporter asked him what that was, and FDR replied, "what Dr. Morgan is guilty of."

That's about as controversial as the TVA has ever been, except during the mid-1960s when I was making my first run for the Senate, and the Republican

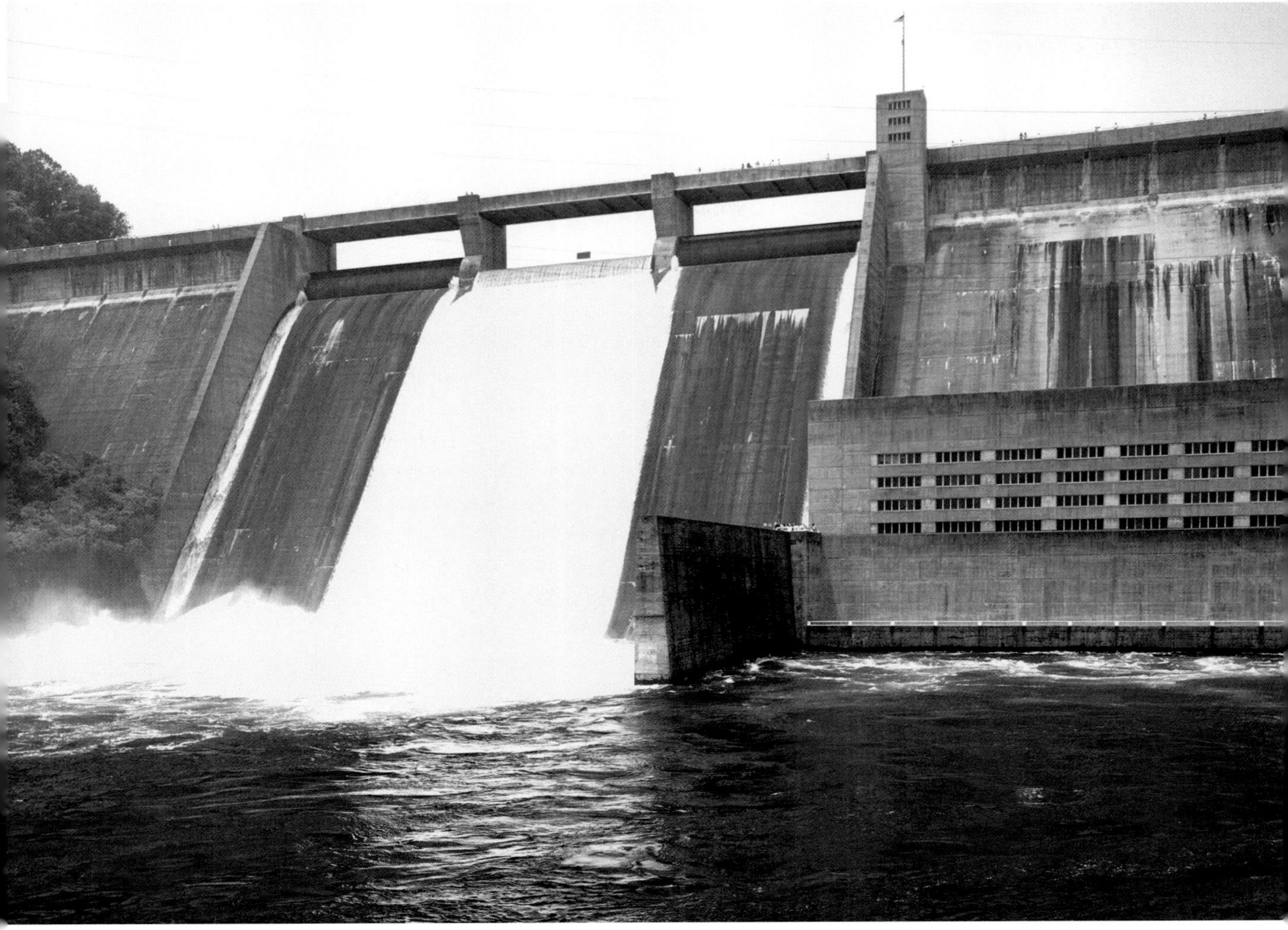

presidential candidate Barry Goldwater came to Tennessee to say he thought we ought to sell the TVA. We both lost, even though I violently disagreed with him. My lifelong friend John Waters, a distinguished chairman of the TVA board for many years, was fond of saying that the TVA was actually very easy to manage. When I would ask him how he could say that of a very large and very complex organization, John's blithe reply was, "the only thing it takes is to keep the lakes high and the rates low."

It is a little more complicated than that. There is an awesome simplicity in the design of the TVA's great structures that admirably reflects the character of the people those structures serve and protect. It is a kinship that has lasted almost seventy-five years and that represents one of the finest public endeavors ever conceived. And as you have seen throughout this volume, the persuasion that the TVA has been a godsend for our region is absolute and universal among the people of the Tennessee Valley.

Appendix: Travel Suggestions

While most of the Tennessee Valley Authority facilities originally featured informative visitor centers, budget reductions following the energy deregulation of the 1990s, coupled with recent heightened security concerns, have led to the closing of many of these centers. At this writing, four visitor centers are in operation: Fontana Dam, Norris Dam, Raccoon Mountain Pumped Storage Plant, and Kentucky Dam.

These four visitor centers correspond roughly to the geographical reach of the Authority, with Fontana Dam at the highest elevation above sea level, in the Appalachian Mountains of North Carolina at the eastern end of the region, and Kentucky Dam, in the flat lands of the west, just above the confluence of the Tennessee and Ohio rivers near Paducah, Kentucky. Fontana and Kentucky represent the range of dam types: Fontana a tall dam on a mountain tributary, Kentucky a broad, main river dam with a navigation lock operated by the Army Corps of Engineers. Norris, the first of the TVA dams, is more like Fontana in setting, though less dramatic.

A visit to the area around Knoxville, Tennessee, affords the most compact introduction to the broadly distributed TVA system. From Knoxville, one can easily visit the following representative TVA sites.

Norris Dam and Norris Town (1933–36)

Norris Dam is located on US 441, about twenty miles northwest of Knoxville. The highway crosses the dam on its way to Lake City, Tennessee. The visitor center is adjacent to US 441 on the Knoxville side of the dam; there is also a road to the bottom of the dam, where one can see (but not enter) the powerhouse. Across the road from the dam is Norris Dam State Park, which offers lodging in cabins originally built as workers' housing by the Civilian Conservation Corps at the time of the dam's construction. On the Lake City side of the dam is a marina, framed by the quarry from which the aggregate for the concrete of the dam was mined.

On the Norris Dam reservation are the Lenoir Museum and the historic Grist Mill and Threshing Barn, operated by the State of Tennessee. Together with the nearby, privately operated Museum of Appalachia, they offer an introduction to the history and culture of the area.

Norris Town, originally built to house construction workers for the dam, is considered to be the United States' first "new town" and has served as a planning model throughout the country. Its original layout survives, as do many of the original houses and the major buildings of the small commercial center.

Cherokee (1940–41) and Douglas (1942–43) Dams

East of Knoxville are Cherokee and Douglas dams, the former on the Holston River, the latter on the French Broad. The facilities of the dams are not open to the public, but both are approachable by car. The two were built from the same plans, as part of the accelerated construction attendant upon the war effort, and it is a striking experience to see what appears to be the same dam in two locations,

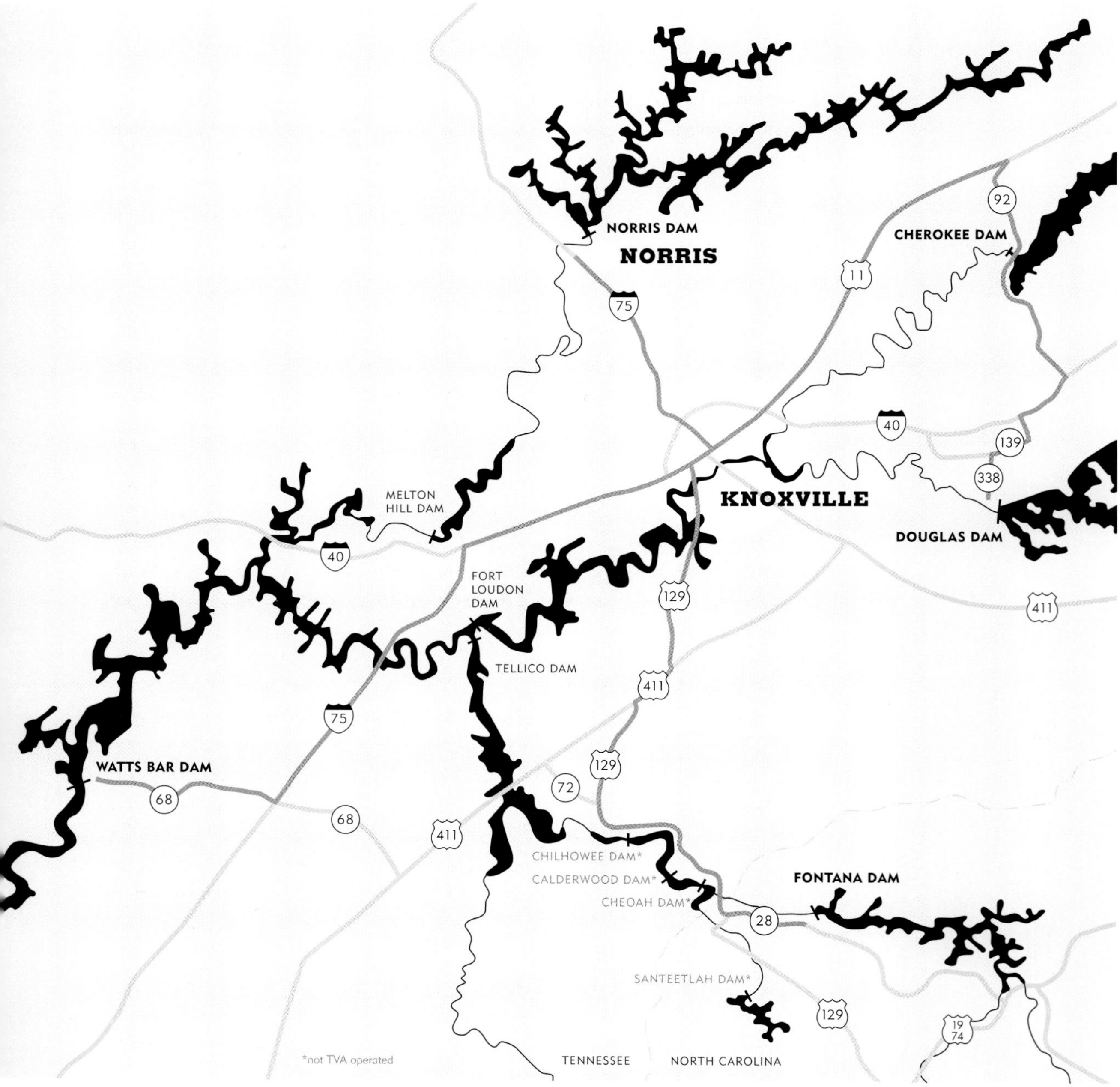
NORRIS DAM
NORRIS
CHEROKEE DAM
92
11
75
MELTON HILL DAM
40
139
338
KNOXVILLE
DOUGLAS DAM
FORT LOUDON DAM
129
411
TELLICO DAM
WATTS BAR DAM
68
72
CHILHOWEE DAM*
CALDERWOOD DAM*
CHEOAH DAM*
FONTANA DAM
28
SANTEETLAH DAM*
19
74
*not TVA operated
TENNESSEE
NORTH CAROLINA

twenty miles apart. Cherokee is on Tennessee State Highway 92, between Jefferson City and Rutledge; Douglas is off route 139, ten miles southwest of Dandridge.

Fontana Dam (1942–45)

About fifty miles south of Knoxville on US 129 is Fontana Dam. (Be aware that 129 joins and then separates from US 441; it's easy to miss where 129 turns off to the east, into the mountains.) The eleven-mile stretch of 129 through the mountains is known as The Tail of the Dragon because of the 318 curves in that short distance. It is a favorite of motorcyclists and sports car drivers and has been featured in several movies, including *Thunder Road* (1958, with Robert Mitchum). Just over the North Carolina border, turn left at Deal's Gap Motorcycle Resort onto North Carolina State 28. Fontana Dam is nine miles from the Resort on 28. The tallest dam in the eastern United States, 480 feet from base to crest, it is dramatic. The visitor center, at the top of the dam, is a handsome modernist interpretation of the dogtrot type, with two enclosed pavilions connected by a covered breezeway. An incline tram originally operated between the visitor center and the turbine room, at the base of the dam, but it is not currently in service. Nearby Fontana Village, like Norris Town, was built originally as worker's housing and now functions as a mountain resort community. As recently as 2002, one of the original prefabricated houses (similar to the demonstration house at Pickwick Dam, shown on page 20) was still standing, but in very dilapidated condition; it is unlikely that it remains today.

Watts Bar Dam (1939–42)

Watts Bar Dam, located on Tennessee State Highway 68 about fifteen miles west of where 68 crosses Interstate 75 at the Sweetwater exit, has perhaps the most dramatically situated visitor center of any of the TVA dams: half-circular in plan, it cantilevers out over the bluff on the downriver side of the dam. It is not, unfortunately, open to the public, but it is readily visible from the roadway. Across 68 from the visitor center and transformer yard is the Watts Bar Resort, a collection of cabins originally built by the TVA for construction workers but subsequently transferred to private hands. This is the dam that first sparked my interest in the TVA.

Before You Travel. Please note that the information given here regarding access to the TVA facilities may change based on security conditions and other factors. You should confirm opening hours with the TVA before traveling; visit www.tva.gov/sites for more information on individual TVA facilities.

Bibliography

Adams, Henry. *The Education of Henry Adams: An Autobiography.* Boston and New York, 1918.

Agee, James. "Tennessee Valley Authority." *Fortune* 8 (October 1933): 81–97.

———. "Tennessee Valley Authority: Work in the Valley/Federal Power." *Fortune* 11 (April 1935): 92–170.

Agee, James, and Walker Evans. *Let Us Now Praise Famous Men: Three Tenant Families.* Boston: Houghton Mifflin Company, 1969.

Architectural Forum, Building, U.S.A., New York: McGraw Hill, 1957.

Banham, Reyner. "Tennessee Valley Authority: The Engineering of Utopia." *Casabella* 542–43 (January–February 1988): 74.

———. *Theory and Design in the First Machine Age.* Cambridge, MA: MIT Press, 1980.

———. "Valley of the Dams." Chap. 37 in *A Critic Writes: Essays by Reyner Banham.* Berkeley and LA: University of California Press, 1996.

Barr, Jr., Alfred H. *Machine Art.* New York: Harry N. Abrams, Inc., 1994. First published 1934 by Museum of Modern Art.

Blau, Eve. *The Architecture of Red Vienna, 1919–1934.* Cambridge, MA: MIT Press, 1999.

Callahan, North. *TVA: Bridge Over Troubled Waters.* South Brunswick, NJ: A. S. Barnes, 1980.

Cogdell, Christina. *Eugenic Design: Streamlining America in the 1930s.* Philadelphia: University of Pennsylvania Press, 2004.

Creese, Walter L. *TVA's Public Planning: The Vision, The Reality.* Knoxville: University of Tennessee Press, 1990.

Creighton, Thomas, Frank Lopez, Charles Magruder, and George Sanderson. *Homes: Small, Medium, Large.* New York: Reinhold, 1947.

Draper, Earle S. *Annual Report of the Land Planning and Housing Division for the Fiscal Year Ended June 30, 1937.* Knoxville: Tennessee Valley Authority, 1937.

———. Earle S. Draper interviews. Oral History Collection, University of Memphis, Tennessee.

Dreyfuss, Henry. *Designing for People.* New York: Simon & Schuster, 1955.

Duffus, R. L., and Charles Krutch. *The Valley and Its People.* New York: Alfred A. Knopf, 1946.

Easterling, Keller, and Richard Prelinger, eds. "New Deal Regional Planning and Greenbelt Towns." *Call It Home: The House That Private Enterprise Built.* The Voyager Company, 1992. CD-ROM.

Field, Gregory B. "'Electricity for All': The Electric Home and Farm Authority and the Politics of Mass Consumption, 1932–35." *Business History Review* 64 (Spring 1990): 32–60.

George P. Palo Papers. The Special Collections Library of the University of Tennessee, Knoxville.

Grant, Nancy L. *TVA and Black Americans: Planning for the Status Quo.* Philadelphia: Temple University Press, 1990.

Gutheim, Frederick A. "Roland Wank: 1898–1970." *Architectural Forum* 133 (September 1970): 59.

———. "Tennessee Valley Authority: A New Phase in Architecture." *Magazine of Art* 33 (September 1940): 516–31. Reprinted as *TVA Architecture, as Shown at the Museum of Modern Art.* Knoxville: Tennessee Valley Authority, 1941.

Hamlin, Talbot. "Architecture of the TVA." *Pencil Points* 20 (November 1939).

Hargrove, Erwin C., and Paul K. Conklin. *TVA: Fifty Years of Grassroots Democracy.* Urbana: University of Illinois Press, 1983.

Hayden, Dolores. *Seven American Utopias: The Architecture of Communitarian Socialism, 1790–1975.* Cambridge, MA: MIT Press, 1976.

Heskett, John. *Industrial Design.* New York: Oxford University Press, 1980.

Huggins, Kay Haire. "Town Planning in the New South: The Work of Earle S. Draper, 1915–1933." Conference paper presented at Citadel Conference on The New South. Charleston, SC, April 20, 1978.

Huxley, Julian. "TVA: an Achievement of Democratic Planning." Special issue of *Architectural Review* 93 (June 1943): 139–66.

———. *TVA: Adventure in Planning*. Cheam, Surrey: The Architectural Press, 1943.

Jordy, William H. *American Buildings and Their Architects: The Impact of European Modernism in the Mid-Twentieth Century.* Garden City, NY: Anchor Press/Doubleday, 1976.

Kaplan, Wendy, ed. *Designing Modernity: The Arts of Reform and Persuasion, 1885–1945*. New York: Thames and Hudson, 1995.

Kasson, John F. *Civilizing the Machine: Technology and Republican Values in America, 1776–1900*. Harmondsworth, England: Penguin, 1977.

Kentgens-Craig, Margaret. *The Bauhaus and America: First Contacts 1919–1936*. Cambridge, MA: MIT Press, 2001.

Lane, Barbara Miller. *Architecture and Politics in Germany, 1918–1945*. Cambridge, MA: Harvard University Press, 1968.

Lawrence, Sidney. "Clean Machines at the Modern." *Art in America* 72 (February 1984).

Lichtenstein, Claude, and Franz Engler, eds. *Streamlined: The Aesthetics of Minimized Drag*. Zürich: Lars Müller, 1995.

Loos, Adolf. "Ornament and Crime." In *Programs and Manifestoes on 20th-century Architecture*, edited by Ulrich Conrads, translated by Michael Bullock, 19–24. Cambridge, MA: MIT Press, 1975.

Macy, Christine, and Sarah Bonnemaison. *Architecture and Nature: Creating the American Landscape*. London: Routledge, 2003.

Marx, Leo. *The Machine in the Garden: Technology and the Pastoral Ideal in America*. London: Oxford University Press, 1964.

McCraw, Thomas K. *TVA and the Power Fight, 1933–1939*. Philadelphia: J. B. Lippincott, 1971.

McDonald, Michael J., and John Muldowny. *TVA and the Dispossessed: The Resettlement of Population in the Norris Dam Area*. Knoxville: University of Tennessee Press, 1982.

Meikle, Jeffrey. *Twentieth Century Limited: Industrial Design in America, 1925–39*. Philadelphia: Temple University Press, 1979.

Miller, Perry. *The Life of the Mind in America from the Revolution to the Civil War.* New York: Harcourt Brace, 1965.

Mock, Elizabeth. *If You Want to Build a House*. New York: Museum of Modern Art, 1946.

"Model T Appliances." *Business Week*, March 17, 1934, 10.

Moffett, Marian. *Built for the People of the United States: Fifty Years of TVA Architecture*. Knoxville: Art and Architecture Gallery, University of Tennessee, 1983.

———. "Looking to the Future: The Architecture of Roland Wank." *Arris* 1: 5–17 (Journal of the Southeast Chapter of the Society of Architectural Historians) (1989).

Morgan, Arthur E. *The Making of the TVA*. Buffalo, New York: Prometheus Books, 1974.

Moutoux, John T. "R. A. Wank, TVA Architect, Sees Worker's Housing as Great Challenge of Tennessee Basin's New Deal." *Knoxville News-Sentinel*, December 2, 1933.

Mumford , Lewis. "The Architecture of Power." *New Yorker*, June 7, 1941, 58.

———. *Technics and Civilization*. New York: Harcourt, Brace and Company, 1934.

Neuse, Steven M. *David E. Lilienthal: The Journey of an American Liberal*. Knoxville: University of Tennessee Press, 1996.

Newton, Norman T. *Design on the Land: The Development of Landscape Architecture*. Cambridge, MA: The Belknap Press of Harvard University, 1971.

Nickles, Shelley. "'Preserving Women': Refrigerator Design as Social Progress in the 1930s." *Technology and Culture* 43 (October 2002): 724–26.

Norman, Donald. *The Psychology of Everyday Things.* New York: Basic Books, 1988.

Nye, David E. *American Technological Sublime.* Cambridge, MA: MIT Press, 1994.

Pound, Ezra. "Machine Art." In *Machine Art and Other Writings: The Lost Thought of the Italian Years*, edited by Maria Luisa Ardizzone. Durham: Duke University Press, 1996.

Reid, Kenneth. "Design in TVA Structures." *Pencil Points* 10 (1939): 44.

Roosevelt, Franklin D. *The Year of Crisis, 1933.* Vol. 2, *The Public Papers and Addresses of Franklin D. Roosevelt, 1928–1945.* New York: Random House, 1938–50.

Schaffer, Daniel. "Benton MacKaye: The TVA Years." *Planning Perspectives* 5 (1990): 9.

Schuman, Tony. "Labor and Housing in New York City: Architect Herman Jessor and the Cooperative Housing Movement." Unpublished typescript available as PDF. *Co-op Village Online Community,* 2005. http://www.lesonline.org/cv/ LABOR%20AND%20HOUSING%20IN%20 NEW%20YORK%20CITY.pdf.

Smith, Terry. *Making the Modern: Industry, Art, and Design in America.* Chicago: University of Chicago Press, 1993.

Sottsass, Ettore. "Menhir, Ziggurat, Stupas, Hydrants & Gas Pumps." In *Ettore Sottsass: Ceramics*, edited by Bruno Bischofsberger. San Francisco: Chronicle Books, 1996.

Tennessee Valley Authority. *The Fontana Project.* TVA Technical Report No. 12. Washington, D.C.: United States Government Printing Office, 1949.

———. *The Norris Project: A Comprehensive Report on the Planning, Design, Construction, and Initial Operations of the Tennessee Valley Authority's First Water Control Project.* Washington, D. C.: United States Government Printing Office, 1940.

Tennessee Valley Authority Library, Knoxville.

TVA Archives, NARA-Southeast Region, Atlanta.

Tobey, Ronald. *Technology as Freedom: The New Deal and the Electrical Modernization of the American Home.* Berkeley: University of California Press, 1996.

"U.S. Monument." *Time* 37 (May 12, 1941): 46.

Wank, Roland. "Nowhere to Go but Forward." *Magazine of Art* 34 (January 1941): 8.

———. "Powerhouses." In *Forms and Functions of Twentieth-Century Architecture*, edited by Talbot Hamlin. New York: Columbia University Press, 1952.

Wilson, Richard Guy. "Gordon B. Kaufmann and Modernism." In *Johnson Kaufmann Coate, Partners in the California Style*, edited by Joseph N. Newland. Claremont, CA: Scripps College, 1992.

———. "The Machine in the Landscape." In *The Machine Age in America, 1918–1941*, edited by Richard Guy Wilson, Dianne H. Pilgrim, and Dickran Tashjian. New York: Abrams, 1986.

Contributor Biographies

Richard Barnes is a photographer who divides his time between commissioned work and personal projects, which he exhibits internationally. He was a 2005–6 fellow at the American Academy in Rome, where he participated in a collaborative exhibition titled Murmur (Flow Room). Barnes's photographs of the Unabomber cabin were included in the exhibition, Down by Law, presented by the Wrong Gallery at the 2006 Whitney Biennial. His photographs are part of the permanent collections of the Metropolitan Museum of Art, the Hirshhorn Museum and Sculpture Garden, the Philadelphia Museum of Art, the San Francisco Museum of Modern Art, the Los Angeles County Museum of Art, as well as numerous other institutions. Barnes is currently working on a book of his recent work to be published in 2008 by Princeton Architectural Press.

Jennifer Bloomer is a writer and architect living in Athens, Georgia. She was born in Knox County, Tennessee, and was educated at Mount Holyoke College, where she earned an AB in Art History. She has a professional MArch., as well as a PhD in architecture history and theory, from Georgia Tech. She taught design and architecture history and theory for twenty years, before leaving academia to practice as principal in an architecture firm. She authored *Architecture and the Text* (Yale University Press, 1993) and has published numerous essays on architecture and on contemporary art in the United States and abroad. She has lectured widely, both nationally and internationally. Bloomer long has been concerned with problems of the homeless and is president of the Nancy Travis House, which provides daycare for homeless children. She raises funds for the Jeannette Rankin Foundation, which offers education scholarships to low-income women over thirty-five. She is currently at work on a novel called *Waiting for the Night Gardener.*

Tim Culvahouse, FAIA, holds a Bachelor of Architecture degree from the Tulane School of Architecture and a Master of Environmental Design from Yale University. His articles have appeared in a wide range of journals, both professional and academic. Since 2000, he has served as editor of *arcCA (Architecture California)*, the quarterly journal of the AIA California Council. He was formerly head of the Department of Architecture, Rhode Island School of Design (1988–93), and associate dean for Design and Architectural Studies, California College of the Arts (1995–99), where he remains an adjunct professor. He leads Culvahouse Consulting Group, Inc., and is a member of the board of Public Architecture, a nonprofit, public-interest architecture group.

Steven Heller is the art director of the *New York Times Book Review* and co-chair of the School of Visual Arts MFA Designer as Author program. He is the editor of *AIGA VOICE: Journal of Design* (online) and contributing editor to *Print, Eye, I.D.*, and *Baseline* magazines. He is the author, editor, or co-author of over one hundred books on design and popular culture, including *Graphic Style: from Victorian to Post-Modern* (Harry N. Abrams, 1994), *Streamline: American Graphic Design Between the Wars* (Chronicle Books, 1996), and *Deco Type: Art Deco Specimens from Between the Wars* (Chronicle Books, 1998).

Barry Katz was educated at McGill University in Montreal and the London School of Economics and holds a doctorate from the University of California at Santa Cruz. He is currently professor of humanities and design at California College of the Arts, consulting professor in the Design Division at Stanford University, and fellow at IDEO, Inc., Silicon Valley's leading design and innovation consultancy. His books include *Herbert Marcuse and the Art of Liberation* (Verso, 1982), *Foreign Intelligence: Research and Analysis in the Office of Strategic Services, 1942–1945* (Harvard University Press, 1989), and *Technology and Culture: A Historical Romance* (Stanford Alumni Association, 1998). A forthcoming book, *The Shape of Things to Come,* studies the history of Silicon Valley design. His writings on the history and philosophy of design have appeared in many academic, professional, and popular journals.

Christine Macy is a professor of architectural design and history at Dalhousie University in Canada. Her research areas include the representation of cultural identity in architecture, public space design, civic infrastructure, and festival architecture. A graduate of the University of California, Berkeley, and the Massachusetts Institute of Technology, she practiced architecture in New York and San Francisco with various firms before establishing her partnership, Filum, with Sarah Bonnemaison in 1990. The firm specializes in lightweight structures and public space design for festivals. Macy's books include *Greening the City: Ecological Wastewater Treatment in Halifax* (Dalhousie, 2001) and the co-authored *Architecture and Nature: Creating the American Landscape* (Routledge, 2003), which received the Society of Architectural Historians' Alice Davis Hitchcock Award in 2005 for the most distinguished work of architectural history by a North American historian. She is currently working on a visual history of dams in the United States and a co-edited volume on the history of festival architecture in Europe.

Todd Smith holds a BA in political science and art history from Duke University, an MA in art history from Indiana University, and a doctorate in art history from Indiana University, with a dissertation on artist Washington Alston (1779–1843). From 2002 through 2005, he was the director of the Knoxville Museum of Art; he previously served as president and CEO of The Plains Art Museum in Fargo, North Dakota. He is currently executive director of the Gibbes Art Museum of Charleston, South Carolina.

Jane Wolff was educated as a documentary filmmaker and landscape architect at Harvard College and the Harvard University Graduate School of Design. She is an assistant professor in the School of Architecture and Environmental Studies at Washington University, St. Louis, Missouri. Wolff's study of Dutch land reclamation practices as a Charles Eliot Traveling Fellow of the Harvard Graduate School of Design in 1994 and as a Fulbright scholar in 1998 has informed her book, *Delta Primer* (William Stout Publishers, 2003), designed to educate broad and varied audiences about the complex and disputed landscape of California's Sacramento–San Joaquin Delta. *Delta Primer* arose from her conviction that designers must find a public voice if they want to affect the rapid, large-scale changes taking place in the contemporary American landscape.